THE HOLY LAND AT THE TIME OF JESUS' MINISTRY

# The Miracles of Jesus

Healing at the Pool of Bethesda, *by Carl Bloch. Courtesy of Brigham Young University Museum of Art. Used by permission.*

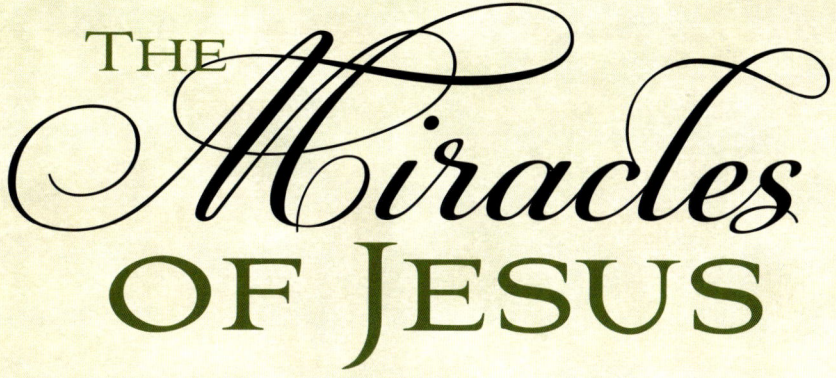
# The Miracles of Jesus

Eric D. Huntsman

Deseret Book

Salt Lake City, Utah

© 2014 Eric D. Huntsman

All rights reserved. No part of this book may be reproduced in any form or by any means without permission in writing from the publisher, Deseret Book Company, P. O. Box 30178, Salt Lake City, Utah 84130. This work is not an official publication of The Church of Jesus Christ of Latter-day Saints. The views expressed herein are the responsibility of the author and do not necessarily represent the position of the Church or of Deseret Book Company.

DESERET BOOK is a registered trademark of Deseret Book Company.

Visit us at DeseretBook.com

**Library of Congress Cataloging-in-Publication Data**
Huntsman, Eric D., 1965– author.
 The miracles of Jesus / Eric D. Huntsman.
   pages cm
 Includes bibliographical references and index.
 ISBN 978-1-60907-916-1 (hardbound : alk. paper)
 1. Jesus Christ—Miracles. 2. Jesus Christ—Mormon interpretations. I. Title.
 BX8643.J4H86 2014
 232.9′55—dc23                                                                 2014006566

Printed in Canada
Friesens, Manitoba, Canada

10  9  8  7  6  5  4  3  2  1

*amicis optimis*
*fratribus veris condiscipulisque Christi*

*To the best of friends*
*true brothers and fellow followers of Christ*

# Contents

Preface . . . . . . . . . . . . . . . . . . . . . . . . . . . . . . . . . . . . . . . . . . . . . . . . . . . . ix

Acknowledgments . . . . . . . . . . . . . . . . . . . . . . . . . . . . . . . . . . . . . . . . xi

A Ministry of Miracles . . . . . . . . . . . . . . . . . . . . . . . . . . . . . . . . . . . 1

1. Power over the Elements . . . . . . . . . . . . . . . . . . . . . . . . . . . . . . 13

2. Healing the Sick . . . . . . . . . . . . . . . . . . . . . . . . . . . . . . . . . . . . . 41

3. Casting Out Devils . . . . . . . . . . . . . . . . . . . . . . . . . . . . . . . . . . . 65

4. Causing the Blind to See and the Deaf to Hear . . . . . . . . . . . . . 87

5. Raising the Dead . . . . . . . . . . . . . . . . . . . . . . . . . . . . . . . . . . . . 105

The Greatest Miracles of All . . . . . . . . . . . . . . . . . . . . . . . . . . . . . 121

Appendixes

   A. Miracles in the Gospels . . . . . . . . . . . . . . . . . . . . . . . . . . . . 127

   B. Our Galilee Miracle . . . . . . . . . . . . . . . . . . . . . . . . . . . . . . . 139

Notes . . . . . . . . . . . . . . . . . . . . . . . . . . . . . . . . . . . . . . . . . . . . . . . 145

Sources . . . . . . . . . . . . . . . . . . . . . . . . . . . . . . . . . . . . . . . . . . . . . 154

Index . . . . . . . . . . . . . . . . . . . . . . . . . . . . . . . . . . . . . . . . . . . . . . . 158

# PREFACE

*The Miracles of Jesus* is a thanksgiving, a scriptural affirmation of the power of Jesus Christ in both the New Testament Gospels and in the lives of believers today. Like *Good Tidings of Great Joy* and *God So Loved the World,* this work is a scriptural exploration of important episodes from the Gospels augmented by art, photos of Holy Land sites, maps, historical details, musical selections, and devotional reflections. This volume focuses on the miracles performed by Jesus during his ministry, culminating in the ultimate miracles that come to all because of his Atonement. As such, it uses the stories of Jesus' miracles to answer the question of Jesus' disciples: "What manner of man is this . . . ?" (Mark 4:41; parallels Matthew 8:27; Luke 8:25). The answer is the same today as it was then: he is the Son of God and the Savior of the World, who has the power to save and help us.

The introduction sets the stage by introducing the meaning of *miracle* in the New Testament and then laying out the role of the premortal Jesus Christ in the creation of the world followed by the miracle of his birth into mortality, both of which are foundational to the miracles he performed during his mortal ministry. Subsequent chapters are organized around the different types of miracles that Jesus performed, such as exercising power over the elements, healing the sick, casting out devils, restoring sight and hearing, and raising the dead.

In addition to examining the textual accounts of these miracles, I explore the meaning and greater symbolism of the miracles, striving to apply them to believers of every age. For example, sidebars in the chapter on healings treat such historical subjects as medicine and healing in the ancient world, and a sidebar in the chapter on casting out devils discusses views of demons in the ancient world. More important, sidebars in each chapter tie the miracles recorded in the Gospels to challenges in today's world. Accordingly, a sidebar in the chapter on healing addresses unseen illnesses, exploring the power of Jesus Christ in helping those who struggle with chronic illness, depression, and emotional struggles. The chapter on casting out devils addresses such contemporary issues as overcoming addictions and how we can deal with flesh-and-blood devils (such as those who perpetrate abuse) in our past. Likewise, the chapter on raising the dead discusses how faith in Jesus Christ helps us accept the death of loved ones.

Two appendixes provide additional information for interested readers. Appendix A provides a survey of the biblical scholarship that lies behind much of this book. In addition to lists of every miracle story, summary, and report in the Gospels, it also examines the unique approach that each of the four Gospels takes in presenting the miracles as well as briefly reviewing how scholars evaluate these stories historically. Appendix B consists of a short personal essay recalling a family experience we had while in the Holy Land on the very sea on and around which so many of Jesus' miracles took place.

The book concludes with a reflection on the truth that the greatest miracles are those that can and do come to everyone through the Atonement of Jesus Christ, celebrating the miracles of a change of heart, forgiveness of sins, healing the soul, and the gift of eternal life. My intent throughout is to increase feelings of gratitude to the Savior by affirming the great things that he has done and continues to do in the lives of his Saints.

# Acknowledgments

As always, I thank my family, without whom I could never have written this, or any other, book. My wife, Elaine, is a steady source of love and support, and my children, Rachel and Samuel, are joys and inspirations to me because of their belief in God and their love of Jesus. Likewise my mother, Marilyn Halversen Huntsman, has always encouraged me with her constant confidence and love.

My assistants Joshua Matson and Stuart Bevan helped me throughout this project, assisting with research, reading early versions of the manuscript, and checking sources. S. Kent Brown and Eric Schetselaar likewise read much of the early draft and made helpful suggestions. I also express appreciation to Camille Fronk Olson, chair of Ancient Scripture at Brigham Young University, for her support. Furthermore, I acknowledge those religious educators who, although differing in style and approach, have been important examples to me of gospel scholarship, teaching, and living. Though I cannot recognize them all, I must mention my friends and colleagues George Durrant, Richard Holzapfel, Andrew Skinner, Kent Jackson, and Bob Millet.

I am grateful to my publisher, Deseret Book Company, for having confidence in this project and helping bring it to print. In particular I thank Jana Erickson, product director; Suzanne Brady, editor; Shauna Gibby, designer; and Malina Grigg and Rachael Ward, typographers.

This volume is dedicated to my best friends, each of whom has encouraged me over the years. Without naming them, I recognize them as the miracles they have been in my life, serving as confidants, examples, and sources of strength. They have made me grateful for the gift of true friendship, the kind that leads me to echo the expression found in Doctrine and Covenants 88:133: "Art thou a brother or brethren? I salute you in the name of the Lord Jesus Christ, in token or remembrance of the everlasting covenant, in which covenant I receive you to fellowship, in a determination that is fixed, immovable, and unchangeable, to be your friend and brother through the grace of God in the bonds of love, to walk in all the commandments of God blameless, in thanksgiving, forever and ever."

My ultimate thanks is to the Lord Jesus Christ himself, who has called us not only his servants but also his friends (John 15:13–15; D&C 84:77). And it is because he so loved us, his friends, that he suffered, died, and rose again, bringing the greatest of miracles into this life and the next.

# Introduction
# A Ministry of Miracles

*For behold, the time cometh, and is not far distant, that with power, the Lord Omnipotent who reigneth, who was, and is from all eternity to all eternity, shall come down from heaven among the children of men, and shall dwell in a tabernacle of clay, and shall go forth amongst men, working mighty miracles, such as healing the sick, raising the dead, causing the lame to walk, the blind to receive their sight, and the deaf to hear, and curing all manner of diseases. And he shall cast out devils, or the evil spirits which dwell in the hearts of the children of men.*

—Mosiah 3:5–6

Foreseen by prophets before Jesus' birth, witnessed by many during his life, and read about by millions since, the miracles of Jesus are a distinguishing aspect of his mortal ministry. Others had also worked mighty acts in God's behalf, but the number and magnitude of Jesus' miracles set him apart from all of them. As Peter later proclaimed, "God anointed Jesus of Nazareth with the Holy Ghost and with power: *who went about doing good,* and healing all that were oppressed of the devil; *for God was with him*" (Acts 10:38; emphasis added). Both then and now these miracles are powerful witnesses that Jesus is the Christ, God's anointed servant and the Savior of mankind.

Whether he was healing the sick, cleansing lepers, casting out devils, providing food and drink, or rescuing his disciples on a stormy sea, Jesus' miracles were mighty blessings to those for whom he performed them. As we read about these miracles and let the Spirit touch our hearts, seeds of faith are planted within us that Jesus can and will perform such miracles even in our day.

The miracles of Jesus are nevertheless more than individual blessings. They are also symbols and types that reveal the full scope of Jesus' identity as the mighty Jehovah, the Creator, the one who provides for his people, and above all the Christ, who wrought the great Atonement, conquering sin and death. For people in every age Jesus can redeem from sin, change hearts and heal souls, strengthen and empower, and bring about a glorious resurrection, which are the greatest miracles of all.

## Jesus' Miracles in the Gospels

Depending on how they are counted, at least thirty-six discrete accounts of miracles appear in the New Testament Gospels.[1] In addition, the evangelists, or authors of the Gospels, summarize Jesus' performance of miracles on thirteen occasions, and they record six other instances of people reporting that Jesus had performed mighty works (see Appendix A). From these figures alone, it is clear that Jesus performed more miracles than any other person who preceded him in scripture, far outstripping the twenty-seven recorded miracles of Moses, the four of Joshua, the nine of Elijah, and the fourteen of Elisha.[2] But Jesus did not just perform more miracles than

*Opposite:* In the Villages the Sick Were Brought unto Him, *by James Tissot. Courtesy of Bridgeman Art Library. Used by permission.*

any other person; his miracles recorded in the New Testament also differ qualitatively from the miracles worked by others because he performed them with his own power. Furthermore, almost all of them pointed to his divine identity as the Son of God and foreshadowed his greater saving work.

The four Gospels are a rich treasure trove of accounts of Jesus' activities as a miracle worker. These accounts share certain literary similarities in how they are written and used in the Gospels (see Appendix A). Nevertheless, each evangelist had a unique approach to the material, often relating the same story with varying degrees of detail and using it to emphasize different points about Jesus' divinity (see Appendix A). Mark's Gospel is widely presumed to have been the first to have been

Healing, *by J. Kirk Richards.*

written, so in cases where there are multiple versions of the same story, references from Mark are listed first in this study, followed by those of Matthew, Luke, and John. This approach allows us to see how each author used this tradition, sometimes adding details or perspective to give different insights into the miracles of Jesus.

The English word *miracle* comes from the Latin *miraculum,* which in turn comes from the verb *mirari,* meaning "to marvel" or "to be amazed at."[3] In both Latin and English, the predominating sense is the amazement or awe felt by witnesses of great acts that go beyond the normal ability of human beings and even seem to contravene the normal pattern or laws of nature. Hence, miracles are usually defined as extraordinary events that manifest some kind of divine intervention.[4] Since the Enlightenment, with its emphasis on reason and science, miracles have been assumed to be impossible acts, and their reality has often been rejected out of hand, particularly by some rationalist philosophers

## Greek Words for Jesus' Miracles

Although the historian Josephus, a nonbiblical ancient source, reports that Jesus "was a doer of startling deeds" (Greek, *paradoxōn*),[5] the original manuscripts of the Gospels in Greek never use *thauma*, which means "an amazing thing" and correlates most closely with our English word *miracle*, in connection with an act of Jesus.[6] A related word, *thaumasion*, or "a marvel," appears only once,[7] as do two similar terms used by Luke. Furthermore, in the synoptic Gospels, miracles are never described as *sēmeia kai terata*, or "signs or wonders." For these authors, that expression is usually pejorative, reflecting a need of or demand for divine proofs by nonbelievers.[8] Instead, in these three Gospels the most common word for miracle is *dynamis*, or "powerful deed."

John regularly uses *sēmeion*, or "sign," whenever he, as the narrator, describes or discusses Jesus' miracles. When John's Gospel describes Jesus as he talks about his own acts, including his miracles, they are described as *erga*, or "works."[9] This use of "works" by Jesus to describe his miracles explicitly connects his deeds during his mortal ministry with the creative and saving acts of God as recounted throughout the Old Testament. Thus Jesus spoke to his opponents after healing the man at the Pool of Bethesda, saying, "My Father worketh hitherto, and I work. . . . For the works which the Father hath given me to finish, *the same works that I do*, bear witness of me, that the Father hath sent me" (John 5:17–36; emphasis added).

The various Greek words that can be translated into English as "miracle" are as follows:

| Greek | English | King James Version Rendering | Scripture Citation |
|---|---|---|---|
| *dynamis* | "powerful deed or work" | "mighty work" | Mark 6:2, 5; Matthew 11:20–21, 23; 13:54, 58; 14:2; Luke 19:37; |
|  |  | "miracle" | Mark 9:39 ("miracle" in 6:52 was understood by translators); |
|  |  | "power" | Luke 5:17; |
|  |  | "virtue" | Mark 5:30; Luke 6:19; 8:46 |
| *endoxon* | "distinguished or splendid deed" | "glorious thing" | Luke 13:17 |
| *ergon* | "work" | "work" | Matthew 11:2; John 5:20, 36; 7:21; 9:3; 10:25, 32; 14:10–11 |
| *paradoxon* | "wonderful or remarkable deed" | "strange thing" | Luke 5:26 |
| *sēmeion* | "sign" | "miracle" | Luke 23:8; John 2:11, 23; 3:2; 4:54; 6:2, 14; 9:16; 10:41; 11:47; 12:18, 37; |
|  |  | "sign" | John 20:30 |
| *teras* | "wonder or portent," usually in *sēmeia kai terata* for "signs and wonders" | "signs and wonders" | None of Jesus, though he warns against seeking signs and wonders in such passages as John 4:48 |
| *thauma* | "amazing thing," closest to our English "miracle" |  | Does not appear in the Gospels |
| *thaumasion* | "wonderful or remarkable thing" | "wonderful thing" | Matthew 21:15 |

*Psalter map of Christ as Creator, ca. 1250, British Library, London.*

and scientists.[10] Since the early days of the Restoration, however, latter-day authorities and commentators have argued against the notion that miracles somehow violate natural laws. Elder James E. Talmage, for instance, wrote: "Miracles cannot be in contravention of natural law, but are wrought through the operation of laws not universally or commonly recognized. In the contemplation of the miracles wrought by Christ, we must of necessity recognize the operation of a power transcending our present human understanding."[11]

This transcendent power exercised by Jesus is reflected in the Greek word commonly used by Mark, Matthew, and Luke when they refer to Jesus' miraculous acts. While those who witnessed the miracles of Jesus were regularly amazed and marveled at what he had done,[12] the so-called synoptic Gospels, rather than use a word that emphasizes amazement or seeming impossibility, most often call a miracle of Jesus a *dynamis*, which in this context means "a mighty or powerful act or deed."[13] As a result, the miracles of Jesus emphasize the power of Jesus—power over the elements, over sickness and other disability, and even over death.

John's Gospel, on the other hand, presents the miracles of Jesus in a very different way. Never using the term *dynamis* for any of Jesus' acts, John instead usually employs *sēmeion*, meaning "sign," for the miracles of Jesus. Thus for John, each miracle, or sign, has more significance than simply how it benefited the recipient. Instead it points to or reveals something about the divine nature of Jesus and his power in the lives of his people, then and now.

## "All Things Were Made by Him"

When Joseph Smith was asked, "What was the first miracle Jesus performed?" he answered, "He made this world."[14] This first miracle occurred when, under the direction of the Father, as *YHWH*, or Jehovah, the premortal Jesus Christ created the heavens, the earth, and everything in them.[15] Accepting this usual identification of the premortal Jesus Christ with the Jehovah of the Old Testament allows Latter-day Saints to see testimonies of Jesus' creative role throughout the Hebrew Bible (see, for example, Genesis 2:4; Psalm 148:5; Isaiah 42:5; 45:18). The Book of Mormon gives further witness of Jesus' identity as the Creator, particularly through its frequent use of the title "Father of heaven and of earth" (2 Nephi 25:12; Mosiah 15:4; Alma 11:39; Helaman 16:18). By that title Jesus is explicitly defined as being the "Creator of all things from the beginning" (Mosiah 3:8; Helaman 14:12).

The clearest statement of Jesus' creative role in the New Testament comes from the testimony of John, who recorded: "In the beginning was the Word, and the Word was with God, and the Word was God. The same was in the beginning with God. All things were made by him; and without him was not any thing made that was made" (John 1:1–3; compare Colossians 1:16). For John, before His birth Jesus was the Divine Word, the means by which God effected his creation and continued to communicate and interact with it. Echoing this understanding is the statement of Hebrews 1:2, which states, "[God] hath in these last days spoken unto us by his Son, whom he hath appointed heir of all things, by whom also he made the worlds."

Many, if not most, of the miracles recorded in the Gospels can, in fact, be directly connected to the earlier miracle of the Creation. The same Being who, as Jehovah, organized the elements and framed the heavens and the earth was thus, as the Man of Galilee, able to control the winds and the waves. He could change water to wine, multiply loaves and fishes, heal bodies, and restore sight by the same power, or *dynamis*, that he had exercised in the beginning. Accordingly, Moroni asked, "Who shall say that it was not a miracle that by his word the heaven and the earth should be; and by the

## From Haydn's *Creation* to "How Great Thou Art"

The miracle of God's creative power has inspired countless pieces of musical literature from classical masterworks to popular hymns. Listening to such music or performing it can stir feelings of awe, reverence, and love within us for God and his Son Jesus, through whom he created this world and continues to sustain it, and from whom we enjoy the miracles of life and needed blessings.

One great masterwork of the classical age in music is the magnificent oratorio *Die Schöpfung*, or *The Creation*, by Franz Joseph Haydn (1732–1809), a foremost composer of the period. For this masterpiece, Haydn drew upon a German rendition of an anonymous English poem, which itself drew from Genesis, the Psalms, and Milton's *Paradise Lost*, to paint in thirty-four powerful movements a vivid picture of the creation of the world and of the first man and woman. In composing the oratorio, Haydn was strongly influenced by the tradition developed by George Frideric Handel (1685–1759). Composed between October 1796 and April 1798, *Creation* uses three soloists, a full chorus, and a symphonic orchestra. The first full official performance of *Creation* took place on April 30, 1798, in Vienna. Its performance in London in 1800 featured a sometimes awkward translation into English, but the oratorio has nonetheless become a staple of musical literature.[16]

Nearly a century later, one of the most popular Christian hymns today, "How Great Thou Art," began as a poem written by the Reverend Carl Boberg in 1886. Reverend Boberg was inspired by the beautiful scenery of the southeastern coast of his native Sweden when he wrote *O Store Gud, nar jag den varld beskådar*, which is translated literally as "O Great God, when I view the world." His poem, which was set to an old Swedish melody, was subsequently translated into German and English. The very literal English translation was subsequently translated into Russian, which version the Reverend S. K. Hind heard and later rendered into the familiar English version we know today. Just as Reverend Boberg had been inspired by the majesty of God's creation in Sweden, so was Reverend Hind moved by the beauty of the mountainous region of Subcarpathian Russia, where he and his wife were preaching.[17]

The well-known first verse testifies of the miracle of creation that God created through his Word, the premortal Jesus Christ. The second verse relates the worshiper's response to the beauty of creation, the third focuses on the miracle of Jesus' sacrifice for us, and the fourth looks forward to his triumphant return. This hymn, popularized during the evangelical crusades of the Reverend Billy Graham, became a particular favorite of President Ezra Taft Benson. After the hymn was included in the 1985 Latter-day Saint hymnal, President Benson frequently requested that it be sung at meetings over which he presided.[18]

Because of the power of such music to engender feelings of worship and gratitude, musical reflections, particularly on well-loved hymns and folk songs, appear throughout this book to help the reader *feel* to some extent what the original recipients of Jesus' miracles must have experienced.

power of his word man was created of the dust of the earth; and by the power of his word have miracles been wrought?" (Mormon 9:17).

## "And the Word Was Made Flesh"

The Light of the World (Nativity), *by François Boucher.*

The Incarnation was the miracle by which the divine Jehovah became the Babe of Bethlehem. The familiar Christmas story, drawn from Matthew 1–2 and Luke 1–2, provides scriptural testimony of the divine conception and miraculous birth of Jesus. In these Infancy narratives, we learn how the Virgin Mary conceived a child who was literally the Son of God (Matthew 1:20–23; Luke 1:31–35), a miracle confirmed by Book of Mormon testimonies (1 Nephi 11:18–20; Mosiah 3:8; Alma 7:10). The subsequent birth and early years of this promised child were accompanied by miracles, including the angelic annunciation to the shepherds (Luke 2:8–14), the prophetic testimonies of Simeon and Anna (Luke 2:25–38), the shining of the new star that led the Magi to the child (Matthew 2:1–2, 9–11), and the prompting that led to the Holy Family's inspired flight to Egypt (Matthew 2:12–15).[19]

But it is the simple, powerful testimony of the prologue of the Gospel of John that describes the miracle of the Incarnation most directly: "And the Word was made flesh, and dwelt among us" (John 1:14). Thus the Divine Word became the man Jesus, and it was as the incarnate Word—deity only thinly veiled in flesh—that he performed the miracles of his ministry. This true identity of Jesus not only explains the power by which he performed his mighty works but it also is the heart of the symbolism of many of the miracles, particularly those miracles that John in his Gospel calls "signs."

## The Hope, Symbolism, and Promise of Miracles

The Creation and Jesus' birth into mortality formed the foundation for his mortal ministry, which, in turn, led to his atoning suffering, death, and resurrection, the fruits of which constitute even greater miracles than calming a storm or restoring the dead to mortal life.[20] Indeed, reading about the miracles Jesus performed during his mortal ministry plants in us the seeds of hope that we too can be the beneficiaries of similar miracles, miracles that symbolically point to the Atonement, which is the miracle that offers us the greatest eternal promise. As Mormon testified, "And what is it that ye shall

Resurrection (fresco), Chora Church (Kariye Camii), Istanbul, Turkey.

hope for? Behold I say unto you that *ye shall have hope through the atonement of Christ and the power of his resurrection,* to be raised unto life eternal, and this because of your faith in him according to the promise" (Moroni 7:41; emphasis added).

That hope does not always arise, however, if we focus simply on the facts of the miracles and fail to see their symbolism as well. I learned the importance of teaching the symbolism of miracles—and particularly their connection to the Atonement—in one of the first New Testament classes I taught at Brigham Young University. I was excited to teach a course on the Gospels, and I was particularly eager to talk about the early miracles of Jesus. While discussing the healing of the man with palsy who was let down through the roof by his friends (Mark 2:1–12; parallels in Matthew 9:1–8; Luke 5:17–26), I confidently testified to the class that if we had faith, Jesus could and would work similar miracles in our lives. Most of the students nodded in agreement, sharing my conviction and faith. But as I moved on to discuss the next story in Mark, I noticed that a few students seemed downcast, sharing neither our smiles nor, apparently, our hope.

At that moment I realized that the very miracle stories that inspire and encourage many of us can have a much different effect on those for whom such miracles do not seem to come when or how they pray they will. In the next few years, experiences in my own life helped me understand this perspective better. Soon afterwards, as my father lay dying, I had a chance to give him a final blessing. He and

## A God of Miracles

When John the Baptist heard of the works of Jesus Christ, he sent some disciples to Jesus to find out whether he was the one who was promised. Jesus told them, "Go and shew John again those things which ye do hear and see: The blind receive their sight, and the lame walk, the lepers are cleansed, and the deaf hear, the dead are raised up, and the poor have the gospel preached to them" (Matthew 11:4–5; Luke 7:22). This combination of miracles and preaching provided the final confirmation that God was with Jesus and working through him. The book of Acts testifies that after Jesus' ascension into heaven, the Spirit of God fell upon his apostles, who then both preached with power and worked miracles in Christ's name. Yet in the world around us, and sometimes even in our own lives, it seems that such miracles are often lacking.

Book of Mormon prophets testified that the Lord is indeed a God of miracles but warned that miracles cease when faith is wanting. To Nephi the Lord declared, "For behold, I am God; and I am a God of miracles; and I will show unto the world that I am the same yesterday, today, and forever; and *I work not among the children of men save it be according to their faith*" (2 Nephi 27:23; emphasis added). Moroni testified, "And who shall say that Jesus Christ did not do many mighty miracles? And there were many mighty miracles wrought by the hands of the apostles.... And the reason why he ceaseth to do miracles among the children of men is because that they dwindle in unbelief, and depart from the right way, and know not the God in whom they should trust. Behold I say to you that whoso believeth in Christ, doubting nothing, whatsoever he shall ask the Father in the name of Christ it shall be granted him; and this promise is unto all, even unto the ends of the earth" (Mormon 9:18–21; compare Moroni 7:27–29, 37).

Faith in Christ can and will bring healing, strength, and temporal blessings. Yet, although we can be confident of miracles in our own lives, we must remember that the Lord answers our prayers in his own way and in his own time. While we can and should hope for miracles now, we must always look beyond the immediacy of mortality to remember that the greatest miracles we can hope for are those that lead us to eternal life (Moroni 7:41).

Mother, both survivors of repeated bouts with cancer and other serious illnesses, had seen real miracles in their lives as remission, healing, and strength had been granted to them. But as I laid my hands on Dad's head for one last blessing, the words that came to me were that it was not permitted for him to live longer than his body could sustain life. Likewise, after our son, Samuel, was diagnosed with autism, my wife, Elaine, and I prayed and fasted repeatedly for a miraculous change in his condition. We were full of faith that the Lord could heal and change him. Yet in this instance, too, the words that came into my mind as I gave him repeated blessings were not what we had hoped and prayed for.

In neither of these personal examples were miracles lacking. Just three days after I voiced that final blessing upon my father, Dad passed easily and comfortably in accordance with promises made in that blessing. Similarly, Elaine and I have seen true miracles in our son's life as he has progressed and adapted far beyond any of our expectations (see Appendix B). No less miraculous has been the strength and comfort that I received in both of these situations.

But it was the question that Jesus posed to the scribes on the occasion of his healing the man with palsy that first helped me see Jesus' miracles as something greater than just the wonderful blessings they were to the people originally involved: "Why reason ye these things in your hearts? Whether is it easier to say to the sick of the palsy, Thy sins be forgiven thee; or to say, Arise, and take up thy bed, and walk?" (Mark 2:8–9). As we shall see in more detail in chapter 2, forgiving this man's sins was, in fact, the greater miracle, making the healing of his body a symbol of the greater spiritual healing that comes from the Atonement. Likewise, I have come to see the healings of individuals in the Gospels as types of the greater, complete healing that will come to all through the miracle of the Resurrection, whether partial or complete healing comes to us during mortality. Like the infirmities of millions of others down through time, the autism of our son, Samuel, will be fully and completely healed when he comes forth from the grave immortal and perfected.[21]

## "I Beheld the Lamb of God Going Forth among the Children of Men"

Nephi received a vision of the Lamb of God going forth among the children of men in which were "multitudes of people who were sick, and who were afflicted with all manner of diseases, and with devils and unclean spirits . . . and they were healed by the power of the Lamb of God; and the devils and the

The Sick Waiting for Jesus to Pass By, *by James Tissot.*

The Raising of Jairus' Daughter, *by Vasily Polenov.*

unclean spirits were cast out" (1 Nephi 11:31). In addition to the miracles of healing and deliverance mentioned in this verse, the ministry of Jesus also witnessed miracles of nature, in which Jesus revealed his control over the physical universe and inexplicably provided food or rescue for those in need. In the chapters that follow, we will examine how his power over the elements revealed his divine identity; his healing the sick demonstrated his compassion as it symbolized the healing that comes through his Atonement; casting out of devils was part of his greater mission of liberating those who are enslaved to forces beyond themselves; restoring sight and hearing allowed people to see and hear spiritually as well as physically; and raising the dead pointed to a greater and more eternal kind of life.

Most important, however, Nephi's vision showed how at the end of his mission, Christ would be "lifted up upon the cross and slain for the sins of the world" (1 Nephi 11:31–33). All the miracles in Jesus' ministry thus necessarily led to the culmination of his mission at his Passion. Likewise, King Benjamin's prophecy of Jesus' ministry of miracles was interwoven into a larger testimony of his incarnation, his birth to Mary, and his salvific suffering and rising from the dead (Mosiah 3:5–10).[22] Indeed, these Book of Mormon witnesses make it clear that the miracles in the New Testament Gospels, though real and unbelievable blessings to the individuals involved, were but a foretaste of the greatest miracles of all that come through the redemption and resurrection of the Lord Jesus Christ.

# 1
# POWER OVER THE ELEMENTS

## *Revealing the Divine Identity of Jesus*

*And there arose a great storm of wind, and the waves beat into the ship,
so that it was now full. . . . And he arose, and rebuked the wind, and said unto
the sea, Peace, be still. And the wind ceased, and there was a great calm.*

—Mark 4:37–39

After Jesus miraculously calmed a tempest on the Sea of Galilee, his disciples "feared exceedingly" (Greek, *ephobēthēsan phobon megan;* literally, "feared a great fear") and exclaimed to each other, "What manner of man is this, that even the wind and the sea obey him?" (Mark 4:41). Similarly, on another occasion when they were caught in a storm, Jesus went to rescue his disciples, walking upon the sea. As he approached them, "they were troubled, saying, It is a spirit; and they cried out for fear [Greek, *apo tou phobou*]" (Matthew 14:26). In both instances, *phobos,* or "fear," referred to more than the alarm they experienced in the face of something they could not understand. The Greek word *phobos* can also connote the awe, reverence, and respect felt in the face of a clear manifestation of Jesus' divinity.[1]

These miracles were two of ten recorded deeds Jesus performed that demonstrated his power over water, the wind and waves, fish, bread, trees, and even the nature and appearance of his own body. As a group, these miracles vary considerably among themselves in subject and literary form, leading some to classify them as nature miracles, gift miracles, miracles of provision, rescue miracles, and even one cursing miracle. Because these miracles do not share all the usual features of a

### Stories of Jesus' Power over the Elements

- Water to wine at Cana (John 2:1–11)
- An astonishing catch of fish (Luke 5:1–11)
- Calming the stormy sea (Mark 4:35–41; parallels Matthew 8:23–27; Luke 8:22–25)
- Feeding the five thousand (Mark 6:32–44; John 6:1–15; parallels Matthew 14:13–21; Luke 9:10–17)
- Walking on water (Mark 6:45–52; John 6:16–21; parallel Matthew 14:22–33, with the addition of Peter's attempt)
- Feeding the four thousand (Mark 8:1–9; parallel Matthew 15:32–39)
- The Transfiguration (Mark 9:2–9; parallels Matthew 17:1–9; Luke 9:28–36)
- The temple tax and the fish with a coin in its mouth (Matthew 17:24–27)
- Cursing the fig tree (Mark 11:12–14, 20–26; parallel Matthew 21:18–22)
- An astonishing catch of 153 fish after the Resurrection (John 21:1–14)

*Opposite:* Christ Walking on Water, *by Ivan Aivazovsky.
Courtesy of Bridgeman Art Library. Used by permission.*

14  THE MIRACLES OF JESUS

Christ Stilling the Tempest, by James Tissot.

miracle story and are often attested in only one source or literary form (see Appendix A), many scholars, even those who otherwise accept that Jesus was known historically as a healer and exorcist, question whether these particular miracles occurred.[2] But these miracles are critical for understanding that Jesus was in fact the incarnate Word, who as the divine Word had first created heaven and earth and continues to sustain and nurture it.

Because creation is effectively an act of divine organization, the Being who first created the elements as the premortal Jehovah necessarily has power to control and reorganize those same elements as the man Jesus. But Jesus' absolute power over nature also sets in high relief the difference in his relationships with men and women, whom he allows their agency, and the rest of his creation, which is always obedient to his commands. As Mormon observed, "O how great is the nothingness of the children of men; yea, even they are less than the dust of the earth. For behold, the dust of the earth moveth hither and thither, to the dividing asunder, at the command of our great and everlasting God" (Helaman 12:7–8).

The prologue of the Gospel of John teaches the same thing, observing that the Word "came unto his own [Greek, *ta idia*], and his own [Greek, *hoi idioi*] received him not" (John 1:11). In this verse *ta idia* is neuter plural, referring to "his own things," or physical creation, while *hoi idioi* is masculine plural, referring to his people.[3] This close connection of Jesus with his creation is also intimated at the time of his triumphal entry into Jerusalem, when, in response to the complaints of some of his opponents about his disciples' enthusiasm, Jesus proclaimed, "I tell you that, if these should hold their peace, the stones would immediately cry out" (Luke 19:40).

But these miracles do more than just make clear Jesus' identity as the Creator. They also symbolize more broadly his godhood in other divine roles, making it clear that he was the divine Word made flesh who came to dwell with his people on the earth as a loving shepherd to feed and sustain his people (John 1:14). Some of these miracles, such as his power over storms on the Sea of Galilee and his transfiguration have been described as epiphanies, or direct revelations of this divine identity. But even miracles in which he provided wine or bread involve symbolism that alludes to his Incarnation and divine status. All of these miracles also reveal Jesus' loving character, as he hastens to help others avoid embarrassment, stave off hunger, or escape danger.

## Turning Water into Wine

The Gospel of John specifically identifies the changing of water to wine as "the beginning of miracles [Greek, *sēmeiōn*]" in Jesus' public ministry (John 2:11). Though rendered as "miracles" in the King James Version, the Greek word here actually means "signs." As a sign, this miracle, like other miracles recorded in John's Gospel, is more than simply a powerful or an amazing act: It is, above all, a sign or symbol of a greater truth about Jesus and his message. This truth was understood by his earliest

This Roman Catholic church in the Arab town of Kafr Kannā commemorates the miracle of Jesus turning the water into wine at Cana.

On the altar of the church at Kafr Kannā are six pots, reminiscent of the vessels holding the water Jesus miraculously changed to wine.

disciples, who were present at Cana: The sign "manifested forth his glory; and his disciples believed on him" (John 2:11).[4]

According to the account preserved only in John 2:1–11, Jesus and some of his disciples were invited to a wedding feast in the small Galilean town of Cana, which has been identified with either Khirbet Qânâ, nine miles north of Nazareth, or, more traditionally, with Kafr Kannā, just under four miles to the northeast.[5] During the course of the festivities, the mother of Jesus told him that the wine for the feast had run out, an occurrence that would greatly embarrass the newly married couple and their families. Mary, who is never directly named in John, did not explicitly ask Jesus to intervene, nor did he immediately act to resolve the problem. She did, however, instruct the servants to do whatever Jesus asked, and he directed them to fill six large stone pots with water. He then told them to draw water from the pots and give it to the master of ceremonies. When they did,

*Depicting the miracle at Cana, this Byzantine mosaic is in the Chora Church (Kariye Camii), Istanbul, Turkey.*

the water had inexplicably become fine wine. Jesus' actions, whether motivated by his mother's implied request or his own compassion for the newly married couple, reveal his loving concern and willingness to help, even though his hour had not yet come (John 2:4).

John describes the six large stone water pots involved in the miracle as ones used "after the manner of the purifying of the Jews" (John 2:6). The number six might be significant because it was one short of seven, the number symbolizing to the Jews perfection and completeness. Stone water pots like these, which could not become impure as clay pots could, were necessary for ritual purity (Leviticus 11:32). As a result, traditional interpretations of this miracle see these pots as symbols of the larger Mosaic law and its requirements, which was incomplete until Christ came, suggesting that Jewish purification and sacrificial rituals were being replaced by the atoning blood of Christ. Wine was also a prominent element in prophetic descriptions of the future messianic banquet (Isaiah 25:6; 55:1; Jeremiah 31:12; Joel 2:18–24; 3:18; Amos 9:13–14), so the wine that replaced the water in these pots could symbolize the new, richer blessings of the gospel that Jesus was bringing.[6] Each of the water pots held between 20 and 30 gallons, which meant that somewhere between 120 and 180 gallons of fine wine were produced by the miracle, underscoring the theme of the abundance that Jesus was providing. The fact

POWER OVER THE ELEMENTS    17

Wedding at Cana, by Carl Bloch.

> ### The Symbolism of the Wedding Feast
>
> John does not disclose the identity of the newly married couple at Cana, leading to speculation about who the bride and groom might have actually been.[7] But leaving pivotal characters unnamed is a common literary device in the Gospel of John, one that allows the evangelist to use certain historical figures as important literary types. John never names Mary, for instance. In the two pivotal scenes in which she appears, at the wedding at Cana at the beginning of Jesus' ministry and at the foot of the cross at its end, she is simply called "the mother of Jesus" (John 2:1, 5; 19:25–26). But the best example of using historical figures as literary types is the author himself, who only refers to himself as "the other disciple" (John 18:15–16) or "the disciple whom Jesus loved" (John 13:23; 19:26; 21:7; 21:20). While there may be several reasons for such anonymity, an important result of not naming the beloved disciple is that readers can put themselves in this figure's place. Just as the beloved disciple rested in the bosom of the Jesus at the Last Supper, so can we recline in the arms of his love during the administration of the sacrament. Similarly, as the beloved disciple stood at the foot of the cross or ran and found the empty tomb, so can we obtain our own witness that Jesus died for us and then rose from the grave.
>
> Likewise, the bride and the groom at the wedding at Cana can serve as broader symbols. In Old Testament prophecy, *YHWH* and his people were in a covenant relationship that drew upon marital terminology to describe it. The failure of Israel to be faithful to the Lord, however, left the full realization of that union to the future. Because the Lord's covenant people had separated themselves from him through sin and apostasy, it was necessary that Jehovah come in the flesh to be with his people so that he could reconcile them to himself.
>
> Accordingly, a wedding feast was an appropriate place for Jesus to begin his public ministry, symbolically revealing himself as Jehovah by his first miracle. By changing water into wine, Jesus not only manifested his power as the Creator, he also signaled that he was the Word made flesh so that he could dwell among and with his people. Later in his ministry, he explicitly characterized himself as a bridegroom with his church as the implied bride (Mark 2:19–20; Matthew 9:15; 25:1–10; Luke 5:34–35; John 3:29). After Jesus' ascension, the bridegroom and the bride are again separated for a season, but not surprisingly the book of Revelation speaks of his glorious return in terms of a marriage of the bride and the Lamb (Revelation 21:2, 9; 22:17).

that wine was later used by Jesus at the Last Supper as a symbol of his blood gives the miracle at Cana a sacramental character as well.[8]

Latter-day Saint commentators have tended to focus on the miracle itself—that is, on the actual transformation of water into wine. Jesus' ability to take water and transmute it into a completely different, organic compound demonstrates that he could control matter even on a subatomic level, changing some hydrogen and oxygen, for instance, into carbon and then completely reorganizing these several elements into wine.[9] Elder James E. Talmage wrote: "The act of transmutation whereby water became wine was plainly a miracle, a phenomenon not susceptible of explanation, far less of demonstration, by what we consider the ordinary operation of natural law . . . [yet] miracles cannot be in contravention of natural law, but are wrought through the operation of laws not universally or commonly recognized."[10] Hence Jesus performed this miracle in accord with higher laws and powers that we cannot understand, let alone exercise. Yet Jesus performed the miracle at Cana with the same knowledge and authority that he had used in creating the world, making this miracle a clear sign that he was, in truth, the Creator.

In the wider context of the Gospel of John, however, the changing of water to wine provides yet another symbol of Jesus' divine identity. In this Gospel, water consistently serves as a symbol of spirit, divinity, and eternal life. Blood, which is frequently represented by wine, represents mortality and earthly life. Thus the transformation of water to wine symbolizes the Incarnation, whereby the divine Word, the premortal Jehovah, became the man Jesus, as articulated in the Gospel's prologue: "the Word was made flesh" (John 1:14). The divine conception and miraculous birth by which the Incarnation occurred may help to explain the prominent role of the mother of Jesus at the miracle of Cana. She was the means, as it were, by which the spirit Jehovah became the flesh-and-blood Babe of Bethlehem.[11] Though already divine and the Creator of heaven and earth, the Lord could not be complete and fulfill his atoning work until he became man. So while the disciples clearly would have been impressed by the outward aspects of Jesus' changing water into wine, the glory which they realized and which caused them to believe in him (John 2:11) may have been manifested in the deeper understanding of his identity symbolized by this miraculous sign. Likewise, our faith and trust in Jesus deepens when we realize who he really is and what abundant, rich blessings he can provide for us.

## Calming the Storm and Walking on Water

The divinity of Jesus that the miracle at Cana symbolized was even more clearly demonstrated in those nature miracles that are the clearest examples of epiphanies, or direct revelations of a divine identity.[12] The twin examples of Jesus' calming a storm on the Sea of Galilee and his later walking on that same body of water are striking illustrations of this direct revelation of a divine identity. These incidents employ common Near Eastern symbols of creation, which often involved a deity defeating the unruly powers of chaos as represented by images of stormy seas.[13] More important, however, because the Hebrew Bible credited *YHWH*, or Jehovah, with the ability to subdue the sea and tread upon the face of the waters, these New Testament miracles directly connect Jesus with the Jehovah of the Old Testament.

Mark 4:35–41 gives the earliest account of Jesus stilling a storm and thereby saving his disciples. His account is followed with only some modifications by Matthew (8:23–27) and Luke (8:22–25).[14] The first part of the episode sets the scene by describing the great storm that arose while Jesus and his disciples were in a small boat crossing eastward on the Sea of Galilee. In Mark's Gospel, journeys from the Jewish western side of the sea to the Gentile eastern side are often portrayed as stormy, perhaps symbolizing the initial difficulty of taking the gospel to the Gentiles.

The disciples' terror contrasts with the unperturbed calm of Jesus, who seemingly would have slept

*Remains of this boat, dated to the first century A.D., were found in 1986 near Kibbutz Ginnosar on the Sea of Galilee. Approximately 27 feet long and 7½ feet wide, it provides an idea of what a boat used by Jesus and his disciples might have been like.*

through the storm had his friends not roused him, begging for his aid. In the second part of the story, Jesus, in a moment of divine majesty, "arose, and rebuked [Greek, *epetimēsen*] the wind, and said unto the sea, Peace, be still. And the wind ceased, and there was a great calm" (Mark 4:39). Jesus' direct rebuke of the storm is followed by an implicit reprimand of his disciples. He asks, "Why are ye so fearful? how is it that ye have no faith?" The conclusion of the story relates the reaction of the disciples: "They feared exceedingly, and said one to another, What manner of man is this, that even the wind and the sea obey him?" (Mark 4:41). The common literary motif of *greatness* weaves the miracle story together, emphasizing the *great* storm that occasions the miracle, the *great* calm that ensues, and the *great* fear of the disciples that results.[15]

This repeated emphasis on greatness underscores Jesus' connection with the Old Testament *YHWH* who could cause the flood to recede (Genesis 8:1), divide the Red Sea (Exodus 14:21; Psalm 106:7–11; Isaiah 51:10), and cause storms to arise and to subside (Jonah 1:4, 15–16; Psalm 89:8–10; 93:3–4; 107:25–30). But though God could be the force behind tempests to accomplish his purposes, some storms result from independently acting forces of nature, which since the Fall can be unpredictable, dangerous, and even contrary to his purposes. As a result, the Lord at times must rebuke the waters (Psalm 104:7), even as Jesus rebuked the wind on the Sea of Galilee (Mark 4:39). This circumstance adds an important element to the image of Jesus as Jehovah: whereas he had originally brought order out of chaos as Creator, since the Fall his creation has become prone to disorder, making it necessary for him to reorganize it. This idea of re-creation is, in fact, a type of Jesus' role as the One who would reverse the effects of the Fall, giving us hope that sickness, disability, age, war, other conflicts, and even the death that characterizes mortality will one day be overcome and set right.[16]

Even beyond being an epiphany that reveals the divine identity of Jesus as Creator and Re-Creator,

Christ Asleep during the Tempest, by Eugene Delacroix.

the mighty act of calming the storm can also be characterized as a rescue miracle.[17] Indeed, in Matthew's version, the disciples cry out, "Lord, *save* [Greek, *sōson*] us: we perish" (Matthew 8:25; emphasis added). Just as the sailors on the ship to Tarshish had to rouse a sleeping Jonah to pray for the Lord to end the storm that threatened them, so Jesus slumbered during the Galilee storm, untroubled, and apparently not in any danger from such a temporal tempest.[18] But whereas Jonah prayed to the Lord, asking him to calm the tempest, Jesus himself rebukes the storm and brings peace. The original audience Mark addressed is generally understood to have consisted of a small, persecuted Christian community in and around Rome.[19] They would have compared their own trials and struggles to being caught in a dangerous storm. They, like the original disciples on the boat with Jesus, might have had a crisis of faith as they waited for the Lord to rescue them but would have taken heart that he would, in fact, save them in time.[20] This is the point at which readers and believers today can find modern application: just as *YHWH* could rescue his people from actual storms on the sea and convey them safely to their port (Psalm 107:23–30), when storms of life arise for us, Jesus will save us if we have faith and will call upon him. Beyond that, the use of the word *save* (Greek, *sōzō*) also connects Jesus' miracle here to the deeper, spiritual salvation that comes through the Atonement.[21]

These same elements appear the second time we are told that Jesus mastered the sea and calmed a storm, but in the story of Jesus walking on the water to rescue his disciples, Jesus' divinity was even more evident (Mark 6:45–52; Matthew 14:22–33; John 6:16–21). Once again, it appears that Mark preserved perhaps the earliest record of this miracle and that his account was followed, and in some points augmented, by Matthew. Although Luke does not include this miracle story,[22] John does. Seemingly from a tradition independent of Mark's, this miracle is recounted in John's Gospel as its fifth miraculous sign. This attestation in two different sources, Mark and John, provides this miracle of Jesus walking on the sea with an even stronger claim to historicity than the earlier story of Jesus' calming the storm recorded in Mark 4:35–41.[23] In both versions, the story begins with the disciples alone on the sea: Jesus had sent them to cross the lake ahead of him, and in the middle of the night a storm arose and made their progress across the lake difficult. In the fourth watch of the night, which would have been between 3:00 and 6:00 A.M., Jesus suddenly appeared, walking upon the water. His appearance frightened the disciples, but after identifying himself

Christ Walking on the Sea, *by James Tissot.*

## "Master, the Tempest Is Raging"

Mary Ann Baker (1831–1921), the author of the well-known hymn "Master, the Tempest Is Raging," about Jesus calming the stormy sea, was buffeted by many storms in her own life. Left an orphan at a young age by the death of her parents, she, together with her sister and brother, were forced to make a life for themselves. Not long afterward, her brother died of tuberculosis, the same disease that had claimed her parents. She later wrote that this series of losses led her to question her faith until "the Master's own voice stilled the tempest in my unsanctified heart, and brought it to the calm of deeper faith and a more perfect trust."[24]

After describing the terror that the Lord's disciples must have felt when they were caught up in a sudden storm on the Sea of Galilee, the chorus proclaims that not only the wind and the waves but also men and devils obey the voice of Christ:

Master, the tempest is raging!
The billows are tossing high!
The sky is o'ershadowed with blackness.
No shelter or help is nigh.
Carest thou not that we perish?
How canst thou lie asleep
When each moment so madly is threat'ning
A grave in the angry deep?

*Chorus*
The winds and the waves shall obey thy will:
Peace, be still.
Whether the wrath of the storm-tossed sea
Or demons or men or whatever it be,
No waters can swallow the ship where lies
The Master of ocean and earth and skies.
They all shall sweetly obey thy will:
Peace, be still; peace, be still.
They all shall sweetly obey thy will:
Peace, peace, be still.

The second verse extends the image of Jesus calming an actual storm to his power to still the metaphoric tempests that arise in our own lives. Finally, the third verse, bringing together Jesus' power over storms, both actual and metaphorical, affirms that he will, at last, convey us to a safe harbor, which is ultimately that heaven where he and God dwell.

Master, with anguish of spirit
I bow in my grief today.
The depths of my sad heart are troubled.
Oh, waken and save, I pray!
Torrents of sin and of anguish
Sweep o'er my sinking soul,
And I perish! I perish! dear Master.
Oh, hasten and take control!

Master, the terror is over.
The elements sweetly rest.
Earth's sun in the calm lake is mirrored,
And heaven's within my breast.
Linger, O blessed Redeemer!
Leave me alone no more,
And with joy I shall make the blest harbor
And rest on the blissful shore.[25]

Saint Peter Attempts to Walk on Water, *by François Boucher.*

and bidding them to not be afraid, he entered their boat. In Mark's account the storm ceased at that moment; in John's Gospel, the boat instantaneously appeared at its destination.

The account of Jesus striding across the water manifests him doing something that no ordinary mortal could do. As with the earlier calming of the sea by his mere command, his mastery of the elements of water and wind here strongly suggests his divinity, but his identification of himself by the statement "It is I" (Mark 6:50; Matthew 14:27; John 6:20) most directly connects him with the Old Testament Jehovah. The phrase "It is I" is a translation of the Greek *egō eimi*, which is itself a translation of the divine name in Hebrew, *'ehyeh 'ašer 'ehyeh*, or "I Am that I Am," by which *YHWH* revealed himself to Moses (Exodus 3:14).[26] This identification of Jesus with Jehovah helps explain the slightly odd reference that when Jesus first appeared, he was "walking upon the sea, and would have *passed by* them" (Mark 6:48; emphasis added). This seems to have been an allusion to two Old Testament epiphanies in which *YHWH* revealed himself first to Moses (Exodus 33:17–23) and later to Elijah (1 Kings 19:11–13), revealing his glory as he *passed by* his prophets.[27] Because of these connections, the revelation of Jesus' divinity by his walking on the Sea of Galilee resonates with powerful Old Testament revelations of Jehovah (Job 9:8; 38:16; Habakkuk 3:15).

Jesus' divinity is thus the focus of this miracle story in both Mark and John. In fact, in contrast to the earlier calming of the storm, the disciples in this second account do not seem to have been in any actual danger; rather, this storm was simply making their crossing slow and difficult. As a result, their fear arose more from the sight of Jesus on the face of the water than it did from the wind and the waves.

Matthew, who largely followed the earlier account preserved in Mark, added an important element, perhaps from his own recollection, which makes this sea miracle a rescue story as well. Matthew 14:28–31 records that Peter, seeing his Lord walking on water, asked whether he could join him. When Jesus bade Peter leave the boat and walk to him, Peter was able at first to walk on the water as well, sinking only when he noticed the strength of the wind whipping up the waves. Crying out to the Lord "save me" (Greek, *sōson me*), Peter was rescued by Jesus, who took his hand and helped him into the boat (Matthew 14:30).

The application to us is clear: When buffeted by the storms of life, we can nonetheless tread the seemingly impossible path of faith. Yet if we take our eyes off Christ or allow ourselves to be distracted by the storms about us, we will sink. Nevertheless, even in moments when our faith may falter, Jesus is still there, ready and able to save us.

## Miracles of Provision

The nature miracles recounted in the Gospels not only emphasize that Jesus is the Creator but also underscore that he sustains and nurtures his creation. In the Hebrew Bible, God is described as providing for both man and beast, giving them plants and fruit for food (Genesis 1:29–30). Similarly, in his own Sermon on the Mount, Jesus affirms that Heavenly Father fed fowls of the air (Matthew 6:25–26). Psalm 104 teaches that *YHWH* provides for the needs of all creation, poetically proclaiming that "he sendeth the springs into the valleys, which run among the hills. They give drink to every beast of the field: the wild asses quench their thirst. . . . He causeth the grass to grow for the cattle, and herb for the service of man: that he may bring forth food out of the earth; *and wine that maketh glad the heart of man,* and oil to make his face to shine, and *bread which strengtheneth man's heart.* . . . These wait all upon thee; that thou mayest give them their meat in due season. That thou givest them they gather: thou openest thine hand, they are filled with good" (Psalm 104:10–11, 14–15, 27–28; emphasis added).

These references to Jehovah's being the source of wine and bread thus serve as models for Jesus' miracles of providing wine and bread during his ministry. Such miracles of provision are often called gift miracles, which are distinguished by two factors from most of Jesus' other miracles. First, while there is an apparent need in each instance, there is no direct request for aid or help, reflecting that the Lord knows that our "heavenly Father knoweth that ye have need of all these things" (Matthew 6:32). Second, the way in which the miracle is actually accomplished is not clearly described, perhaps symbolizing that God's efforts in providing for us often go unrecognized.[28]

The first recorded miracle of provision after the miracle at Cana is the astonishing catch of fish at Capernaum that accompanied the call of Simon Peter, recorded in Luke 5:1–11. *Kfar Naḥûm,* or

Cana, where Jesus turned water into wine, was just north of Nazareth, where he was raised. Capernaum, on the northwestern shore of the Sea of Galilee, became the headquarters of his northern ministry.

Christ Calling Peter and Andrew, *by Harry Anderson.*

"Nahum's village," is not attested in the Old Testament, but this Hasmonean fishing village had become a prosperous town by the first century A.D. and was part of the tetrarchy of Herod Antipas during Jesus' ministry. Near the border of the territory of Philip, brother of Herod Antipas, Capernaum attracted from nearby Bethsaida such fishermen as Simon Peter and Andrew. Capernaum also became the headquarters for much of Jesus' Galilean ministry, so much so that it came to be known as Jesus' hometown (Mark 2:1; Matthew 4:13; 9:1). More miracles are recorded as having happened at Capernaum than at any other single site.[29]

In this story, Jesus entered the boat of Simon, who had been fishing all night without catching anything. After Jesus instructed him to lower his nets one more time, Simon Peter immediately caught so many fish that his nets began to break. He reacted in fear and awe, as did his partners James and John, and when Jesus called upon them to become fishers of men, they forsook everything and followed him. Inasmuch as Simon Peter was a fisherman by trade, Jesus' helping him obtain such a great catch certainly demonstrates that he can help and support each of us in our chosen vocations. Because Peter left his

The Miracle of the Loaves and Fishes, *by Harold Copping.*

*This church at Tabgha, on the north shore of the Sea of Galilee, commemorates the miracle of feeding the five thousand.*

*A Byzantine mosaic from an earlier church at Tabgha depicts two fish with a basket containing five loaves of bread.*

boat and nets, however, this miracle clearly serves a different purpose in Luke's narrative. There the miracle serves as a sign that strengthened Simon's faith so that he could accept his commission and follow Jesus.[30] As becomes more obvious from a similar story in John that is set after Jesus' resurrection (John 21:4–14), the image of catching fish was an important symbol of Peter's apostolic role in gathering disciples to Christ. Still, the very real fact that Jesus could provide fish, which could be used for food or for sale, underscores that he can provide for his own while they are in his service.

When large crowds followed Jesus into a rural area (KJV, "desert place"), Jesus took five loaves of bread and two fish and with them fed more than five thousand people (Mark 6:32–44; John 6:1–14; parallels Matthew 14:13–21; Luke 9:10–17).[31] This astounding feat is the only miracle besides the Resurrection that appears in all four Gospels.[32] None of the Gospels describe how Jesus actually performed this miracle: he simply took the loaves, offered the standard type of blessing offered before eating bread, and had his disciples distribute the bread among the crowds that were present. John's account is alone in noting that these five loaves were made of barley, which connects Jesus' miracle with that of Elisha, who fed one hundred men with twenty barley loaves (John 6:9; compare 2 Kings 4:42–44). After all ate and were satisfied, the disciples gathered twelve baskets of leftover fragments, thereby emphasizing the amount of bread that Jesus had provided.

By tradition the feeding of the five thousand took place at Tabgha, a site northwest of the Sea of Galilee not far from Capernaum, though Luke seems to place the miracle in the vicinity of Bethsaida, just over the upper Jordan River north of the sea (Luke 9:10).[33] Mark 6:34 notes that Jesus had compassion on the hungry crowd there "because they were as sheep not having a shepherd." This phrasing is an allusion to Numbers 27:17, which records Moses' similar observation about the hosts of Israel towards the end of their wilderness wanderings. On that occasion the Lord selected Joshua (Hebrew, *Yəhôšūaʿ*) as

Moses' successor, a detail that becomes significant when we realize that the Greek form of the Hebrew name Joshua is *Iēsous,* or Jesus. Through his allusion to Numbers, Mark invites us to see that just as God, through Moses, had provided manna to feed the Israelites in the wilderness, so on this occasion Jesus, the new Moses, furnished ample bread to those who sought him here on the shores of the Sea of Galilee.

By the time of Jesus, the miracle of manna feeding the children of Israel had become associated with God's giving the law at Sinai, making Jesus' multiplication of the five loaves a symbol of how his gospel fulfilled and expanded the Law, contained in the five books of Moses.[34] The feeding of the five thousand is thus about spiritual as well as physical feeding. Further, the use of actions and words similar to those used by Jesus at the Last Supper connects this miracle with the ordinance of the sacrament, as does the discourse on the bread of life that follows the miracle as it is recounted in John 6:26–59. In this sermon, Jesus teaches that eating this bread symbolized "eating his flesh" and "drinking his blood" (John 6:50–58). These images are more than just anticipations of the sacrament that Jesus would later institute; rather, they teach how we must fully accept the atoning death of Christ by actually internalizing and making it an integral part of our lives.[35]

Mark 8:1–9, followed by Matthew 15:32–39, recounts a second miraculous feeding, this time of four thousand. While some maintain that this story is a variant or doublet of the earlier feeding of five thousand, enough details are different to suggest that Jesus did in fact perform two different miracles. Because Luke records only one miraculous feeding, that of the five thousand, it is possible that his reference to a miraculous multiplication of loaves and fishes in the vicinity of Bethsaida might actually refer to this miracle of feeding the four thousand rather than to the earlier one usually placed at Tabgha. While the feeding of the five thousand took place on the western side of Galilee, which was solidly Jewish territory, Mark places this second feeding on the eastern shore, which, though mixed, was predominately Gentile. This placement might explain the difference in the number of baskets of fragments that were collected at the two different feedings. After the feeding of the five thousand, the disciples gathered twelve baskets (Greek, *kophinōn,* typical Jewish baskets) of fragments, perhaps symbolizing how the apostles were sent forth to gather the twelve tribes of Israel into the Church of Christ. After the feeding of the four thousand, however, they gathered seven baskets (Greek, *spyridas,* a more general term for baskets). Because seven and seventy were numbers sometimes associated with the Gentile nations, the number seven, taken together with the placement in Gentile territory of the second feeding of a multitude, might represent how *all* peoples were called to feast at the table of Christ, accepting the sacrifice of Jesus and being spiritually fed by him.[36]

In both miracles, Jesus was "moved by compassion." The Greek word rendered here as "compassion" is *splanchnizomai,* which means "being stirred in the *splanchna,* or viscera." This word makes Jesus' compassion in these two miracles of provision very close to the Book of Mormon expression "having the bowels of mercy" (Mosiah 15:9; Alma 7:12; 3 Nephi 17:6–7).

Another miracle, the miracle of the fish with a coin in its mouth (Matthew 17:24–27), completes the list of recorded miracles of provision.[37] Like the astonishing catch of fish recorded in Luke, this

## "My Shepherd Will Supply My Need"

The text of "My Shepherd Will Supply My Need," a tender hymn attesting to the Lord's provision and care, was written by Isaac Watts (1674–1748). It was first published in 1719 in a collection of paraphrased scriptures entitled *The Psalms of David Imitated in the Language of the New Testament*. Reformed Christians in England before Watts's time restricted their congregational singing to the exact words of scripture, but the passages did not often lend themselves well to musical settings. Watts's purpose in producing such paraphrases of scripture was to produce more pleasing texts that would not only help singers understand what they were singing but also cause them to be moved more deeply by the lyrics.[38]

The words of Watts's paraphrase are a resetting in common meter of Psalm 23, which begins, "The Lord is my shepherd; I shall not want. He maketh me to lie down in green pastures: he leadeth me beside the still waters." In the first four verses of Watts's rendering, the psalm's original assertion of the Lord's provident care for David becomes even clearer as it is applied more broadly to each of us.

My Shepherd will supply my need:
Jehovah is His Name;
In pastures fresh he makes me feed,
Beside the living stream.

He brings my wandering spirit back
When I forsake his ways;
And leads me for his mercy's sake,
In paths of truth and grace.

When I walk through the shades of death,
Thy presence is my stay;
A word of thy supporting breath
Drives all my fears away.

Thy hand, in spite of all my foes,
Doth still my table spread;
My cup with blessings overflows,
Thine oil anoints my head.

The final verses introduce a new concept, noting how the house of the Lord becomes the home of his Saints, who are no longer guests but children of God in his temple. This sentiment resonates particularly with the story of the temple tax and the fish with a coin in its mouth (Matthew 17:24–27), in which Jesus compares the children of the kingdom to the children given place in the palace of a king.

The sure provisions of my God
Attend me all my days;
O may thy house be mine abode,
And all my work be praise!

There would I find a settled rest,
(While others go and come)
No more a stranger or a guest,
But like a child at home.[39]

Originally set to the hymn tune HOPEWELL, this lovely text about the miracle of God's care has appeared in many arrangements. One familiar to many Latter-day Saints may be Mack Wilberg's 1995 arrangement of this text set to an American folk melody taken from *Southern Harmony*,[40] which beautifully connects Jesus' miracles of provision with the even greater miracle of the heavenly home he is preparing for us.

The Tribute Money, by Massacio.

story, which is recorded only in Matthew, features the apostle Peter. In this episode, collectors of tribute came to Peter and asked whether Jesus paid a religious tribute called in Greek the *didrachma*. Not a political tax to Herod Antipas or even the Roman overlords, the didrachma was the equivalent of the annual half-shekel payment that every Jewish male paid toward the maintenance of the temple in Jerusalem.[41] When Peter asked Jesus about this payment, he replied that only foreigners paid tribute to a king. The king's children, on the other hand, did not. Because the children here represent members of Christ's Church, the implication is that Peter and other followers of Jesus were no longer obligated to pay the annual temple tax; for them, as children of God, the temple was, in effect, their home.

To avoid causing offense, however, Jesus directed Peter to catch a fish and predicted that it would have a piece of money (Greek, *statēr,* a coin worth a full shekel) in its mouth. The coin would be sufficient to pay the temple tax for both of them. This episode does not completely follow the standard miracle story form, because neither the miracle itself nor any reaction to it is recorded. The reader assumes, however, that Peter followed through with Jesus' instructions and found the coin as promised.[42]

This implied miracle story is important in Matthew's narrative because it serves as a segue, or bridge, into the sermon on the Church that follows it (Matthew 18). In that sermon, Jesus instructs Peter and the other disciples on how to handle affairs in the Church, especially relations with and between other children of the kingdom. This sermon thus serves as the conclusion to the miracle story, showing the results of membership in the kingdom obtained by Jesus' paying for our entrance into his Father's house.

## The Transfiguration

While Jesus' power over the elements and his ability to provide for his people revealed him as Creator and Sustainer, the Transfiguration serves as a very different kind of epiphany or revelation of his divine nature. On that occasion, Jesus took Peter, James, and John alone onto a mountain, which traditionally has been identified as Mount Tabor, a conical mountain set by itself that rises above the Jezreel Valley.[43] A location that is perhaps more likely, however, is Mount Hermon, at the northern border of the Holy Land. The highest mountain in the Holy Land, Mount Hermon is near Caesarea Philippi, the last place the synoptic Gospels mention Jesus being before the Transfiguration.[44] Wherever it occurred, however, somewhere on a mountain Jesus miraculously changed the appearance of his own body: "And he was transfigured before them. And his raiment became shining, exceeding white as snow; so as no fuller on earth can white them" (Mark 9:2–3). While the glory that Peter, James, and John witnessed may have been a vision of Jesus' premortal glory as Jehovah, it can also be seen as a foretaste of the splendor that he would have as the risen, glorified Lord, especially when he returns with power to rule upon the earth. John refers to this incident only obliquely, when his prologue declares, "We beheld his glory, the glory as of the only begotten of the Father" (John 1:14). Of the synoptic Gospels, Mark records the earliest and most straightforward account, with Matthew and Luke providing important additional insights.

All three synoptic accounts are prefaced by Jesus' prophecy to his disciples: "For the Son of man shall come in the glory of his Father with his angels; and then he shall reward every man according to his works" (Matthew 16:27; parallels Mark 8:38; Luke 9:26). To that prophecy Jesus added the promise that "there be *some* [Greek, *tines*] standing here, which shall not taste of death, till they see the Son of man coming in his kingdom" (Matthew 16:28; emphasis added; parallels Mark 9:1; Luke 9:27).

Although John's having been translated certainly means that he will be present when the Lord returns (John 21:22–23; 3 Nephi 28:6–8; D&C 7:1–3), *tines* ("some") in the Greek text is masculine plural and therefore must refer to more than one person. Because the description of the Transfiguration

The traditional site of the Transfiguration, Mount Tabor rises beyond the modern village identified with the New Testament site of Nain.

The Church of the Transfiguration on the summit of Mount Tabor.

The Transfiguration of Christ, *by Titian (Tiziano Vecellio).*

immediately follows the promise of "some standing here" not tasting death until the Second Coming, the most likely meaning is that Peter, James, and John were the "some" standing there who saw Jesus' future glory.[45] That suggests that Jesus' miraculous transformation on the Mount of Transfiguration was an advanced revelation of the glory he will have at his second coming.

As soon as Jesus was transformed in front of his three closest disciples, two other persons, Elijah (Greek, *Ēlias;* KJV, "Elias")[46] and Moses, appeared. Then the voice of God himself proclaimed, "This is my beloved Son: hear him" (Mark 9:7).

This testimony of the divine identity of Jesus as the very Son of God is the focus of the account in Mark's Gospel (Mark 9:2–8). The immediate disappearance, in the next verse, of Moses and Elijah, whose personification of the Law and the Prophets represents the twin sources of authority in Judaism, leaves the divine Son as the only source of authority and salvation.[47] As a result, in addition to being a

> ## Foretastes of Future Glory
>
> In the Olivet discourse shortly before his crucifixion, Jesus prophesied about his second coming, saying, "Then shall they see the Son of man coming in the clouds with great power and glory" (Mark 13:26; see also Matthew 24:30). Just as Peter, James, and John received a foretaste of that glory at the Transfiguration, so did other visions of the glorified Jesus reveal to his servants the power that he will wield when he returns to rule and reign upon the earth.
>
> One of these epiphanies was the first vision that John received in the book of Revelation: "And in the midst of the seven candlesticks one like unto the Son of man, clothed with a garment down to the foot, and girt about the paps with a golden girdle. His head and his hairs were white like wool, as white as snow; and his eyes were as a flame of fire; and his feet like unto fine brass, as if they burned in a furnace; and his voice as the sound of many waters. And he had in his right hand seven stars: and out of his mouth went a sharp two-edged sword: and his countenance was as the sun shineth in his strength" (Revelation 1:13–16).
>
> A similar vision was given to Joseph Smith and Oliver Cowdery soon after the dedication of the Kirtland Temple: "We saw the Lord standing upon the breastwork of the pulpit, before us; and under his feet was a paved work of pure gold, in color like amber. His eyes were as a flame of fire; the hair of his head was white like the pure snow; his countenance shone above the brightness of the sun; and his voice was as the sound of the rushing of great waters, even the voice of Jehovah, saying: I am the first and the last; I am he who liveth, I am he who was slain; I am your advocate with the Father" (D&C 110:2–4).
>
> Such visions, preparing us as they do for the Lord's glorious return, remind us that the mission of Jesus Christ is not yet complete. The power that he demonstrated in his mortal ministry of miracles will be fully evident at the great and last day. As Paul wrote, "Then cometh the end, when he shall have delivered up the kingdom to God, even the Father; when he shall have put down all rule and all authority and power. For he must reign, till he hath put all enemies under his feet. The last enemy that shall be destroyed is death" (1 Corinthians 15:24–26).

foretaste of Jesus' future glory, Mark's account of the Transfiguration serves as a powerful witness of Jesus to both his closest disciples and to later readers.

The larger literary context of Matthew's account (Matthew 17:1–8) adds another implicit symbolism of the Transfiguration. In Matthew 16:18, Peter was promised that the Church would be built upon the rock of an apostolic testimony of Christ, a testimony that Peter had just received from the Spirit and which was then sealed by the more sure testimony from the Father at the Transfiguration (Matthew 17:5; 2 Peter 1:17–19). Peter was then promised that he would receive the keys of the kingdom of heaven to bind and loose in heaven and earth (Matthew 16:19). In the chapter following the account of the Transfiguration, Peter and others of the Twelve seem to have already received these keys (Matthew 18:18), making the Transfiguration the most reasonable occasion for Peter, James, and John to have received this authority, which they could afterwards share with the other apostles. Indeed, Joseph Smith taught, "The Savior, Moses, and Elias, gave the keys to Peter, James and John, on the mount, when they were transfigured before him."[48] Further, President Joseph Fielding Smith suggested that at the same time these three apostles received on the mount the endowment and keys associated with temple ordinances.[49]

Luke's account (Luke 9:28–36) adds several more details that connect the Transfiguration directly with the Atonement that Jesus was soon to perform in Jerusalem. Luke 9:28–29 notes that Jesus took Peter, James, and John onto the mountain *to pray,* much as he would take these three with him to Gethsemane while he prayed during the last night of his mortal life (see Mark 14:32–33; Matthew 26:36–37). With this connection in mind, the presence of Moses and Elijah on the mount may be seen as parallel with the appearance of the angel who came to strengthen Jesus in the garden (Luke 22:43).[50] More explicitly, Luke 9:30–31 reveals that Moses and Elijah "appeared in glory, *and spake of his decease which he should accomplish at Jerusalem*" (Luke 9:31; emphasis added). From this passage we can conclude that the Transfiguration also prepared and strengthened Jesus for the Atonement.

The accounts of the Transfiguration can bless and strengthen believers today. We too can gain a testimony that Jesus is in fact the Son of God and gain an assurance that he will come again in glory. As members of his Church, we can receive the blessings of the sealing power and the other ordinances of the temple. But above all, we can know—and be saved by—the reality of Jesus' salvific suffering, death, and resurrection.

## The Fig Tree and the 153 Fish

Not long after the Transfiguration, Jesus concluded his Galilean ministry and began his final journey to Jerusalem (Mark 8:31–10:52; Matthew 19:1–20:34; Luke 13:22–19:28). Although he performed several healings and an exorcism along the way, the number of miracles recorded in the synoptic Gospels noticeably drops off after Jesus arrived in Jerusalem. Particularly in Mark's account, Jesus' ministry in the holy city is characterized by a lack of miracles, perhaps because in that final phase of his earthly mission he needed to descend below all things (D&C 88:6), becoming powerless as he submitted fully to the Father as a sacrifice for sin and death.[51] As a result, only two nature miracles are recorded after the Transfiguration. One is the curious cursing of the fig tree on the Mount of Olives, and the other is the miraculous catch of 153 fish, which occurs in a postresurrection appearance on the shore of the Sea of Galilee.

Although punitive miracles occur in the Old Testament (see, for example, Exodus 7–14; Deuteronomy 6:22; 2 Kings 2:24) and even in the New Testament (Acts 5:1–11), the cursing of the fig tree is the only example of a destructive miracle in the mortal ministry of Jesus. This glaring divergence from the usual pattern of Jesus' actions, let alone the annoyance that the Savior seems to exhibit when he finds the fig tree without fruit, has led some scholars to question its historicity.[52] Nevertheless, both the symbolism of the miracle and the use to which Jesus puts it in teaching his disciples about

The Accursed Fig Tree, by James Tissot.

the power of faith argue for its legitimacy. Matthew puts the cursing of the fig tree and its withering together, which emphasizes the immediacy and power of Jesus' word (Matthew 21:18–19). Mark's account, on the other hand, places the cursing on the morning of Jesus' cleansing of the temple and the effect of the curse on the morning of the next day (Mark 11:12–14, 20–21). This interweaving of one story with another encourages us to use the two stories to interpret each other. As a result, in Mark's account the fig tree and its lack of fruit symbolize that both the temple and the people of Israel were fruitless and worthy of condemnation in Jesus' time.[53] The casting out of the unworthy merchants and the overturning of their tables thus become symbols of the destruction that awaited both the temple and Jerusalem in A.D. 70 at the hands of the Romans. Both accounts point us to a nearly contemporaneous demonstration of Jesus' divine power and to a later demonstration of that power, for the fig tree and its fruitlessness also serve as types of the final destruction of the wicked at the end of the world. The cursing of the fig tree thus reveals Jesus as the One who will be the divine Judge.

The final nature miracle recorded in the Gospels does not happen during Jesus' mortal ministry.

According to John's Gospel, at some point after Jesus' resurrection, he appeared to a group of seven of his disciples who had returned to Galilee, apparently to resume their former work as fishermen (John 21:1–14). The traditional site of this appearance, during which Jesus reaffirmed Peter's position as the first among the apostles is called the Primacy of St. Peter and lies on the northwestern coast of the Sea of Galilee. It is very near Tabgha, the site traditionally considered that of the miracle of the feeding of the five thousand, and not far from Capernaum, where Peter was first called.[54] There, in a story similar in many ways to the story in Luke 5:1–11 of an astonishing catch of fish,[55] the disciples toiled all night and caught nothing. Jesus, who at first was not recognized by any of the men, appeared on the shore and told them to cast their nets on the right side of the boat. When they did, they were unable to draw in the amazing catch. The miracles of the fish recorded in John and in Luke share the symbolism of discipleship and missionary labor, but there are some important details that differ.

In Luke's account, the new disciple Peter is called to follow Jesus in a ministry of gathering his elect, but at that point both the mission and the man are imperfect. When Peter is first called, his nets break and the boats begin to sink (Luke 5:6–7). In the Galilean ministry that follows, many who are gathered into the gospel net stumble and are lost (see, for example, John 6:60–66). Peter

*The waterfront below the traditional site of the Primacy of St. Peter on the Sea of Galilee evokes the scene of Jesus' post-resurrection appearance to some of the disciples, in which Jesus reiterated Peter's calling as the first apostle.*

POWER OVER THE ELEMENTS  39

The Franciscan Church of the Primacy of St. Peter on the shores of the Sea of Galilee.

Before the altar inside the church is a large rock claimed to be the Mensa Christi, or table of Christ, on which he served a meal of fish to his disciples.

himself falters at the time of Jesus' arrest, apparently denying for a time his association with the Lord (Mark 14:66–72; Matthew 26:69–75; Luke 22:54–62; John 18:17–27).[56] But as a newly recommitted disciple of the risen Lord at the time of the second miracle of the fish, Peter never turns back, which is perhaps symbolized by the fact that this time the nets do not break and the disciples are able to take all of the fish, carefully numbered to the exact sum of 153, to the shore and present them to the resurrected Jesus (John 21:8–11).[57]

This miracle symbolically has Peter and the other disciples take their catch of souls to the risen Lord, who accepts them and receives his servants into his presence for what may be a type of a messianic banquet as they proceed to share a meal that Jesus has provided them (John 21:12). Thus from the first nature miracle, the changing of water to wine at Cana, to the last, the astonishing catch of 153 fish, Jesus is revealed as the incarnate Word; the Creator of the world; its sustainer and the one who provides for his people; the future Judge; and, finally, the divine Master who will welcome his faithful servants into his kingdom. As we recognize these aspects of our Savior's identity and mission, we open ourselves to receive all the miracles that he can and will perform for us.

# 2
# HEALING THE SICK
## *He Had Compassion on Them*

*And Jesus went forth, and saw a great multitude, and was moved with compassion toward them, and he healed their sick.*

—Matthew 14:14

Not counting instances of restoring sight to the blind and hearing to the deaf, which are treated separately in chapter 4, the New Testament Gospels record twelve discrete stories of Jesus healing individuals. In addition, the synoptic Gospels provide eleven summaries of Jesus healing groups of people, and as recorded in Matthew 11:2–6 and Luke 7:18–23, Jesus himself spoke of his healing activities to emissaries from John the Baptist (see Appendix A). From these statistics alone, it is clear that historically Jesus had a reputation as a healer, with healings of the sick and afflicted constituting the most common type of miracle attested in the New Testament Gospels. Indeed, the number and variety of sources for Jesus' healings has persuaded even scholars who look at the biblical record from solely a historical perspective that the case for these particular miracles is quite strong.[1]

Jesus' restoring health to the sick and ability to the crippled, together with his

### Healings of Jesus

- Royal official's son (John 4:46–54; compare with the account of the centurion's servant)
- Simon Peter's mother-in-law (Mark 1:29–31; parallels Matthew 8:14–15; Luke 4:38–39)
- Cleansing a leper (Mark 1:40–45; parallels Matthew 8:1–4; Luke 5:12–15)
- Centurion's servant (Matthew 8:5–13; parallel Luke 7:1–10; compare with the account of the royal official's son)
- Paralytic forgiven and healed (Mark 2:1–12; parallels Matthew 9:1–8; Luke 5:17–26)
- Man at the Pool of Bethesda (John 5:5–16)
- Man with the withered hand (Mark 3:1–6; parallels Matthew 12:9–14; Luke 6:6–11)
- Woman with a hemorrhage (Mark 5:25–34; parallels Matthew 9:20–22; Luke 8:43–48)
- Bent woman (Luke 13:10–17)
- Man with dropsy (Luke 14:1–6)
- Ten lepers (Luke 17:11–19)
- Servant of the high priest, whose ear had been severed (Luke 22:50–51)

Summaries of Jesus' healings are found in Mark 1:32–34 (parallels Matthew 8:16–17; Luke 4:40–41); 3:7–12 (Matthew 12:15–16; Luke 6:17–19); 6:2, 5 (Matthew 13:54, 58); 6:53–56 (Matthew 14:34–36); Matthew 4:23–25; 9:35; 14:13–14 (Luke 9:10–11; John 6:2); 15:29–31; 19:1–2; 21:14; and Luke 8:2. Jesus' account to disciples of John the Baptist of his work as a healer is found in Matthew 11:2–6 and Luke 7:18–23.

*Opposite: Jesus Heals the Crippled, by Yongsung Kim (http://www.taemen.co.kr/). Used by permission.*

He Did No Miracles but He Healed Them, *by James Tissot.*

The Healing of the Officer's Son, *by James Tissot.*

cleansing individuals of the scourge of leprosy, were great blessings for those who were healed. But they have even greater significance in what they symbolized about his larger mission—how he had come to heal, strengthen, and purify us. The Gospels attest that on occasion Jesus would forgive sins even as he healed the body, revealing that his mission was ultimately about saving us from sin. This larger mission is seen particularly when those being helped expressed faith or when Jesus sent them away, noting that their faith had "saved" them. Accordingly, these healing miracles are as much about spiritual healing as they are physical healing. They also reveal a vital aspect of Jesus' character: the evangelists are frequently explicit that Jesus healed because he had compassion for those who were suffering, regardless of whether they asked for help or ever expressed faith.

As is the case with so many of Jesus' miracles, those healed or otherwise blessed are rarely named, and often other details, such as where the miracles took place and even the specifics of the illness or condition, are left out.[2] This feature of miracle stories has two results. First, the absence of such particulars focuses more attention on Jesus and the power he exercises. Second, by refraining from focusing on the specific individuals helped, the miracles remain more general types, allowing readers to put themselves in the place of those to whom Jesus ministered. By seeing these miracles as symbols of all that he can do for us, modern believers gain greater trust and confidence in the love of Jesus, as well as his ability to heal us, physically and spiritually, today.

## The Royal Official's Son and the Centurion's Servant

According to John, the second miraculous "sign" (Greek, *sēmeiōn*) that Jesus performed was the healing of the son of a royal official (John 4:46–54; Greek, *basilikos;* KJV, "nobleman"). Returning from

Jerusalem by way of Samaria, Jesus went again to Cana, where the royal official met him. Because this Cana is in Galilee, the nobleman was probably an official of Herod Antipas and thus probably Jewish, though not necessarily observant. When the official met Jesus and asked that He heal his son, who was close to death, Jesus warned him against seeking "signs and wonders" (Greek, *sēmeia kai terata*), meaning portents or impressive manifestations designed to cause belief. The royal official did not ask for such a sign; rather he simply asked that Jesus go to his home to see what he could do for his son. The man's persistence led Jesus not only to agree to help him but also to announce that his son was alive—that is, that he had been healed. Returning to his home at Capernaum, which was not far from Tiberias, the new capital of Herod Antipas, the father found that the boy's fever had broken at the very moment Jesus had told him his son would live, which led the nobleman and his entire household to believe in Him.

That the nobleman went to Jesus already believing that He could heal his son suggests that this was not literally the second miracle Jesus performed in his ministry. Clearly the nobleman had heard about or perhaps witnessed other mighty works that Jesus had performed. But in John's Gospel, this miracle of healing is simply the second *sign* that John has elected to narrate in some detail.[3] Because in the Gospel of John signs are more about revealing something about Jesus than they are accounts of miraculous acts themselves, with this second sign, John moves us from the understanding of Jesus given by the first sign to a deeper understanding of the Lord's identity. The first sign taught that Jesus was both the Creator and the incarnate Word. The second sign adds the understanding that Jesus was also the ultimate Healer. John underscores the connection between these two signs by beginning the story by noting that the royal official met Jesus in "Cana of Galilee, where he made the water wine" (John 4:46).

Bearing in mind the connections between the Creation and healing, sickness can be viewed as a type of the Fall, by which the original, perfect Creation became subject to all kinds of imperfection, especially mortality with its attendant problems of illness, age, disability, and eventually death. As a

*This dirt road through the hills, above the Sea of Galilee (left), is reminiscent of the road on which the royal official would have traveled as he hurried from Capernaum to Cana through the hills seen here at Karnei Hattin (right).*

result, the divine Word who originally created, or organized, the world is also the one who can, as the incarnate Word, reorganize it, or set it back in order. This symbolism makes healing miracles powerful symbols of the atoning mission of Jesus Christ. Accordingly, when Jesus responded to the official by saying, "Go thy way; thy son *liveth* [Greek, *zē*]" (John 4:50; emphasis added), the use of the word "liveth" rather than "is healed" may be significant. It may, in fact, intimate that this miracle is about something much greater than simply restoring good health: the Gospel of John frequently uses the concept of having life to also mean obtaining the eternal life that Jesus came to bring.[4]

Christ Heals the Centurion's Servant, *by Sevastiano Ricci.*

Jesus healed the royal official's son when He was far away from the boy. A similar encounter that involved Jesus healing at a distance is the story of the centurion's servant (Matthew 8:5–13; Luke 7:1–10). In fact, the similarities have led some to suggest that John's account of the royal official's son and the story of an army officer's servant are different versions of the same event.[5] The Greek word translated as "servant" (*pais*) in Matthew and Luke can mean either "servant" or "child," in which case the person healed could have been a child, both in the story of the nobleman's son and in the story of the centurion's servant. On the other hand, the Greek terms for royal official (*basilikos*), which was an administrative post, and centurion (*hekatonarchos*), a military position, are clearly different. Further, although the military officer probably worked for Herod Antipas and may not have been an actual Roman centurion, he is nonetheless presented as a Gentile, who was apparently posted in Capernaum in charge of Herod Antipas's police there.[6] The foreign identity of the military officer is established in his subsequent dialogue with Jesus. When the officer declined Jesus' offer to go to his house to heal his servant and bade Jesus to simply "speak the word only, and my servant shall be healed," Jesus responded approvingly, saying, "Verily I say unto you, I have not found so great faith, no, *not in Israel.* And I say unto you, That *many shall come from the east and west,* and shall sit down with Abraham, and Isaac, and Jacob, in the kingdom of heaven" (Matthew 8:8, 10–11; emphasis added).

As a result, if the stories of the royal official and the centurion are taken as separate episodes, they provide parallel examples of Jesus helping both a Jew and a Gentile, showing his love and gift of healing extended to each. Yet the two men acquired their faith and showed it differently. The royal official's

> ### "There Is a Balm in Gilead"
>
> Jesus' ability to heal was anticipated by an ancient liniment or salve that was famous in the ancient world for its healing and comforting properties. It was made from the gum of a bush called *Commiphora opobalsamum*, which was particularly plentiful in Gilead, an area in the modern kingdom of Jordan. The balm of Gilead is mentioned several times in the Bible, most famously in Jeremiah 8:22, which asks, "Is there no balm in Gilead; is there no physician there? why then is not the health of the daughter of my people recovered?"
>
> This balm of Gilead became the subject of what is known historically as a Negro spiritual, a musical form that was popularized for wider audiences after the Civil War by the Fisk Jubilee Singers of Fisk University in Nashville, Tennessee.[7] "There Is a Balm in Gilead" illustrates the healing power of Jesus for each one of us even as it, and other spirituals, preserve the struggles, pain, faith, and hope of untold numbers of oppressed African-Americans who yearned for their Savior to make them whole.
>
>> There is a balm in Gilead, to make the wounded whole;
>> There is a balm in Gilead, to heal the sin sick soul.
>>
>> Sometimes I feel discouraged, and think my work's in vain,
>> But then the Holy Spirit revives my soul again.
>>
>> If you can't preach like Peter, if you can't pray like Paul,
>> Just tell the love of Jesus, and say He died for all.[8]

belief grew *after* his son's healing, whereas the centurion expressed solid faith even *before* Jesus performed the miracle. Nevertheless, both stories employ the motif of healing at a distance, which teaches us that Jesus Christ does not need to be physically present to heal us or for us to benefit from the fruits of his Atonement. Though perhaps far away at the moment, his power can still be felt in our lives now.

## Cleansing Leprosy

An early miracle recorded in the synoptic Gospels is the cleansing of a leper (Mark 1:40–45; parallels Matthew 8:1–4; Luke 5:12–15). Leprosy in the biblical world was not necessarily the disease known today as Hansen's disease; rather, the term *leprosy* was a catch-all description for a spectrum of conditions that affected a person's skin or even clothing and dwellings (Leviticus 13). Though some cases may have involved considerable deformity and sickness, every instance of biblical leprosy, however minor, had significant ritual, and hence social, implications because the sufferer was excluded from religious life and often even the company of others. Hence, the leper who first approached Jesus needed help and attention beyond simply being healed of his disease.

The earliest version of the story, preserved by Mark, has textual problems that might raise questions about how to interpret aspects of the story,[9] but in all three synoptic Gospels it is clear that the leper broke social conventions in his desperate attempt to get help. Regulations governing those suffering from leprosy required that they keep distant from those who were not afflicted, but this man walked right up to Jesus and boldly, or perhaps despairingly, entreated him for help, saying, "If thou wilt, thou canst make me clean" (Mark 1:40).[10] Rather than recoiling from the leper, as many of his contemporaries might well have done, Jesus instead compassionately put forth his hand, touched him, and said, "I will; be thou clean" (Mark 1:41). The man was immediately cleansed from his leprosy, and Jesus helped arrange for his social reintegration by directing him to go through the steps mandated by the law of Moses (Mark 1:44; Leviticus 14:1–32).[11] The prophet Elisha's healing the Syrian Naaman of leprosy is clearly a precedent for Jesus' act here (2 Kings 5:10–14), but Jesus' miracle is more direct, more immediate, and, consequently, more powerful.

Reinforcing this assertion of Jesus' power, Luke preserves an account of Jesus healing ten other lepers (Luke 17:11–19), which illustrates Jesus' superiority to Elisha, who had healed only one leper. Luke places this miracle late in Jesus' ministry, when he was traveling to Jerusalem for the final week of his mortal mission. He encountered ten lepers, but these men, unlike the first leper he had healed, "stood afar off," keeping the conventionally required distance between the unclean and the clean. When the lepers pleaded for mercy, Jesus instructed them to show themselves to a priest. As they were traveling, they were miraculously cleansed of their leprosy, making this another instance of Jesus healing at a distance. Of the ten, only one, who happened to be a Samaritan, glorified God and returned to thank Jesus, leading Jesus to commend him. Significantly, when Jesus says, "Arise, go thy way: thy faith *hath made thee whole*" (Luke 17:19; emphasis added), the phrase translated here as "hath made thee whole" is in Greek *sesōken se,* which means "has saved you."[12] All ten were cleansed (Greek, *ekatharisthēsan*) and healed (Greek, *iathē*) (Luke 17:14–15), but only the one who expressed gratitude was saved.[13] As

Healing of the Lepers at Capernaum, *by James Tissot.*

Christ among the Lepers, *by J. Kirk Richards.*

one of several instances when a healing of Jesus is described not only in terms of the miraculous cure of a disease but also in the broader terms of salvation, the saving of the grateful Samaritan leper suggests a deeper, spiritual healing.

In addition to these specific cases of Jesus curing lepers and making them clean, Jesus mentions this kind of healing when he instructs envoys from John the Baptist to report to the prophet that "the blind receive their sight, and the lame walk, *the lepers are cleansed,* and the deaf hear, the dead are

> ### Leprosy in the Bible
>
> Modern portrayals of leprosy in biblical movies often stress the horror of the condition, noting the disfigurement it caused in the victim and the revulsion it aroused in others. These depictions are based upon the characteristics of the better-known Hansen's disease, which is caused by a bacteria that primarily attacks the nerves and the mucosa of the respiratory tract, though skin lesions are the chief external sign of the illness. Secondary infections lead to the disfigurement, including loss of extremities.
>
> Although the Hebrew *ṣāra'aṯ* is commonly translated as "leprosy" in the Old Testament, the term refers to a collection of conditions that affected human skin, clothing, and even the walls of houses. Rather than matching the symptoms of Hansen's disease, the descriptions of *ṣāra'aṯ* in Leviticus 13–14 seem to suggest a range of flaky and scaly skin conditions such as psoriasis, eczema, or certain fungal infections of humans and mildew or mold of clothing or homes. Under the Mosaic system, more detrimental than any physical aspects of the condition was the ritual uncleanliness that *ṣāra'aṯ* brought, which separated the sufferer from participating in religious life as well as in the wider community.
>
> The Septuagint, or Greek translation of the Hebrew Bible, regularly translated Hebrew *ṣāra'aṯ* with the Greek *lepra*, which describes a similar set of skin conditions. As a result, many scholars maintain that the leprosy described in the New Testament was the same condition as that described in Leviticus—not as horrific and disfiguring as Hansen's disease but still entailing significant social and religious restrictions.
>
> Nevertheless, an ancient version of Hansen's disease is attested in India as early as the sixth century before Christ. Soldiers of Alexander the Great returning from India might have brought the disease to the Near East, where the Greeks gave it the name *elephantiasis* (not to be confused with another condition, called tropical elephantiasis, which is caused by a parasitic worm).[14]
>
> In 2009 the remains of a first-century corpse found in a tomb outside the Old City of Jerusalem revealed the earliest proven case of Hansen's disease.[15] While Greek authors were generally careful to distinguish between *lepra* and *elephantiasis*, it is possible that in Judea this new disease might have been subsumed under the broader umbrella of "leprosy."[16] It is possible, then, that some of the lepers Jesus cleansed might have been suffering from Hansen's disease after all.

raised up, and the poor have the gospel preached to them" (Matthew 11:5; parallel Luke 7:22). The expression "lepers are cleansed" points to the greater symbolic significance of healing leprosy. None of these lepers is named, allowing the cleansing of lepers to serve as a powerful type of how Jesus makes us clean and pure. Just as biblical leprosy made individuals ritually unclean and unable to join in normal human society, so our fallen state and especially our willful sins make us spiritually unclean and unworthy to enter the presence of God (see, for instance, 1 Nephi 10:21; 15:34; Alma 7:21; 11:37; 40:26). In this regard, Luke's example of the Samaritan leper is of particular importance. Two great miracle-working prophets, Moses and Elisha, both cured leprosy (Numbers 12:10–15; 2 Kings

Christ among the Lepers, by J. Kirk Richards.

one of several instances when a healing of Jesus is described not only in terms of the miraculous cure of a disease but also in the broader terms of salvation, the saving of the grateful Samaritan leper suggests a deeper, spiritual healing.

In addition to these specific cases of Jesus curing lepers and making them clean, Jesus mentions this kind of healing when he instructs envoys from John the Baptist to report to the prophet that "the blind receive their sight, and the lame walk, *the lepers are cleansed,* and the deaf hear, the dead are

> ### Leprosy in the Bible
>
> Modern portrayals of leprosy in biblical movies often stress the horror of the condition, noting the disfigurement it caused in the victim and the revulsion it aroused in others. These depictions are based upon the characteristics of the better-known Hansen's disease, which is caused by a bacteria that primarily attacks the nerves and the mucosa of the respiratory tract, though skin lesions are the chief external sign of the illness. Secondary infections lead to the disfigurement, including loss of extremities.
>
> Although the Hebrew ṣārāʿat is commonly translated as "leprosy" in the Old Testament, the term refers to a collection of conditions that affected human skin, clothing, and even the walls of houses. Rather than matching the symptoms of Hansen's disease, the descriptions of ṣārāʿat in Leviticus 13–14 seem to suggest a range of flaky and scaly skin conditions such as psoriasis, eczema, or certain fungal infections of humans and mildew or mold of clothing or homes. Under the Mosaic system, more detrimental than any physical aspects of the condition was the ritual uncleanliness that ṣārāʿat brought, which separated the sufferer from participating in religious life as well as in the wider community.
>
> The Septuagint, or Greek translation of the Hebrew Bible, regularly translated Hebrew ṣārāʿat with the Greek lepra, which describes a similar set of skin conditions. As a result, many scholars maintain that the leprosy described in the New Testament was the same condition as that described in Leviticus—not as horrific and disfiguring as Hansen's disease but still entailing significant social and religious restrictions.
>
> Nevertheless, an ancient version of Hansen's disease is attested in India as early as the sixth century before Christ. Soldiers of Alexander the Great returning from India might have brought the disease to the Near East, where the Greeks gave it the name *elephantiasis* (not to be confused with another condition, called tropical elephantiasis, which is caused by a parasitic worm).[14]
>
> In 2009 the remains of a first-century corpse found in a tomb outside the Old City of Jerusalem revealed the earliest proven case of Hansen's disease.[15] While Greek authors were generally careful to distinguish between *lepra* and *elephantiasis*, it is possible that in Judea this new disease might have been subsumed under the broader umbrella of "leprosy."[16] It is possible, then, that some of the lepers Jesus cleansed might have been suffering from Hansen's disease after all.

raised up, and the poor have the gospel preached to them" (Matthew 11:5; parallel Luke 7:22). The expression "lepers are cleansed" points to the greater symbolic significance of healing leprosy. None of these lepers is named, allowing the cleansing of lepers to serve as a powerful type of how Jesus makes us clean and pure. Just as biblical leprosy made individuals ritually unclean and unable to join in normal human society, so our fallen state and especially our willful sins make us spiritually unclean and unworthy to enter the presence of God (see, for instance, 1 Nephi 10:21; 15:34; Alma 7:21; 11:37; 40:26). In this regard, Luke's example of the Samaritan leper is of particular importance. Two great miracle-working prophets, Moses and Elisha, both cured leprosy (Numbers 12:10–15; 2 Kings

5:8–14), but Luke's telling of the story provides a most powerful type: Our faith in Christ not only makes us clean but saves us.

## A Paralytic Forgiven and Healed

Another early miracle, the healing of the paralyzed man at Capernaum (KJV, "one sick of the palsy"), who was lowered through the roof by his friends, appears in all three synoptic Gospels (Mark 2:1–12; Matthew 9:1–8; Luke 5:17–26). The scene is set with Jesus teaching inside a private home, which overflowed with people who came to hear him. The only way that the paralyzed man's friends could get him close to Jesus was to tear open the roof of the house and lower him through the hole. Jesus acknowledged these efforts as a sign of their faith, but before healing the man, he made a pronouncement that provoked contention from some of the Jewish scribes present: "Son, thy sins be forgiven thee" (Mark 2:5). When the scribes began to think to themselves that Jesus' statement was blasphemous, he perceived their thoughts and set the healing of this paralyzed man into a larger, more symbolic setting: "Why reason ye these things in your hearts? Whether is it easier to say to the sick of the palsy, Thy sins be forgiven thee; or to say, Arise, and take up thy bed, and walk? But that ye may know that the Son of man hath power on earth to forgive sins, (he saith to the sick of the palsy,) I say unto thee, Arise, and take up thy bed, and go thy way into thine house" (Mark 2:8–11).

The story of the restoration of the paralyzed man is one of several instances in which Jesus healed those who were crippled, a promise associated with the coming messianic age (Isaiah 35:6). While we know that the story took place in Capernaum, reminding us of the historicity of the event, neither the paralytic nor his friends are named. Thus the emphasis remains on Jesus and his restoring the man's strength, making being crippled a type of the disabilities, impediments, and infirmities that accompany our fallen state. In fact, when the King James Bible teaches that Jesus cured people of their "infirmities," the Greek word is usually *astheneia,* which is often translated as "sickness,

*An aerial view of the site of Capernaum, the town that was the headquarters of Jesus' Galilean mission and where many of his miracles were performed.*

*The historical reconstruction of a first-century house in the Nazareth Historical Village provides an idea of what the house might have looked like in which Jesus healed the man with palsy.*

disease, or infirmity" but literally means "weakness" or "lack of strength."[17] This meaning connects such physical infirmities with the Book of Mormon teaching on weakness—the lack of power to accomplish anything good on our own, which characterizes our mortality. Such weakness can become strength only through grace, or the strengthening and enabling power of Christ's Atonement (Jacob 4:7; Ether 12:27).[18]

Pairing the healing of the paralyzed man with the forgiveness of sins and an emphasis on faith connects it to the Atonement beyond its power to strengthen us and heal us from the effects of the Fall. Many in this period associated sickness or other ailments, such as blindness, with sin (see, for instance, John 9:2).[19] In such cases removing the cause of a disease would also remove its symptoms. But Jesus' opponents focused not on Jesus' extension of forgiveness as a medically therapeutic technique but on his taking a prerogative that

The Palsied Man Let Down through the Roof, *by James Tissot.*

they viewed as belonging solely to God. Beyond making a Godlike pronouncement, Jesus' asking which was harder, forgiving sins or curing paralysis, raised a significant question that we can see as being connected to his Atonement: Which one is, in fact, more difficult? Though curing paralysis with a word seems impossible to us, to actually forgive the man for his sins required that Jesus take upon himself those sins, suffer for them, and die for them.

Perhaps no other miracle of healing is more directly and unambiguously connected to the Atonement of Jesus Christ than is this one. Jesus' directly forgiving the paralyzed man's sins is even more powerful than the spiritual cleansing he provided through the physical cleansing of the lepers. And just as the paralyzed man's friends had exercised faith in taking him to Jesus,[20] so the man himself exercised faith when at the words "Arise, and take up thy bed, and go," he immediately stood up and walked (Mark 2:11). So, too, it takes faith for us to come to Jesus, to allow him to heal our souls and forgive our sins, but so it also takes faith for us to go forward and trust that he has, in truth, paid for our sins and made us clean.

## Medicine and Healing in the Ancient World

Health and sickness are generally seen in the Hebrew Bible as signs of God's blessing or punishment. Indeed, the principal healer is *YHWH* himself, as when he promised that if his people kept his commandments, "I will put none of these diseases upon thee, which I have brought upon the Egyptians: for I am the Lord *that healeth thee*" (Exodus 15:26; emphasis added). Likewise, the Lord declared, "See now that I, even I, am he, and there is no god with me: I kill, and I make alive; I wound, and I heal: neither is there any that can deliver out of my hand" (Deuteronomy 32:39). Perhaps as a result, references to human physicians and medicines in the Old Testament are rare and primarily negative (2 Chronicles 16:12; Job 13:4; Jeremiah 46:11).[21] The best human agents of health were *YHWH*'s representatives, especially prophets such as Moses, Elijah, or Elisha.

In the Greek world, on the other hand, medicine became relatively advanced. Some ancient cultures around Israel—such as the Egyptians and Babylonians—had established medical professions, but the Greeks developed a rational approach to sickness and health based upon careful observation and systematic treatment. Hippocrates (ca. 460–370 B.C.), known as the Father of Medicine, distinguished the practice of medicine from other careers and disciplines and maintained that diseases arose from natural causes, not spiritual ones. He and his school left a significant body of medical writings, known as the Hippocratic Corpus. Still, outside obvious external causes of disease, such as wounds, Greek physicians were left to speculate on the causes of illness. For the greater part of their history, theories about the cause of disease revolved around theories of four bodily humors and how the combination of these wet, dry, hot, and cold fluids inside the body affected health.[22]

Greek medicine and related theories spread throughout the Near East in the Hellenistic period and throughout the rest of the Mediterranean during the Roman Empire. As a result, many Jews at the time of Jesus were aware of Greek medicine and physicians. The woman with the issue of blood, for instance, "had suffered many things of many physicians, and had spent all that she had, and was nothing bettered, but rather grew worse" (Mark 5:26; parallel Luke 8:43). And even Jesus could refer to contemporary medical practitioners with his aphorism, "They that are whole have no need of the physician, but they that are sick" (Mark 2:17; parallels Matthew 9:12; Luke 5:31). Presumably most of those in Galilee and Judea with whom Jesus came in contact would have relied more on traditional home remedies and, when in great need, on the services of recognized healers.[23]

Particularly in regard to traditional healers, we must recognize an important difference in perception and approach between the ancient view of health and sickness and our own understanding. The modern approach focuses on causes and seeks to find *cures* for *diseases*. The most common ancient view focused on symptoms, trying to alleviate *illness* with *healing*, so that "meaning [was] restored to life and the sufferer [was] returned to purposeful living."[24] On the surface, the miracles of Jesus fall into the view of his time: he restored mobility, purity, sight, hearing, and even life so that suffering individuals could return to an active role in their society. But the symbolism of so many of Jesus' miracles also addresses the *cause* of all evil and difficulty—the Fall—by truly curing it through the even greater miracle of the Atonement.

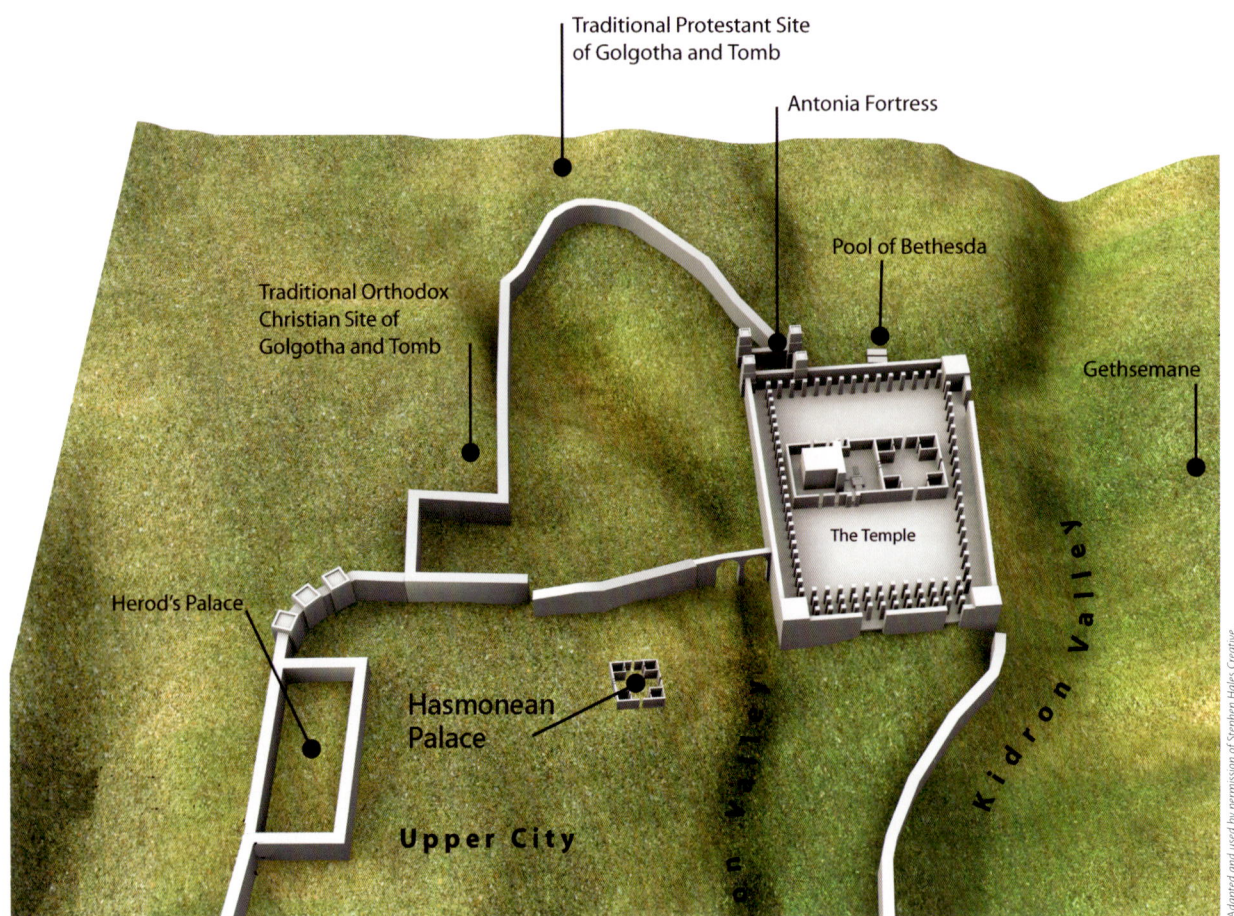

## THE MAN AT THE POOL OF BETHESDA

John records that soon after Jesus arrived in Jerusalem for a festival, he healed a man who had suffered with an infirmity for thirty-eight years (John 5:5–16). This miracle is the third of the seven miraculous signs (*sēmeia*) in that Gospel's narrative, and it combines important symbols from both the first and the second signs. We have suggested that the first sign, the changing of water to wine at Cana, symbolized that the divine Word, or Creator, was made flesh (John 2:1–11). In the second sign, healing the royal official's son at a distance, the incarnate Word healed, or reorganized, even as he had previously organized the world.

That Jesus was in fact divine and thus associated with the Creation is represented in the setting of the scene at a pool north of the temple mount. In the porches surrounding this pool, called Bethesda, or "House of Mercy,"[25] "a great multitude of impotent folk, of blind, halt, withered," had gathered, "waiting for the moving of the water" (John 5:3). Though the details that an angel troubled the water and that only the first person who entered the pool was healed may be later insertions into the text,[26]

> ## Waiting for the Moving of the Waters
>
> When we read the story of the Pool of Bethesda, we naturally focus on the man whom Christ healed. After suffering with his infirmity for thirty-eight years, he was at last restored. But as President Boyd K. Packer noted in a tender general conference address directed to the parents of children who are disabled or otherwise handicapped, many others at the Pool of Bethesda that day were *not* healed. They remained beside the pool, waiting for the moving of the waters.
>
> As the father of a child who suffers from the challenges of autism, I know something of waiting and of dreams postponed. Sometimes knowing that all will be made right in the resurrection is *not* enough. Despair can set in. But miracles come even to those who are not healed when and how we want them to be healed. They come in the form of added strength, deepened faith, and comfort in times of sadness. They come from recognizing precious minds and beautiful spirits in those who are not cured in this life (see Appendix B). They come from the miracle of learning joy in serving those who endure physical challenges of all kinds and taking pleasure in small, simple successes.
>
> To the parents, friends, and other loved ones of the disabled, President Packer taught: "That day of healing will come. Bodies which are deformed and minds that are warped will be made perfect. In the meantime, we must look after those who wait by the Pool of Bethesda. You parents and you families whose lives must be reordered because of a handicapped one, whose resources and time must be devoted to them, are special heroes. You are manifesting the works of God with every thought, with every gesture of tenderness and care you extend to the handicapped loved one. Never mind the tears nor the hours of regret and discouragement; never mind the times when you feel you cannot stand another day of what is required. You are living the principles of the gospel of Jesus Christ in exceptional purity. *And you perfect yourselves in the process.*
>
> "I bear witness of the restoration which will come. Each body and mind will be restored in perfect frame. However long and unfair mortality may seem, however long the suffering and the waiting may be, he has said: 'After that cometh the day of my power; then shall the poor, the lame, and the blind, and the deaf, come in unto the marriage of the Lamb, and partake of the supper of the Lord, prepared for the great day to come. Behold, I, the Lord, have spoken it.' (D&C 58:11–12.)"[27]

the symbol of the moving of the water itself is vital for understanding the symbolism of this miracle. The image of still water that is stirred up resonates with some of the opening lines of the creation story, when "darkness was upon the face of *the deep*. And the Spirit of God *moved upon the face of the waters*" (Genesis 1:2; emphasis added). In this passage the Hebrew creates the image of God's Spirit sweeping across the primeval waters,[28] an image of uncreated chaos that was about to be organized by divine creative effort.

The healing of the infirm man picks up the imagery of the second sign, the healing of the royal official's son (John 4:46–54), in which the sickness of the son can be taken as a type of the effects

Christ at the Pool of Bethesda, *by Bartolomé Esteban Murillo.*

of the Fall, by which the original Creation had been disturbed and was becoming increasingly more disorganized. In the healing of the infirm man, he is specifically said to have been ill for thirty-eight years, which was the period of time that Israel wandered between Kadesh-barnea and Wadi Zereb (Deuteronomy 2:14). This was the time when the rebellion of the children of Israel led to the death of all but two of the original generation.[29] The forty years of wandering in the wilderness also frequently serve as a type of mankind's mortal sojourn on the earth, a representation of our struggle to arrive in heaven, our promised land. The man at the Pool of Bethesda, therefore, can represent all of us in mortality, particularly in our state of rebellion and sin. When Jesus speaks with this invalid, the man complains that he has no one to carry him into the water when it is troubled. But while the man

# HEALING THE SICK   55

*The remains of the Pool of Bethesda can be found today under and around the ruins of early Byzantine and Crusader churches that were built to commemorate Jesus' healing of the man who had been ill for thirty-eight years.*

*This model of the Pool of Bethesda shows the double pool surrounded by colonnades, which created the five porches described in John 5:2.*

has been waiting for someone to take him to the water, Jesus, the Living Water, has come to him. Interestingly, Jesus does not wait for the man to express any faith or to do anything; instead, he simply commands him, "Rise [Greek, *egeire*], take up thy bed, and walk" (John 5:8). The man is immediately healed and begins to walk.

John underscores the connection between the initial Creation and Jesus' re-creation by noting that the healing took place on the Sabbath (John 5:9). In the subsequent discourse on the divine Son (John 5:17–47), Jesus emphasizes his connection to and similarity with the Father in a number of ways. Significantly, when his Jewish opponents go as far as seeking to kill him because he had healed on the Sabbath, Jesus says definitively, "My Father worketh hitherto, and I work" (John 5:17). Whereas the Creation under the direction of the Father had taken six "days," at which point he completed his work and rested on the seventh day (Genesis 2:2), Jesus maintained that his ongoing work of re-creation, or Atonement, had not yet been completed. Indeed, although the major components of his work were accomplished with his own suffering, death, and resurrection, his work will not be completely finished until death is completely conquered with the final resurrection. This truth is anticipated in Jesus' healing words to the man at the Pool of Bethesda: the word "rise" (*egeire*) is also the verb used most commonly in Greek to refer to resurrection.[30]

## Healing Women

In a culture and time that were so male centric, the attention that Jesus paid to women is noteworthy. All four of the Gospels, and especially Luke, contain stories of Jesus healing women, teaching them, including them in his parables, and even allowing them to become part of his ministry. In addition to three individual stories about Jesus healing women, Luke includes a summary that notes how Jesus was accompanied in his Galilean ministry by a group of women "which had been healed of evil spirits and infirmities," including Mary Magdalene, Joanna, Susanna, "and many others, which ministered unto him of their substance" (Luke 8:2–3). All this is particularly striking in the cultural context of the Gospels, in which Jewish men would be wary of interaction and especially any kind of physical contact with women to whom they were not related.[31] That many of these women are not named allows them to serve as types of all women, whom Jesus invites to come to him and be healed.

*The house of Peter, in which Peter's mother-in-law was healed by Jesus, would have been like one of the dozens of other small, first-century houses in Capernaum, the remains of whose foundations may be seen today.*

The first of these stories of women, the curing of Simon Peter's mother-in-law of a dangerous fever in Capernaum (Mark 1:29–31; parallels Matthew 8:14–15; Luke 4:38–39), is one of the first miracles recorded in the synoptic Gospels, occurring early in Mark and Luke. This day, which has been called a "paradigmatic day," a day that seems to have served as a model of Jesus' activities throughout his ministry, was a Sabbath. It was on this Sabbath that he taught in the synagogue, cast out a devil, healed Peter's mother-in-law, and then at sunset healed and cast out devils from a large crowd of needy people (Mark 1:21–34; Matthew 8:14–17; Luke 4:33–41). According to each of the synoptic accounts, upon being healed, Peter's mother-in-law immediately begins "to serve" (Greek, *diēkonei;* KJV, "waited on") those present, presumably serving them a meal and providing for their other needs in a domestic context. Her service, however, might also be intended to illustrate how all women, when they are made whole by Jesus, are called to serve in a broader sense.

The three synoptic Gospels tell this story with subtle differences that emphasize different aspects of what Jesus did on that occasion. According to Mark, when Jesus entered Simon's home, those present told him that his mother-in-law was lying sick with a fever. Without any concern about touching an unrelated woman who might, depending upon the nature of her illness, also have been ritually impure, Jesus raised her up by the hand, whereupon her fever left her. The Greek word Mark uses for "raised," *ēgeiren,* is a form of the same word used in John 5:8, which records that Jesus bade the man at the Pool of Bethesda "to rise." In Mark, too, it may likewise symbolize the eventual final healing that comes to all in the resurrection.[32] In Matthew's account, no one tells Jesus of the woman's sickness; rather, he comes into the house on his own to look for her. When Jesus touches her hand, she rises and

*A mosaic depicting the healing of Peter's mother-in-law, created in the fourteenth century for the Church of the Holy Saviour in Chora (Kariye Camii), Istanbul, Turkey.*

begins to serve Jesus specifically, whereas in the other accounts she served all present. This one-on-one interaction between the woman and Jesus gives this healing story the feel of a call or commission story, suggesting that it is perhaps a metaphor for how women can be called to serve Christ.[33] Luke, on the other hand, heightens the scope of Jesus' healing, noting that the woman's fever was "severe," and rather than having Jesus touch her or raise her from her bed, Luke reports that Jesus stood over her and "rebuked" (Greek, *epitimēsen*) the fever, using the same word with which Jesus reprimanded the storm in Mark 4:39 and with which he also rebuked devils as he cast them out (Mark 1:25; 9:25; Matthew 17:18; Luke 4:35; 9:42). There is no report that faith was expressed by Peter's mother-in-law. Although in Mark and Luke those who asked Jesus to see her presumably felt some confidence that he would be able to help her, her healing is portrayed primarily as an act of compassionate intervention on the part of Jesus.

On the other hand, the woman who suffered from a persistent hemorrhage of some kind (Mark 5:25–34; parallels Matthew 9:20–22; Luke 8:43–48) had such faith that she said to herself, "If I may touch but his clothes, I shall be whole" (Mark 5:28). At the moment she touched the hem of his garment, she was immediately healed. So strong was her faith that Jesus sensed power (Greek, *dynamin*; KJV, "virtue") flow out of him when she touched him (Mark 5:30; Luke 8:46). The word translated

I Shall Be Whole, by Al R. Young.

"power" here is the same one the synoptic Gospels generally use for "miracle." In other words, a miracle seems to have occurred almost entirely because of the woman's faith without the direct volition of Jesus (compare the faith of the brother of Jared, as recorded in Ether 3:6–20). But Jesus did not seem concerned about the woman's touching him, revealing that he was more concerned about her well-being than he was about contemporary Jewish rules about purity. A woman with that kind of affliction would have been socially and religiously marginalized,[34] but rather than rebuke her for possibly defiling him, he instead made her an example of faith, declaring, "Daughter, be of good comfort; thy faith *hath made thee whole* [Greek, *sesōken se*]" (Matthew 9:22; emphasis added). Significantly, in this passage Matthew uses the phrase that means literally "has saved you" (compare Matthew 8:25; 14:30;

## Unseen Illnesses

The illness of the woman with a hemorrhage was not one that many others would easily have been aware of. Although a challenge for her personally and one that may well have weakened her physically, it was by definition a private struggle. But if and when word of her condition circulated, her ritual uncleanliness would have immediately isolated her from most of the people around her and kept her from religious participation. Even if she managed to keep her condition secret, her own feelings about herself, and perhaps her own scruples about religious expectations, might have kept her apart.

In a sense, this woman's plight typifies the situation of so many who endure unseen illnesses, including such physical conditions as chronic pain or sickness that others may not see or empathize with. Even more strikingly, they may be any number of emotional, psychological, or mental challenges that make one feel alone, different, or inadequate and which may cause discomfort or even suspicion in others. Chronic depression and discouragement can even make one feel distant from the Lord.

As Elder Jeffrey R. Holland taught, major depressive disorder (MDD) is not about "bad hair days, tax deadlines, or other discouraging moments we all have." While not always understood by others, chronic depression is a real affliction that restricts one's ability to function fully. In light of this truth, Elder Holland counseled, "If things continue to be debilitating, seek the advice of reputable people with certified training, professional skills, and good values. Be honest with them about your history and your struggles. Prayerfully and responsibly consider the counsel they give and the solutions they prescribe. If you had appendicitis, God would expect you to seek a priesthood blessing *and* get the best medical care available. So too with emotional disorders. Our Father in Heaven expects us to use *all* of the marvelous gifts He has provided in this glorious dispensation." Through both professional help and the blessings of God, Elder Holland continues, "broken minds can be healed just the way broken bones and broken hearts are healed. While God is at work making those repairs, the rest of us can help by being merciful, nonjudgmental, and kind."[35]

*The Woman with an Infirmity of Eighteen Years, by James Tissot.*

To those who suffer from unseen illnesses, the words of the hymn "Lord, I Would Follow Thee" speak directly: "In the quiet heart is hidden / *Sorrow that the eye can't see.*" This same hymn challenges those of us whom the Lord has put into their lives to emulate the Savior in loving and helping them:

> *I would be my brother's keeper*
> *I would learn the healer's art. To the wounded and the weary*
> *I would show a gentle heart. I would be my brother's keeper*
> *Lord, I would follow thee.*[36]

Luke 17:19),[37] reminding us again that such healings are often types of the much greater spiritual healing that comes through Christ.

A third healing of a woman appears only in Luke, in which miracle Jesus helped a woman who was bent over with some crippling disease, perhaps an extreme form of osteoporosis (Luke 13:10–17). Though not exclusive to women, this disease is more common among women, particularly in antiquity when so many women subordinated their nutritional and other needs to their children and husbands.[38] This woman entered the synagogue on the Sabbath, and Jesus, unconcerned about touching a woman to whom he was not related or appearing to work on the Sabbath, laid his hands upon her. Immediately she straightened herself and was healed. Luke notes that she had suffered from this condition for eighteen years, the same amount of time that Israel had been in bondage to their enemies the Moabites, Philistines, and Ammonites (Judges 3:14; 10:8). Jesus preceded this healing by proclaiming, "Woman, thou art *loosed* [Greek, *apolelysai*] from thine infirmity" (Luke 13:12; emphasis added), and the Greek word here means "released, set free, or liberated."[39] As a result, the healing of the infirm woman becomes a symbol of how Jesus liberates us from sickness, from sin, and from oppression. Her response was to glorify God, which Luke describes using the imperfect tense (Greek, *edoxazen*), which suggests that she began and then continued to glorify God. These interwoven ideas of restoration to proper physical form, liberation, and glorifying God make the healing on the Sabbath particularly appropriate, because the Sabbath was not just a day to abstain from work but a day that represented God's finishing his work and pronouncing it good, a weekly recollection of Israel's deliverance from Egypt, and a regular opportunity to praise God.[40]

## Other Healings

The motif of Jesus healing on the Sabbath day—which occurred in the case of the man at the Pool of Bethesda, Peter's mother-in-law, and the bent woman—is also a feature of two other miracle stories. One of them, the healing of the man with a withered hand (Mark 3:1–6; parallel Matthew 12:9–14; Luke 6:6–11), is found in all three of the synoptic Gospels. Before healing the man, Jesus anticipates the argument of his opponents by asking, "Is it lawful to do good on the sabbath days, or to do evil? to save life, or to kill?" (Mark 3:4). In Matthew, he goes further, asking rhetorically, "What man shall there be among you, that shall have one sheep, and if it fall into a pit on the sabbath day, will he not lay hold on it, and lift it out? How much then is a man better than a sheep? Wherefore it is lawful to do well on the sabbath days" (Matthew 12:11–12). In healing the man with a withered hand, Jesus does not touch him or do anything that could be possibly construed as work;[41] he simply tells the man to stretch forth his hand, and as soon as he does, he is healed.

Luke preserves a similar incident later in the ministry, while Jesus was on the road to Jerusalem, when he recounts the healing of the man with dropsy (Luke 14:1–6). While the precise medical condition meant by the term "dropsy" (Greek, *hydrōpikos*) is unknown, it is generally understood to have been a case of severe, painful edema or swelling. Also a case of Jesus healing on the Sabbath, the

HEALING THE SICK  61

The Man with the Withered Hand, *by James Tissot.*

healing of the man with dropsy is somewhat parallel to the story of the man with the withered hand. Luke reports that Jesus asked his observers the same question about saving a donkey or an ox that fell into a pit, a question that Matthew recorded Jesus asking at the earlier incident of healing the man with the withered hand. But in Luke the account of the healing of the man with dropsy follows and balances the story of the bent woman, serving as another example of Luke's use of gender pairs in his text. Taken together, the healing of the bent woman and of the man with dropsy thus illustrates that Jesus helps and saves all, both male and female.[42]

This inclusive approach of Luke, which reflects so well how Jesus himself cared about women, the poor, Gentiles, and others who were marginalized, is also found in the fact that Luke alone of all four

All the City Was Gathered at His Door, by James Tissot.

Gospel writers preserves the healing of the ear of the high priest's servant (Luke 22:50–51).[43] All four record how Peter, in an attempt to protect Jesus, cut off this man's ear as the servant and the rest of the arresting party laid hold of Jesus, but only Luke notes that Jesus healed the man on the spot. While the Gospel of John names the man Malchus (John 18:10), he remains unnamed in Luke, which allows him to serve as a more general type of all those whom Jesus heals. This healing is one of the few miracles reported during the Passion week, and Jesus' immediate helping of a presumed enemy reminds us of his compassionate, forgiving attitude on the cross, when he forgave those who crucified him and dealt kindly with the repentant thief (Luke 23:34, 43). From these stories we can take heart that Jesus will reach out to us and is willing to heal us, even at times when we are rebellious or fighting against him.

In addition to all these discrete stories of Jesus' healings, his report to the disciples of John the Baptist (Matthew 11:2–6; Luke 7:18–23), together with eleven summaries of Jesus healing groups of people (see Appendix A), makes it clear that healing was a significant part of Jesus' ministry. Often, when Jesus saw multitudes who were sick and afflicted, the Gospels are clear that "he was moved with compassion on them [Greek, *esplanchnisthē*]" (Matthew 9:36). And Mark notes a powerful episode when the people "ran through that whole region round about, and began to carry about in beds those that were sick, where they heard he was. And whithersoever he entered, into villages, or cities, or country, they laid the sick in the streets, and besought him that they might touch if it were but the border of his garment: and as many as touched him *were made whole* [Greek, *esōzonto*]" (Mark 6:55–56; emphasis added). As we have seen, the word the King James Version often renders as "made whole" comes from the Greek verb *sōzō,* which means "to save." Thus when we become impatient, complaining that the healing of our own bodily afflictions seems slow in coming, we can remind ourselves of two things. First, the forgiveness of sins and greater spiritual healing that Christ has promised us can come now. And second, all our physical, emotional, psychological, developmental, and other challenges will, in fact, be made right in the resurrection.

# 3
# CASTING OUT DEVILS
## *Liberating the Captives*

*But if I cast out devils by the Spirit of God, then the kingdom of God is come unto you.*

—Matthew 12:28

The Gospels record six stories, together with several summaries and reports, about Jesus' casting out devils, making this the most frequent type of miracle, after healings (see Appendix A).

The act of casting out a devil is commonly called an *exorcism*. This English word comes from the Greek verb *exorkizō*, meaning "command," "compel," or "adjure by an oath," though this verb and its noun form are rarely used in the New Testament (Matthew 26:63; Acts 19:13).[1] Despite reports of demonic possession today, particularly in developing countries,[2] exorcisms are difficult for most modern readers and believers to understand. Many historians and some biblical scholars, in fact, have tried to rationalize exorcism phenomena recorded in the Bible, suggesting that perhaps it was a nonmedical way of explaining mental illness, psychological challenges, or even such physical disorders as epilepsy.[3] Nevertheless, Jesus himself is portrayed as accepting the reality of demonic possession, not just healing those so afflicted but speaking to the demons involved. In addition, the first miracle of the restored Church was the casting out of a devil from Newel Knight in April 1830.[4]

Focusing too much on the exorcisms themselves, however, can overshadow the greater symbolism of Jesus' success in casting out devils. Indeed, the Gospels portray the exorcisms that Jesus performed as part of his larger, successful battle with the power of Satan.[5] One well-respected biblical scholar wrote: "The

### Jesus' Power over Devils

- Capernaum demonic (Mark 1:21–28; parallel Luke 4:33–37)
- Gadarene demonic (Mark 5:1–20; parallels Matthew 8:28–34; Luke 8:26–39)
- Mute demonic (Matthew 9:32–34)
- Blind and mute demonic (Matthew 12:22–23; parallel Luke 11:14)
- Daughter of the Syrophoenician woman (Mark 7:24–30; parallel Matthew 15:21–28)
- Demonic or epileptic boy (Mark 9:14–29; parallels Matthew 17:14–21; Luke 9:37–42)

Summaries of Jesus' exorcisms are found in Mark 1:32–34 (parallels Matthew 8:16–17; Luke 4:40–41); 3:7–12 (Matthew 12:15–16; Luke 6:17–19); Matthew 4:23–25; and Luke 8:2. Reports of them are found in Mark 3:22 (Matthew 9:34); Matthew 11:2–6 (Luke 7:18–23); and 12:24–30 (Luke 11:15–26).

Opposite: The Possessed Man in the Synagogue, by James Tissot. Courtesy of Bridgeman Art Library. Used by permission.

expelling of demons was the infallible sign of the coming of the kingdom. . . . The reason for this is that in the New Testament demonical possession is not so much the result of a league with Satan as an expression of bondage under Satan's dominion."[6] Likewise, wondering how exactly the devil or his minions possess individuals obscures the truth that there are many ways in which Satan misleads us, seeks to control our lives, or otherwise impedes our spiritual progress. His techniques include temptations small and great, addictions, and even discouragement and depression. In this light, one of the few references in the Book of Mormon to Jesus' casting out devils is particularly insightful: "And he shall cast out devils, *or the evil spirits which dwell in the hearts of the children of men*" (Mosiah 3:6; emphasis added). The suggestion here seems to be that casting out devils has as much to do with eliminating any degree of influence or control that the forces of evil seek to exercise over our hearts as it does with healing cases of demonic possession.

*Jesus driving out the unclean spirit. Tenth-century relief in which the demon being cast out is portrayed as a winged spirit emerging from the sufferer's mouth. Hessisches Landesmuseum, Darmstadt, Germany.*

Perhaps the best way to view exorcism in the New Testament Gospels is through the lens of the prophecy of Isaiah that Jesus quoted in the synagogue at Nazareth: "The Spirit of the Lord is upon me, because he hath anointed me to preach the gospel to the poor; he hath sent me to heal the brokenhearted, *to preach deliverance to the captives,* and recovering of sight to the blind, *to set at liberty* them that are bruised, to preach the acceptable year of the Lord" (Luke 4:18–19; emphasis added). The synoptic Gospels present our deliverance from the power of Satan as a two-stage process: it began in the ministry of Jesus as he delivered individuals from the grip of demons and will continue until the end of the world, when the forces of evil will finally be vanquished.[7] Of the three synoptic authors, Luke uses the motif of exorcism the most broadly, applying it not only to cases of demonic possession but even to cases of clearly physical healings, such as when Jesus "rebukes" the fever of Simon Peter's mother-in-law (Luke 4:39) or frees the bent woman from "a spirit of infirmity" (Luke 13:11).[8] It is possible to interpret Luke's usage to mean that for him all the effects of the Fall—sin, death, and even physical ailments—were part of the bondage that Satan has imposed upon mankind. Curiously, the Gospel of John never mentions Jesus' performing exorcisms, though on four occasions opponents of Jesus accuse him of having a demon himself (John 7:20; 8:48, 52; 10:20). Although there may be literary or theological reasons for the absence of exorcisms in the Gospel of John, the best explanation may be that for John the power of Satan was broken by Jesus' sacrificial death on the cross.[9] Thus in the Gospels, including Luke, it is ultimately through the Atonement of Jesus Christ that all captives are liberated from Satan and saved from the effects of the Fall. As Jacob in the Book of Mormon wrote, "O how great the goodness of our God, who prepareth a way for our escape from the grasp of this awful monster; yea, that monster, death and hell, which I call the death of the body, and also the death of the spirit" (2 Nephi 9:10).

### What Demonic Possession Is Not

Some modern commentators have sought to explain cases of demonic possession in the scriptures with physiological, psychological, or mental illnesses that are better understood today than they were in biblical times. According to this view, a person portrayed as suffering at the hands of an evil spirit might actually have been experiencing epileptic seizures or struggling with a psychological illness, such as schizophrenia or dissociative identity disorder. Although it is true that many at the time of Jesus might have wrongly understood such cases as these, we can be confident that the Lord himself understood the difference between a spiritual condition and a physical or mental illness.

What today's believer in scripture must *not* do is wrongly attribute demonic origins to real physiological or psychological conditions, especially when properly diagnosed. Sometimes giving in to certain temptations and making certain life choices can affect our health and allow the adversary to have greater influence over us, and it may well be true that Satan can encourage discouragement and exploit depression. Nephi, for instance, poured out his heart to the Lord, asking why he, like all of us, at times allowed "the evil one [to] have place in my heart to destroy my peace and afflict my soul" (2 Nephi 4:27). But we should never look at another person and assume that his or her struggles are the result of sin or demonic possession. That is particularly true in the case of mental illness.

Regarding that challenge, Elder Alexander B. Morrison of the Seventy wrote: "Among the most painful trials an individual or family can face is that of mental illness. By mental illness I do not mean the temporary social and emotional concerns experienced as part of the normal wear and tear of living. Rather, I mean a disorder that causes mild to severe disturbances in thinking and behavior. If such disturbances are sufficiently severe and of sufficient duration, they may significantly impair a person's ability to cope with life's ordinary demands. These illnesses may even threaten life itself, as in severe depression, or be so debilitating that the sufferer is unable to function effectively.

"Some blame their problem on demonic possession. While there is no doubt that such has occurred, let us take care not to give the devil credit for everything that goes awry in the world! Generally speaking, the mentally ill do not need exorcism; they require treatment from skilled health-care providers and love, care, and support from everyone else."[10]

## Overthrowing the Kingdom of Satan

John presents the changing of water to wine as the first miracle of Jesus' public ministry, but the first miracle recorded in both Mark and Luke is the casting out of a devil from a man in the synagogue at Capernaum (Mark 1:21–28; Luke 8:26–39). Matthew, on the other hand, uses a summary of Jesus' healing all manner of sickness and disease as his first formal miracle (Matthew 4:23) and omits the story of the Capernaum demonic completely. Instead, he moves directly to the healing of Peter's mother-in-law (Matthew 8:14–15), which is the first description of the healing of an individual in that Gospel. For Mark and Luke, however, the placement of the exorcism in Capernaum soon after the story of Jesus' forty days in the wilderness where he was "tempted of Satan" is significant (Mark 1:13; Luke 4:2–13). Having successfully resisted Satan's tests in the desert, Jesus went on the offensive, taking the battle directly to Satan.

Mark begins his account of the Galilean ministry by stating that "Jesus came into Galilee, preaching the gospel [Greek, *euangelion*, or "good news"] of the kingdom of God" (Mark 1:14). Though many Jews of Jesus' time were awaiting a temporal savior who would deliver them politically from Herodian collaborators and militarily from Roman occupiers, Jesus' good news signals that the salvation he brings is on a much more cosmic scale. The kingdom of God itself is bursting into the world, but the actual enemy is Satan and his false kingdom, not any particular political adversary.[11] In that setting, Jesus entered the synagogue at Capernaum, where he astonished those present by teaching with authority. The content of Jesus' teaching on that day, however, is not reported. Rather, Mark, who often emphasizes deeds over teachings, moves

*This monumental synagogue in Capernaum, dated by some archaeologists to the third century and by others to the fourth or even early fifth century, was built considerably after the time of Jesus, but it still affords an opportunity to pilgrims to remember what Jesus did in Capernaum.*

*The black basalt foundation under the partial wall of a, white synagogue might mark the spot of a much earlier synagogue, perhaps even the one visited by Jesus.*

directly to the story of the demonic, which allows him to illustrate Jesus' victorious assault on the kingdom of Satan.

While Jesus was in the synagogue, "a man with an unclean spirit" cried out, asking that Jesus leave him alone but also declaring that he knew that Jesus was, in fact, "the Holy One of God" (Mark 1:23–24). While "unclean spirit" is a standard biblical way of describing a demon or evil spirit, the description also loosely connects this episode with Jesus' subsequent healing of a leper. In both cases, mortals are unclean because of circumstances in mortality, but Jesus can free them from their impurity and prepare them for the presence of God.

The method Jesus employed for casting out the devil was to "rebuke" it (Greek, *epetimēsen*, also meaning "to vanquish" or "to defeat"),[12] telling it to be quiet (Greek, *phimōthēti*; KJV, "hold thy peace") and commanding that it

The Man Possessed of a Devil in the Synagogue, *by James Tissot.*

come out of the afflicted man. The word that Jesus used to silence the demon speaking through the man, however, is not the word usually translated "be quiet." A strong word, perhaps more akin to the verb *muzzle* in this context, *phimoō* also has the connotation of binding and overpowering, indicating that Jesus was in fact subduing the demon as well as silencing him.[13] After the evil spirit had convulsed (Greek, *sparazan*; KJV, "torn") its victim, it cried out and immediately came out of him.

This action caused amazement in all who witnessed the miracle, leading them to exclaim, "What thing is this? what *new doctrine* is this? for *with authority* commandeth he even the unclean spirits, and they do obey him" (Mark 1:27; emphasis added). The authority with which Jesus cast out the devil was no doubt amazing, but because Mark did not relate the details of Jesus' preaching on this occasion, we cannot be certain what the "new doctrine" was. Perhaps, given the context and what had just happened, the new teaching was the good news that the kingdom of God was at hand, which was then illustrated by the new king's driving out the forces of his opponent. Characteristically, the Gospel writer does not name or otherwise identify the man liberated on this occasion. Thus while being freed from demonic oppression was a welcome and wonderful blessing to that individual in particular, this story is as important, or perhaps more important, for what it symbolizes in general about Jesus' power over evil.

Another example of a possible exorcism representing how Jesus frees us from the power of Satan might be found in the case of Mary Magdalene, "out of whom went seven devils" (Luke 8:2; Mark

16:9). One of the more prominent women in the Gospels, she is unusual in being identified, apparently, by the name of her hometown, Magdala,[14] rather than by the name of a father, husband, or son. As is always the case in the Gospels with demonic possession, no direct reason is given for why Mary had been afflicted with seven evil spirits. Despite the later tradition of identifying her, probably wrongly, with the woman who was a sinner (Luke 7:36–50) or the woman taken in adultery (John 8:2–11),[15] there is no reason to assume that she had done anything wrong that made her subject to demonic attack or possession. In fact, the only other detail given in this brief summary is that Mary was one of a larger group of women who began to follow Jesus in his Galilean ministry.[16] All of these "had been healed of evil spirits and infirmities," with Luke making no distinction between the spiritual and the physical ailments they had suffered (Luke 8:2).

It may be that trials from evil spiritual sources are somehow equated in the Gospels with physical

*Left: Magdala road sign.*

*Below: The site of Magdala today.*

## Views of Demons in the Ancient World

Many, if not most, ancient cultures accepted the reality of spiritual powers in and around the physical world perceived by the senses. Some of these powers were beneficent, some were hostile, and some could be either helpful or harmful, depending upon the situation or their own changing inclination. These spiritual powers largely represented the uncertainty that prevailed in a prescientific world, where so many natural phenomena were not understood and yet needed explanation. But throughout much of the Near East, particularly in Sumerian, Akkadian, Assyrian, and Egyptian belief systems, the world was seen as being filled with hostile powers that might inflict suffering and even possess the bodies of their victims.[17]

Although the patriarchs before Moses and many prophets afterwards understood the true origin of man and other spirits, a clear idea of the role and nature of Satan and his followers had been lost when many of the early books of the Old Testament were being transmitted and some of the later ones were being written. As a result, demons are rarely mentioned in the Old Testament, the evil spirit who tormented Saul (1 Samuel 16:14–23; 18:10–11; 19:9–10) being one of the few exceptions. Enigmatic, rare references to figures called in Hebrew šēdîm, usually associated with foreign or false gods (Deuteronomy 32:17; Psalm 106:37; KJV, "devils"), and śə'îrîm, spirits who inhabited ruins (Isaiah 13:21; 34:14; KJV, "satyrs"), have been taken as dim, confused memories of demons.[18] But even the figure of Satan was poorly understood throughout much of the period of the Old Testament. In Hebrew, sātan means "accuser," "adversary," or at times "slanderer," and in most surviving references, his appearance is as HaSātan, "the accuser," the divinely appointed prosecutor working for God in the heavenly court (Job 1–2; Zechariah 3). Only in a text written as late as the fourth century B.C. does the term Satan appear, without the definite article, as a proper name, when Satan is named as the individual spirit who tempts David to sin by taking a census (1 Chronicles 21:1, Chronicles having been written after the Jews' return from the Babylonian exile).

The Persians espoused a heavily dualistic system of belief that featured an ongoing cosmic battle between the forces of light, led by the god Ahura Mazda, and the hosts of darkness, led by the evil deity Angra Mainyu. Some scholars feel that exposure to the Persian system influenced the Jews during the Exile; regardless, Judaism witnessed an explosion of speculation about demons and angels in the intertestamental period. This move was probably encouraged by the repeated subjugation of the Jews to foreign powers during this period, which saw the rise of apocalypticism as an attempt to explain their trials in the context of an ongoing cosmic struggle.[19]

For the Greeks, the term daimōn, from which we get the English word demon, was originally neutral, referring to any unseen spiritual or divine power. As Greek was increasingly used for writing Jewish and other Near Eastern texts, the term came to mean evil spirits, exclusively,[20] and that usage was adopted by New Testament authors.[21]

# 72 ❧ THE MIRACLES OF JESUS

challenges, such as those that come with disease, age, and death. Because of the Fall, we are subject to both, and this may explain the number seven in association with the devils in Mary's case. In Jewish numerology, seven is the number of completion or totality. This number thus suggests that before Jesus came into her life, Mary, like all of us, was completely in the thrall of Satan. But through Jesus, she, and we, can be set free.[22] As Abinadi taught in the Book of Mormon, fallen men and women "are carnal and devilish, *and the devil has power over them;* yea, even that old serpent that did beguile our first parents, which was the cause of their fall; which is the cause of all mankind becoming carnal, sensual, devilish, knowing evil from good, *subjecting themselves to the devil*. Thus all mankind were lost; and behold *they would have been endlessly lost were it not that God redeemed his people* from their lost and fallen state" (Mosiah 16:3–4; emphasis added).

## Casting Out Legion

While the casting out of the demon in Capernaum took place in a Jewish synagogue, the next, and arguably best known, exorcism occurred in a very different setting. The synoptic Gospels report that Jesus and his disciples crossed the Sea of Galilee, where he encountered an entire legion of devils possessing a man who was dwelling among tombs (Mark 5:1–20; Matthew 8:28–34; Luke 8:26–39). Although there is some textual question as to the actual location of this episode,[23] it has usually been associated, especially in the King James Version, with the Greek city of Gadara, and the man possessed by demons is usually called the Gadarene demonic. Though Gadara's territory extended to the southeastern corner of the Sea of Galilee, the city itself was some five miles from the sea, which would be a rather long way for the herd of pigs described in the story to run to their deaths; neither does this stretch of land have steep slopes near the sea, down which swine

*Mary Magdalene, whom Jesus freed from seven devils, came from Magdala, a prosperous fish-processing town between Capernaum and Tiberias, Antipas's capital. On the eastern (Gentile) side of the Sea of Galilee, Jesus cast out the legion of devils from a man who dwelt in tombs near Gergesa, or Gadara, or perhaps even farther south, near Gerasa.*

*The steep hillside down which the swine are believed to have run into the sea.*

*View of the Sea of Galilee from the hillside at Kursi.*

could stampede into the water. Some Greek manuscripts of the Gospels place the event in Gerasa (modern Jerash), a city that was even farther from the sea—thirty-seven miles.[24] As a result, the site of this exorcism has come to be identified with Kursi, a location in the Golan that does have a hillside sloping steeply into the Sea of Galilee, which early Christians venerated as the site of Gergesa, a third name for the location of this miracle, which appears in some Gospel manuscripts.[25] Kursi is about four miles north of the ancient city of Hippos (Susita, in modern Hebrew), which was near the sea. Hippos, Gadara, Gerasa were all cities of the Decapolis, a group of ten cities in eastern Palestine that were culturally more Greek than Semitic. This setting of the exorcism in Gentile territory is important both for the story and its interpretation, because it shows that the power of the devil was a challenge for both Jews and Gentiles and, perhaps more important, that Jesus was the source of liberation for both peoples.[26]

Another difference in the setting between the Capernaum demonic (Jewish) and the so-called Gadarene demonic (Gentile) is that the Jewish episode happened in a synagogue while the Gentile example occurred among tombs. Whereas a synagogue represents sacred space, tombs were, for the Jews, a place of ritual defilement.[27] But just as Jesus neither recoiled at the touch of a leper nor feared being defiled by contact with the woman with an issue of blood, his concern for individuals consistently outweighed any worry about issues of ritual purity. The accounts in Mark and Luke thus agree that Jesus met a man possessed by a demon who lived in the tombs, naked, violent, and unable to be restrained. Curiously, Matthew's account suggests that there were two men in this condition, though this is probably an example of what has been termed "Matthean doubling," in which Matthew sometimes uses two figures in Gospel stories to fulfill the Old Testament requirement for two or more witnesses (Deuteronomy 17:6; 19:15).[28] In any case, the Joseph Smith Translation corrects the figure in Matthew to one.[29]

*The Swine Driven into the Sea*, by James Tissot.

In the exorcism at Capernaum, only one demon was involved, but all three synoptic Gospels agree that multiple demons were present in the case of the Gadarene demonic. Mark and Luke, in fact, suggest as many as six thousand because in their accounts, when Jesus asks their name, they reply, "My name is Legion: for we are many" (Mark 5:9; Luke 8:30). The Roman military division known as a *legio* could include up to six thousand men, though the name "Legion" may not have been intended to represent a precise number. Instead, it likely meant simply a great number and has the important effect of transforming this encounter between Jesus and the minions of Satan into a military engagement. As a result, some scholars have suggested a political interpretation for this episode, seeing Jesus' subsequent delivery of the man as a symbol of a promise of liberation from Roman imperialism.[30] But because the synoptic Gospels portray this as an exorcism, the primary interpretation remains that of a spiritual

> ## Overcoming Addictions
>
> Elder Russell M. Nelson observed: "From an initial experiment thought to be trivial, a vicious cycle may follow. From trial comes a habit. From habit comes dependence. From dependence comes addiction. Its grasp is so gradual. Enslaving shackles of habit are too small to be sensed until they are too strong to be broken. Indeed, drugs are the modern 'mess of pottage' for which souls are sold."[31]
>
> Addiction is a chemical dependency of the brain that is caused both by substance abuse and by repeated behaviors that produce such neurotransmitters as dopamine. As a result, individuals can become addicted to tobacco, alcohol, and drugs and also to overeating, gambling, pornography, sex, compulsive video gaming, and other activities that similarly stimulate the brain. Both substance and behavior addictions result in patterns of tolerance and withdrawal, meaning that the brain needs more of the same stimulation to gain the desired effect and then reacts negatively when the stimulant is removed. Because of the neurochemical aspect of addiction, those who suffer from addictions find it increasingly difficult, even impossible, to control their use of substances or their negative behaviors. They become, quite literally, slaves to their addictions. Such slavery can be the modern equivalent of the demonic possession of ancient times.
>
> Overcoming addiction requires hard work and outside help, whether from family, friends, or support groups. Nor can the need for professional medical intervention be ignored while the brain is weaned off its chemical dependency.[32] And spiritual intervention is likewise crucial. Elder M. Russell Ballard observed: "Medical research describes addiction as 'a disease of the brain.' This is true, but I believe that once Satan has someone in his grasp, it also becomes a disease of the spirit. But no matter what addictive cycle one is caught in, there is always hope.... If anyone who is addicted has a desire to overcome, then there is a way to spiritual freedom—a way to escape from bondage—a way that is proven. It begins with prayer—sincere, fervent, and constant communication with the Creator of our spirits and bodies, our Heavenly Father.... There is hope for the addicted, and this hope comes through the Atonement of the Lord Jesus Christ and by humbling oneself before God, pleading to be freed of the bondage of addiction and offering our whole soul to Him in fervent prayer."[33]

victory over the devil: Jesus has come to vanquish the forces of Satan, just as he will at the end of time, by casting them "into the bottomless pit [Greek, *eis tēn abysson*]" (Revelation 20:1–3, 9–10).

This imagery of Jesus' final victory over the forces of evil may explain one of the most perplexing details of the story. When Jesus first approaches the demonic, the devils cry out, "What have we to do with thee, Jesus, thou Son of God? art thou come hither to torment us before the time?" (Matthew 8:29). This fear of torment no doubt referred to their final defeat and imprisonment at the end of time. This connection is strengthened in the account of Luke, in which the demons beg Jesus "that he would not command them to go out *into the deep* [Greek, *eis tēn abysson*]" (Luke 8:31; emphasis added). This passage uses the same Greek word for "the deep" as Revelation does for "the bottomless pit."

In all three synoptic accounts the demons ask to be cast into a nearby herd of swine (Mark 5:12; Matthew 8:31; Luke 8:32). Oddly, Jesus gives permission, and when the demons enter the pigs, some two thousand of them rush down a steep bank *into the sea,* where they drown. Various explanations have been suggested for this action, such as the idea that one man is worth more than thousands of swine or even that a Jewish audience would not have felt sorry for pigs, seeing some poetic justice in unclean spirits destroying unclean animals.[34]

When we remember that in Near Eastern cosmologies, seas represented both the disorganized chaos that preceded creation and were also connected to the watery deep under the earth,[35] the meaning of the fate of the demons who are plunged into the depths of the Sea of Galilee with their swine hosts becomes clear. Jesus has the power to deliver anyone from the power of Satan, even Gentiles, who were sometimes associated by Jews with dogs and even swine, the prototypical unclean animal. The delivered demonic, almost certainly a Gentile, is promptly cleansed, clothed, and returned to his right mind; he then desires to follow Jesus. Significantly, in Luke, he is described as "having been saved [Greek, *esōthē;* KJV, 'was healed']" (Luke 8:36). The eventual fate of the demons, however, is to be plunged into the bottomless pit; before that time comes, however, they are free to continue their work among others who are still impure, as symbolized by the pigs. It is generally assumed that the pigs plunged themselves to their doom to escape the demons, but their stampede into the sea may represent the fate of those who are not delivered by Jesus, as is the case of those who persist in wickedness and run from, rather than to, him. If they do not repent and come to Christ, they could be punished as the devil and his hosts will be when they are at last cast out "into the deep."

## Imprisoned by Infirmities

Two stories of individuals afflicted by demons involve persons whose possession resulted in their being rendered mute, and in one case, blind. Notably, neither of these cases appears in Mark, the Gospel presumed to be the earliest. Instead, they appear first in Matthew, which generally downplays exorcisms.[36] For instance, Matthew completely passes over the story of the Capernaum demonic and drastically trims the story of the Gadarene demonic, relating it in a mere seven verses compared to the account in Mark, which takes twenty. Further, Matthew avoids some of the more sensational aspects of demonic possession, such as the convulsions and crying out that in other accounts accompanies the departure of a devil from its victim (compare Matthew 17:18 with Mark 9:20, 26 and Luke 9:42). Still, Matthew recognizes that exorcisms were part of Jesus' healing ministry, as can be seen in a number of summaries, reports, and other teachings regarding the casting out of evil spirits (Matthew 4:23–25; 7:22–23; 10:1; 11:2–6; 12:22–30, 43–44). Significantly, these examples may be more akin to the pattern found in Luke, where physical illnesses and demonic afflictions are depicted as two aspects of the same fallen experience. Just as these mute men were bound by their infirmities, so are we all imprisoned by Satan until we are delivered by Christ.

The story of the mute demonic is attested only in Matthew's Gospel (Matthew 9:32–34).[37] A man who either could not speak or suffered from a severe speech impediment (Greek, *kōphos*)[38] was taken to Jesus. When the devil was cast out, the mute man began to speak, causing the crowds who witnessed the miracle to marvel. Though some details may have well been lost in the processes of Matthew's concise rendering, the fact that this victim manifested none of the typical behaviors associated with demonic possession makes this exorcism seem more like a healing than the casting out of a devil.

Perhaps the key to the symbolism here is found in Jesus' later direction to his disciples to "take no thought how or what ye shall speak: for it shall be given you in that same hour what ye shall speak. For it is not ye that speak, *but the Spirit of your Father which speaketh in you*" (Matthew 10:19–20; emphasis added; Mark 13:11; Luke 12:11–12). This promise has an important parallel in 2 Nephi 32:2–3, which teaches that those who receive the Holy Ghost speak with the tongue of angels, for "angels speak by the power of the Holy Ghost; wherefore, they speak the words of Christ." While we generally think of a devil as causing someone to speak blasphemously or to lie (see, for

The Blind and Mute Man Possessed by Devils, *by James Tissot.*

example, Revelation 13:5–6), the image of a demon binding someone's tongue shows that its power is opposite that of the Holy Ghost.

The later story of the mute and blind demonic illustrates that the inability to speak could represent the absence of the Holy Ghost as much as it does the restraining power of an evil spirit (Matthew 12:22–23; Luke 11:14). The similarity of this episode to the story of the mute demonic in Matthew

> ### "Where Can I Turn for Peace?"
>
> In a moment of great discouragement, Nephi cried out that he desired that the evil one no longer "have place in my heart *to destroy my peace* and afflict my soul" (2 Nephi 4:27; emphasis added). This desire for peace, which comes in part by overcoming the influence of Satan, is beautifully expressed in the hymn "Where Can I Turn for Peace?" This moving hymn has deep meaning for Emma Lou Thayne, the author of its lyrics.
>
> As members of the Young Women general board, Sister Thayne and Joleen G. Meredith were asked to write a musical number for a Laurel conference in 1971. At the time, Sister Thayne and her family were facing considerable health and other trials. She reflected, "Who of us has not had Gethsemane times? And how often has each of us reached for the calm and the kindness that only the Savior can offer?" Sister Meredith's music for this hymn is peaceful and full of hope. Together, the words and music are "a mental health hymn in many ways," Sister Meredith commented. Having served for many years on such state boards as the Substance Abuse and Mental Health Board, Sister Meredith certainly understands the power of beautiful music and inspired lyrics in healing hearts and soothing troubled minds.[39]
>
> > *Where can I turn for peace?* Where is my solace
> > When other sources cease to make me whole?
> > When with a wounded heart, anger, or malice,
> > I draw myself apart, Searching my soul?
> >
> > Where, when my aching grows, Where, when I languish,
> > Where, in my need to know, where can I run?
> > Where is the quiet hand to calm my anguish?
> > Who, who can understand? He, only One.
> >
> > He answers privately, Reaches my reaching
> > In my Gethsemane, Savior and Friend.
> > *Gentle the peace he finds for my beseeching.*
> > Constant he is and kind, Love without end.[40]
>
> Whether sung from the hymnbook or listened to as arranged by Mack Wilberg in 2000 and sung by the Mormon Tabernacle Choir,[41] this simple but penetrating hymn brings solace, just as Jesus brought peace to so many tormented souls during his ministry.

9:32–34 presents the possibility that this is a doublet, or literary repetition, of the earlier episode, a possibility perhaps strengthened by the fact that the parallel in Luke makes the sufferer only mute, not mute and blind.[42] Although Luke uses standard exorcism terminology, such as "he was *casting out* a devil" (Greek, *ekballōn*) and "when the devil *was gone out*" (Greek, *exelthontos*), Matthew tellingly writes, "he *healed him* [Greek, *etherapeusen auton*], insomuch that the blind and dumb both spake and saw" (Matthew 12:22; emphasis added). Thus for Matthew this miracle was more about delivering a man from his infirmities and less about the devil that was at some level the root of his suffering.

In both Gospels, however, this miracle story is followed by the report that Jesus' opponents accused him of accomplishing such exorcisms not with the power of God but by being in league with Beelzebub (Hebrew, *Ba'al Zəḇûḇ,* literally "Lord of the Flies"), a figure seen as either a prince of the devils or even Satan himself. This accusation leads Jesus to respond with two parables: the house divided against itself and the story of the strong man (Mark 3:23–27; parallels Matthew 12:25–30; Luke 11:17–23), both of which reveal the lack of logic in the charge against Jesus. Between these two parables Jesus declares that if he by the power, or "finger," of God has been casting out devils,[43] then the kingdom of God has come upon them. This assertion underscores the overall idea that exorcisms can be seen as part of the wider victory of the kingdom of God over the current reign of Satan in this world. In that context, various infirmities and handicaps that bind people in this life, of which muteness and blindness are just two examples, are both consequences of the Fall and symbols of Satan's efforts to restrain us and hinder our progress.

## When Children Suffer

Two final stories of exorcisms vividly illustrate Jesus' power to deliver even the most helpless from the grasp of Satan. Although the story of the Syrophoenician woman who interceded for her daughter (Mark 7:24–30; Matthew 15:21–28) and the story of the man who begged for help for his suffering son (Mark 9:14–29; Matthew 17:14–21; Luke 9:37–43) share the obvious feature of a parent desperate to help a child, they are different in other significant ways. The woman's story takes place in Gentile territory, while the man's is set in Jewish Galilee. The daughter is not present herself and her healing takes place at a distance; the father takes his son first to Jesus' disciples and then to the Lord himself. The boy's suffering is described in terrible detail before Jesus casts

Christ and the Canaanite Woman, *by Jean-Germain Drouais.*

80   THE MIRACLES OF JESUS

out the devil and at last grants peace to the boy. But the common feature that is the most poignant in both cases is that children are the ones who suffer. The background of neither child is known, but the word used for "young daughter" (Greek, *thygatrion*) means a very young girl, and the son's affliction was "from childhood" (Greek, *ek paidothen;* KJV, "of a child"). In both cases the clear impression is that the sufferers have not done anything to warrant the distress they are experiencing.

Because the daughter was not present, the focus in the first story is on the encounter between Jesus and the girl's mother. Mark describes her as a "Greek, a Syrophenician by nation" (Mark 7:26). Matthew emphasizes her Gentile status by calling her "a woman of Canaan." The Phoenicians were descended from Canaanites whom the children of Israel had not destroyed, and in the Old Testament they represented the spiritually lethal danger of idolatry. Thus this woman represents not only Gentiles but also false and dangerous religion. This episode, set in the countryside around Tyre, immediately follows a heated debate in Galilee between Jesus and some scribes and Pharisees about what ritually defiled a person. Because Gentiles were seen as being unclean, this debate puts in context Jesus' seemingly gruff response to the woman when

The Woman of Canaan, *by Harold Copping.*

she begs him to help her daughter: "Let the children first be filled: for it is not meet to take the children's bread, and to cast it unto the dogs" (Mark 7:27). The woman persists, however: "Yes, Lord: yet the dogs under the table eat of the children's crumbs" (Mark 7:28). This exchange constitutes one of the so-called "hard sayings of Jesus,"[44] but in both Jesus' pronouncement and the woman's response, the reference to dogs has to do with the unclean and, in the eyes of some Jews in that period, the unworthy state of both the woman and her daughter.[45]

Attempts to explain this exchange have focused on either the woman's persistence, which is taken as a sign of faith and resolute determination to help her daughter, or on the meaning of the Greek word translated here as "dogs." In regard to this latter point, some commentators have noted that the word used by both Jesus and the woman is the equivalent of "little dogs" (Greek, *kynarion*), suggesting that somehow using a term denoting small house dogs, presumably pampered pets, would have been

### Recovering from Abuse and Betrayal

Many, too many, people in the world today suffer from the continuing effects of abuse. Whether emotional, physical, sexual, or verbal abuse, such mistreatment leaves unseen scars that continue to affect lives long after the abuse has ended. Often such abuse also involves betrayal when those closest and dearest to us, those who are charged to love and protect us, instead hurt us or allow harm to come upon us. Betrayal also includes infidelity, whether sexual or emotional, that destroys trust in a marriage, leaving the victim feeling worthless, afraid, and abandoned. In all these cases future relationships and the ability to be happy can be severely impaired. Such devastation makes perpetrators into flesh-and-blood devils in the lives of those whom they hurt.

Resolving complex issues and deep healing do not usually come from prayer and priesthood blessings alone. Recovery from abuse requires three components: professional help, spiritual strength, and personal resolve and effort. But because Satan often exploits the circumstances of abuse to inhibit healing, we must never forget the role of divine help in recovery.

Elder Richard G. Scott taught: "If you have been abused, Satan will strive to convince you that there is no solution. Yet he knows perfectly well that there is. Satan recognizes that healing comes through the unwavering love of Heavenly Father for each of His children. He also understands that the power of healing is inherent in the Atonement of Jesus Christ. Therefore, his strategy is to do all possible to separate you from your Father and His Son. Do not let Satan convince you that you are beyond help.

"Healing may begin with a thoughtful bishop or stake president or a wise professional counselor. If you had a broken leg, you wouldn't decide to fix it yourself. Serious abuse can also benefit from professional help. There are many ways to begin healing, but remember that a full cure comes through the Savior, the Lord Jesus Christ, our Master and Redeemer. Have faith that with effort His perfect, eternal, infinite Atonement can heal your suffering from the consequences of abuse."[46]

less rude than referring to the woman and her daughter as mongrel dogs.[47] Even the diminutive term, however, was likely to have been offensive.[48] Matthew's expanded account clarifies the situation by recording that Jesus prefaced his declaration to the woman by saying *to his disciples,* who have already asked Jesus to send the woman away, "I am not sent but unto the lost sheep of the house of Israel" (Matthew 15:24). Knowing that, the disciples may well have let their conventional attitudes about Gentiles, which may not have been much different from those of the Pharisees and scribes whom Jesus had already corrected, interfere with their view of the woman. In fact, Jesus' willingness even to talk to an unfamiliar woman, especially a Gentile, reveals that he was not bound by social conventions of the time. This and the fact that he immediately grants the woman's request may suggest that his use of a term that Pharisees and perhaps his own disciples might have used for a Gentile woman may have been an implicit criticism of that very attitude.[49]

Despite the focus on the woman, the important result of this episode is that Jesus does, in the end, heal her daughter. Matthew's account closes by recording, "Then Jesus answered and said unto her, O woman, great is thy faith: be it unto thee even as thou wilt. And her daughter was made whole from that very hour" (Matthew 15:28).

In addition to emphasizing the role of faith in saving ourselves and others, this example of healing at a distance underscores that even today, when Jesus is not physically present, he can and will act to deliver us and the ones we love from the power of Satan. Furthermore, this deliverance of the innocent is open to all, not just the house of Israel.

The second example of a suffering innocent takes place in Jewish Galilee soon after Jesus descended from the Mount of Transfiguration with Peter, James, and John. In the account of Mark, which is the most detailed, Jesus finds his other disciples arguing with a crowd. A man from the group quickly explains that he had brought his son, who suffered from "a spirit" (Greek, *pneuma*) that not only made his son mute but also threw him into convulsions and caused him to foam at the mouth, grind his teeth, and stiffen uncontrollably (Mark 9:17–18). The symptoms that all three synoptic Gospels describe are much like those experienced by many epileptics, and the fact that both Mark and Luke initially call the spirit simply a *pneuma* and neither an unclean spirit nor a demon have led some to think that this is more of a case of healing than an exorcism. Matthew, in fact, uses the Greek word meaning "moonstruck" (Greek, *selēniazetai*; KJV, "lunatic"), which was a term often used anciently for epilepsy.[50]

Nevertheless, after Jesus secures an expression of faith from the father, Mark and Luke record, He rebuked the spirit, which is now called a "foul" or "unclean spirit" (Mark 9:25; Luke 9:42); Matthew and Luke explicitly also call it a devil (Matthew 17:18; Luke 9:42). In other words, in the end, all three synoptic Gospels portray the boy's malady as a possession. Still, the idea of healing is as strong in this episode as is the concept of exorcism. Matthew notes that after Jesus rebuked the devil, the boy "was cured" (Greek, *etherapeuthē*), and Luke writes that Jesus "healed the child" (Greek, *iasato ton paida*).

It is the imagery in Mark's account, however, that probably speaks most strongly of the power of

The Possessed Boy at the Foot of Mount Tabor, by James Tissot.

> ### "Help Thou My Unbelief"
>
> A few years ago I spoke at the annual women's conference at Brigham Young University. The topic that my co-presenter, Wayne Brickey, and I were assigned was how to better understand the New Testament Gospels. Toward the end of the hour, I was to address the issue of faith in Mark 9. As I opened my scriptures and glanced again at the story of the demonic or epileptic boy (Mark 9:14–29), the Spirit led me in a totally unexpected direction.
>
> Just that week, my son, Samuel, had been formally diagnosed with autism. At that point he was severely affected with severe sensory processing disorder (SPD), considerable communication handicaps, and a lack of emotional self-regulation. He was four years old but knew and used only about twenty words. The greatest challenge he had then was communicating his frustrations and anxieties, and he was subject to frequent meltdowns, in which he threw himself on the floor and screamed uncontrollably. As I read the story of the man who took his son with a "dumb spirit" to Jesus in the hope that he would heal him, I was constrained to tell the women there that day that in a very real way, *I* was that father.
>
> The turning point of the story in Mark is no doubt when Jesus says to the desperate man, "If thou canst believe, all things are possible to him that believeth" and "straightway the father of the child cried out, and said with tears, Lord, I believe; *help thou mine unbelief*" (Mark 9:23–24; emphasis added). I consider myself to be a man of faith. I believe in Jesus and his ability to heal and change lives, but at that time of great sorrow in my life, I was in great need of deeper, stronger faith.
>
> Even those of us with faith can always use more faith—not always faith to receive a particular miracle in a specific way but sometimes more of that faith that is simply trust and confidence in a loving God. My son was not healed that day, nor has he been completely healed since. Yet God has worked miracles in his life and perhaps even more miracles in the lives of the rest of us in our family as we have been comforted in times of discouragement and sadness and been given the strength to accept our situation—and even find great joy in it.

Jesus to ultimately deliver us from the power of the devil *and* heal us from our infirmities. When Jesus rebuked the spirit and commanded it to depart, "the spirit cried, and rent him sore, and came out of him: and *he was as one dead;* insomuch that many said, He is dead. But Jesus took him by the hand, and *lifted him up* [Greek, *ēgeiren*]; and *he arose* [Greek, *anestē*]" (Mark 9:26–27; emphasis added). Although both verbs used here literally mean to "raise, lift up, or rise," they are also regularly used in the New Testament in the sense of raising the dead.[51] Therefore, while Mark's and Luke's endings to this story can reflect the healing from mortal conditions that can come to us in this life, we see in Mark's conclusion how *all* disabilities and mortal frailties are ultimately overcome and healed in the resurrection, when "the spirit and body shall be reunited again in its perfect form; both limb and joint shall be restored to its proper frame" (Alma 11:43).

The Gospels portray the power of Satan and his legions as real. Demonic possessions occurred, and Jesus had the power to deliver those who were held captive in that way. Although both can also occur today, Satan has other effective tools adapted to our time to lead people into bondage and make them miserable. Addictions can enslave almost as powerfully as can demons, and flesh-and-blood devils can torment the innocent and haunt them long after the abuse is over. But all of us, even the otherwise blameless, are also subject to the effects of the Fall. As natural men and women, subject to physical needs and desires, we can easily be led astray by temptations. And as all of us are mortal, we can all—even the young and the innocent—be imprisoned by infirmities or hampered by sickness. The answer to all of these challenges, demonic and natural, is the miraculous delivering and healing power of Jesus Christ.

# 4
# Causing the Blind to See and the Deaf to Hear

## *Opening Spiritual Eyes and Ears*

*Since the world began was it not heard that any man opened the eyes of one that was born blind.*

—John 9:32

Often instances of Jesus' healing the blind and the deaf are grouped with his other miraculous healings, but the cases of restoring senses are different from other healings in two important ways. First, though many of Jesus' miracles—even the raising of the dead—had some precedent in the Old Testament, there are no clear examples in the Hebrew Bible of someone restoring sight or hearing.[1] There were some other examples of such healings in antiquity to be sure,[2] but none of the prophets who served as types of Christ are reported to have miraculously restored sight or hearing to a blind or deaf person. Perhaps the closest thing to curing blindness mentioned in the Old Testament is when Elisha prayed the Lord would open the eyes of his servant that he could see the angelic hosts that were protecting them (2 Kings 6:17).[3] Nevertheless, the blind were expected to receive their sight in the messianic age (Isaiah 35:5; LXX, or Septuagint, Isaiah 61:1, as quoted in Luke 4:18),[4] making Jesus' miracles in this regard a particular sign of his being the Messiah. Second, these miracles focused on the restoration of the senses, producing markedly different symbolism than healing the crippled or unclean. Restoring a paralytic's ability to walk or a man's ability to use a previously withered hand can represent the strengthening and enabling power of the Atonement as well as anticipating the full healing of the resurrection. Cleansing a leper symbolizes the redeeming power of Jesus' sacrifice that can purify our hearts and souls. But returning the ability to see and hear symbolizes the deeper meaning of opening our spiritual eyes to see things as they are and opening our ears to hear the word of the Lord.

Individuals who refuse to respond to God and come unto Christ are spiritually blind and deaf. Referring to apostate Judah, the Lord told Ezekiel, "Son of man, thou dwellest in the midst of a rebellious

### Restoring Sight and Hearing

- Two blind men (Matthew 9:27–31)
- A deaf-mute (Mark 7:31–37)
- The blind man at Bethsaida (Mark 8:22–26)
- The man born blind (John 9:1–12)
- Blind Bartimaeus (Mark 10:46–52; parallels Matthew 20:29–34; Luke 18:35–43)

Summaries of Jesus healing the blind and mute are found in Matthew 15:29–31 and 21:14. A report of such healings is found in Matthew 11:2–6 (parallel Luke 7:18–23).

*Opposite:* Healing the Blind Man, *by Carl Bloch. Courtesy of Intellectual Reserve, Inc.*

house, *which have eyes to see, and see not; they have ears to hear, and hear not:* for they are a rebellious house" (Ezekiel 12:2; emphasis added). A similar rebuke appears in the Book of Mormon, when Jacob warns, "And wo unto the deaf *that will not hear;* for they shall perish. Wo unto the blind *that will not see;* for they shall perish also" (2 Nephi 9:31–32; emphasis added). Conversely, Jesus commended his disciples for understanding the parables that he taught them, saying, "But blessed are your eyes, *for they see:* and your ears, *for they hear*" (Matthew 13:16; emphasis added). Jesus repeatedly stressed the need for such spiritual understanding, not just physical perception, when he said, "He that hath ears to hear, let him hear" (Mark 4:9, 23; 7:16; 8:18; Matthew 11:15; 13:9, 43; Luke 8:8; 14:35).

When the Lord opened the spiritual eyes of Elisha's servant, he was able to understand the truth that those who were with them were more than those who were against them (2 Kings 6:16). Likewise, the message of these New Testament miracles of the restoration of senses is that just as Jesus was able to restore sight and hearing to the physically blind and deaf, so can he open our spiritual eyes and ears to recognize the things of God, be enlightened, and have our understanding enlarged (D&C 76:12; 88:11).

The Blind of Capernaum, *by James Tissot.*

## Two Blind Men and a Deaf-Mute

As Jesus left the house of Jairus after raising his daughter from the dead, two blind men followed him, calling him the Son of David and begging for mercy (Matthew 9:27–31). Of the four Gospels, Matthew uses the title Son of David the most frequently, to emphasize Jesus' status as the Messiah. Although contemporary messianic expectations often centered on a political savior or a military deliverer, all but two of these references to Jesus as the Son of David are connected in Matthew to healings.[5]

Jesus Healing the Deaf Man, *a fourteenth-century mosaic in the Chora Church (Kariye Camii), Istanbul, Turkey.*

After Jesus asked the blind men whether they believed that he could heal them, he touched their eyes, saying, "According to your faith be it unto you. And their eyes were opened" (Matthew 9:29–30). A physical gesture such as touching their eyes is an action more commonly recorded in Mark, who is usually much more descriptive of miracles, than in Matthew, but Matthew's mention of it here underscores that Jesus often did use his hands in healing. And the record of two men receiving their sight is in line with Matthew's understanding that two witnesses are necessary to establish a truth, in this case the truth being that Jesus did, in fact, have the power to restore sight.

Two details suggest that this episode of restoring the sight of two blind men is about discipleship and not just regaining sight. First, when the men first called upon Jesus, Matthew emphasizes that they "followed him [Greek, *ēkolouthēsan autō*]" (Matthew 9:27). Matthew frequently uses *follow* in his Gospel as an expression of discipleship, since believers are to follow Jesus (see, for example, Matthew 8:19, 22; 9:9; 10:38; 16:24; 19:21).[6] Second, Jesus specifically predicated the miracle upon their faith (Matthew 9:28–29), belief and trust in Jesus being prerequisites of true discipleship. As a result, given that curing blindness can also represent opening one's spiritual eyes, the message may be that these two men came to see and know Jesus for who he really was.

Immediately after the story of the Syrophoenician woman, Mark writes that Jesus entered the territory of the Decapolis, where "one that was deaf [Greek, *kōphon*], and had an impediment in his speech [Greek, *mogilalon*]" was brought to him (Mark 7:31–37). As in the case of the mute demonic in Matthew 9:32–34, the word translated "deaf" here applied both to those who were unable to hear and to those who were unable to speak, perhaps because being unable to hear prevents one from learning to speak by imitation.[7] When this man tried to communicate, apparently he spoke unclearly and with difficulty, which is the meaning of *mogilalos.*

Jesus' method of healing is typical of Mark's Gospel: It is descriptive and straightforward in recording actions and words of Jesus that others might wrongly compare to contemporary magic practices. First, Jesus placed his fingers in the man's ears. Next, he touched the man's tongue with some of his own spittle, an action that had some parallel in ancient medical and magical practices.[8] Finally, after looking up to heaven and sighing as if in prayer, he uttered the command, "Ephphatha, that is, Be opened" (Mark 7:34).

Noting that Matthew and Luke both omit this episode, some biblical scholars suggest that these evangelists were uncomfortable with the methods used to describe Jesus' healing of this man.[9] Nonetheless, each element Jesus employed in this miracle has clear symbolism in line with his mission. Inserting a finger into previously stopped ears could be symbolic of opening the ears so they could hear; the significance of Jesus doing it with his own finger emphasizes that he alone was able to restore the man's hearing. Understanding the application of saliva might be found in noting that it was Jesus' spittle: inasmuch as he was the one with authority to speak God's word, he was the only one able to give this man the ability to speak. By using his own saliva, he was, in effect, imparting some of himself to the man. Finally, pronouncing *ephphatha* was not akin to a magical incantation, which usually consisted of unknown words or nonsense gibberish; this word was simply the Aramaic term meaning "be open," an expression that would be understood by Jesus, the man being healed, and any witnesses who were nearby.[10] Each of these acts immediately had a result, as "straightway his ears were opened, and the string [Greek, *desmos,* meaning 'impediment'] of his tongue was loosed, and he spake plain" (Mark 7:35).

Those who witnessed this healing, which is without Old Testament precedent, immediately

Jesus Heals a Mute Possessed Man, *by James Tissot.*

"were beyond measure astonished, saying, *He hath done all things well:* he maketh both the deaf to hear, and the dumb to speak" (Mark 7:37; emphasis added). Yet while there was no prophetic precedent for restoring hearing, Isaiah had foretold that this would be a clear sign of the messianic age: "Then the eyes of the blind shall be opened, and *the ears of the deaf shall be unstopped*" (Isaiah 35:5; emphasis added).[11] And the crowd's acclaim that "he hath done all things well" echoes the summary of God's creative work at the end of the sixth day: "And God saw every thing *that he had made,* and, behold, it was very good" (Genesis 1:31; emphasis added). In other words, Jesus was accomplishing a new creation, or re-ordering the original Creation that had become flawed through the Fall. Finally, use of the term *mogilalos,* meaning impeded speech rather than absolute muteness, adds another level of symbolism for those who become converted to Christ and then grow in his gospel. Before our ears are opened to hear the word of the Lord, we can speak and preach at best imperfectly. As the Lord instructed Hyrum Smith through his brother Joseph, "Seek not to declare my word, but first seek to obtain my word, and *then shall your tongue be loosed;* then, if you desire, you shall have my spirit and my word, yea, the power of God unto the convincing of men" (D&C 11:21; emphasis added).

Other specific examples of healing muteness, deafness, and blindness (Mark 9:17–27; Matthew 12:22–32; Luke 11:14–26) have been treated in our previous discussion of exorcisms, in which the power of Satan was interpreted as restraining people from being inspired to speak the word of the Lord or to see with their spiritual eyes. While there remain in the Gospels three other specific and powerful examples of healing blind men (Mark 8:22–26; 10:46–52; and parallels John 9:1–14), the only other clear reference to Jesus' healing the deaf is his report to the disciples of John the Baptist that in his ministry, "the blind receive their sight, and the lame walk, the lepers are cleansed, and *the deaf hear,* the dead are raised up, and the poor have the gospel preached to them" (Matthew 11:5; emphasis added; Luke 7:22).

## A Blind Man Healed in Stages

A richly symbolic healing of a blind man appears in the account of Mark shortly after the feeding of the four thousand. After crossing the Sea of Galilee back to Dalmanutha on the Jewish side of the sea, some Pharisees went to Jesus, tempting or testing him by seeking "a sign from heaven [Greek, *sēmeion apo tou ouranou*]" (Mark 8:11). Although signs are positive revelations of Jesus in the Gospel of John, in Mark and the other synoptic Gospels, the term is always negative. Just as these opponents of Jesus failed to understand who he was by asking for a sign, in the episode that immediately follows, Jesus' own disciples are portrayed as not fully understanding his true identity when they have a discussion with him about bread (Mark 8:14–21). After Jesus warned them of the leaven of the Pharisees and of Herod, they thought he had rebuked them for having failed to bring any bread. Discerning their thoughts, Jesus questioned them, asking, "Why reason ye, because ye have no bread? perceive ye not yet, neither understand? have ye your heart yet hardened? *Having eyes, see ye not? and having ears, hear ye not?*" (Mark 8:17–18; emphasis added). This comparison of failing to understand with being unable

> ### The Blind in the Ancient World
>
> Although a lame man might be able to perform a productive occupation in the ancient world, such as being a blacksmith, the plight of the blind in the ancient world was particularly grave.
>
> A person could be blind from birth or become blind through injury, disease, or purposeful maiming as punishment. Being blind was widely agreed to be one of the most serious misfortunes that could befall a person. Later, in fact, the Talmud characterized being blind as being only a little less serious than being dead.[12]
>
> Some blind people could make a living through singing or creating and reciting poetry. In the Greek tradition, blind poets such as Homer were considered to have been especially inspired, almost prophetic, and blind prophets, such as the mythic Teiresias, were able to see with spiritual eyes what seeing people could not discern with their physical eyes. But for most of the blind and many of the deaf, begging was the only way of supporting themselves that was open to them.
>
> To make matters worse, blindness was often seen as a punishment for sin,[13] as witnessed in the question of the disciples to Jesus before he healed the man born blind: "Master, who did sin, this man, or his parents, that he was born blind?" (John 9:2). Jesus' response was clear: "Neither has this man sinned, nor his parents: but that the works of God should be manifest in him" (John 9:3). Although choices can result in accident, disease, or disability, the fact is that most such infirmities are no one's fault. The course of nature in a fallen world often results in unfortunate conditions. Yet in this life or the next, such conditions will be remedied, and in this life the works of God can be manifest as we lovingly serve and help those so challenged.

to see or hear provides the context for the miracle of Jesus healing a blind man at Bethsaida, the story of which follows (Mark 8:22–26).

According to Mark's account, after performing the miracle of feeding the four thousand, Jesus and his disciples crossed the Sea of Galilee to Bethsaida, on the northern end of the sea just east of the Upper Jordan River in the tetrarchy of Philip. Because of the difficult terrain around the mouth of the Upper Jordan as it flowed into the Sea of Galilee, the Gospels note that Jesus sometimes crossed to Bethsaida by boat from Capernaum or other sites on the western side of the lake rather than traveling by land.

The original settlement of Bethsaida was a Jewish fishing village on the coast, though at the time of Jesus' ministry, the tetrarch Philip had built just north of the earlier, smaller town a new, Roman-style city, which he named Julias in honor of the empress Livia, who had taken the name Julia Augusta in A.D. 14.[14] Bethsaida appears to have been the hometown of three of Jesus' disciples, Peter, Andrew, and Philip (John 1:44), and we have noted that one of the miraculous feedings of a multitude might have occurred there. Although the healing of the blind man is the only specific miracle recorded as having taken place in Bethsaida, a saying of Jesus notes that many mighty works were done here and

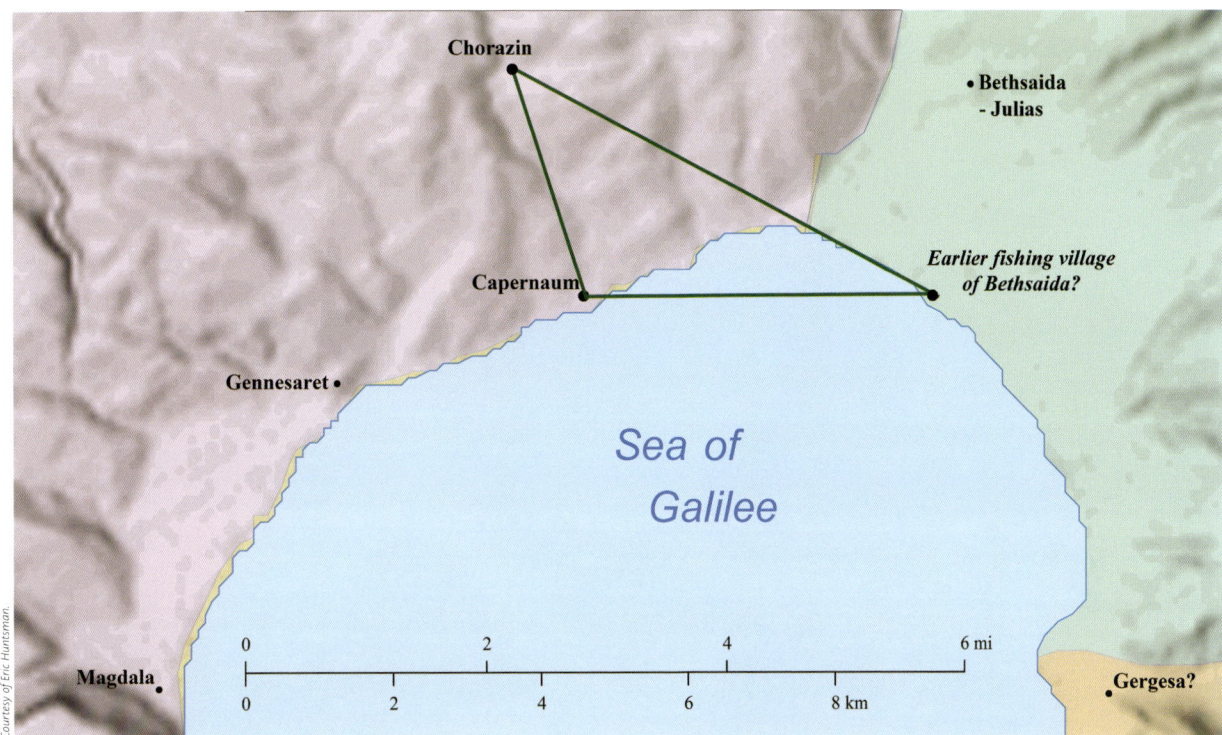

*The region at the northern end of the Sea of Galilee defined by the three important towns of Capernaum, Chorazin, and Bethsaida is sometimes called the "evangelical triangle," because so many of Jesus' miracles and teachings took place there.*

*Ruins of Bethsaida-Julias, the city built by the tetrarch Philip, which probably was not far from the Jewish fishing village of Bethsaida, where Jesus healed the blind man.*

Sight Restored, by J. Kirk Richards.

in the town of Chorazin (Matthew 11:21; Luke 10:13), which together with Capernaum delineated the so-called evangelical triangle where much of Jesus' Galilean ministry took place.

As Jesus entered the village of Bethsaida (Greek, *komē;* see Mark 8:22–23, 26), some of its residents took a blind man to him. Jesus led the man out of the town, applied saliva to his eyes, laid his hands on him, and asked him whether he saw anything. The man looked up and said, "I see men as trees, walking" (Mark 8:24), which led Jesus to again touch his eyes, whereupon the man could see clearly. That the man could describe men as looking like trees indicates that he had not been born blind, for he knew what both men and trees looked like.[15] Still, the fact that Jesus healed the man in stages seems, at first, to be an odd detail.

The explanation for this feature of the story may be found in the role this story plays in Mark's narrative as a whole. The story of the healing of the blind man at Bethsaida begins the second principal section of Mark (Mark 8:22–10:52), which is usually called "On the Road to Jerusalem" but has also been called "The Spiritually Blind Disciples."[16] The episode in Mark's narrative immediately following the miracle of the healing of the blind man is Peter's famous declaration at Caesarea Philippi, where the chief disciple testified that Jesus was the Christ (Mark 8:27–30; Matthew 16:13–20; Luke 9:18–20). Matthew's fuller account of this episode makes it very clear that Peter's knowledge of Jesus' identity and role had come to him by revelation (Matthew 16:16–17), meaning that Peter's eyes had been opened in regard to *who* Jesus was. But in all three synoptic Gospels, it is clear that the disciples

### Seeing and Hearing Things as They Really Are

In an 1832 revelation to Joseph Smith and Sidney Rigdon, the Lord promised to reveal his mysteries to those who fear and serve him, declaring, "For by my Spirit will I enlighten them, and by my power will I make known unto them the secrets of my will—yea, even *those things which eye has not seen, nor ear heard*, nor yet entered into the heart of man" (D&C 76:10; emphasis added). Using the language of seeing and hearing to describe revelation gives the stories of Jesus' healing the blind and the deaf an important symbolic meaning: When he opens our spiritual eyes and ears, he does so to reveal new truths to us. We can then see and hear things as they really are far better than we can through physical sight and hearing.

In 1833 another revelation gave an important definition of truth: "And truth is knowledge *of things as they are, and as they were, and as they are to come*" (D&C 93:24; emphasis added). In the book of Revelation, the glorified risen Lord is described as the One "which is, which was, and which is to come" (Revelation 1:8; 4:8; 11:17). Knowing the identity and role of Christ is one of the greatest truths we can know. Indeed, to his disciples Jesus declared, "I am the way, *the truth*, and the life: no man cometh unto the Father, but by me" (John 14:6; emphasis added), and when Pilate later asked whether Jesus was a king, he testified, "To this end was I born, and for this cause came I into the world, that I should bear witness unto the truth. Every one that is of the truth *heareth my voice*" (John 18:37; emphasis added).

As we come to know who Christ is and learn to hear his word, we are set on the path to one of the most vital revelations that we can receive. In our dispensation, the Lord has promised, "Inasmuch as you strip yourselves from jealousies and fears, and humble yourselves before me, for ye are not sufficiently humble, the veil shall be rent and *you shall see me and know that I am*—not with the carnal neither natural mind, but with the spiritual. For no man has seen God at any time in the flesh, except quickened by the Spirit of God" (D&C 67:10–11; emphasis added).

still did not have a clear idea of *what* Jesus had come to do. Woven into the subsequent events are three Passion predictions,[17] in which Jesus proclaimed to his closest followers that they were going to Jerusalem, where "the Son of man must suffer many things, and be rejected of the elders, and of the chief priests, and scribes, and be killed, and after three days rise again" (Mark 8:31; Matthew 16:21; Luke 9:22). Each time Jesus made this prediction to his disciples, one or more of them misunderstood his meaning or otherwise acted inappropriately. The most glaring example occurred after the first prediction, when Peter began to rebuke Jesus, telling him that this would never happen, which caused Jesus to reprimand him (Matthew 16:22–23; Mark 8:32–33). Like the blind man at Bethsaida, Peter had begun to see who Jesus was, but his vision of the Lord and his mission was yet unclear and incomplete.[18] Only when they had arrived at Jerusalem and the disciples had witnessed the Passion and Resurrection of Jesus did they come to fully see and understand who Jesus was and what he had come to do.

## The Man Born Blind

The sixth miraculous sign in the Gospel of John is the story of Jesus healing a man who had been blind since birth (John 9:1–12). This story represents a greater miracle than other cases of restoring sight because, as the man who was healed testified, "Since the world began was it not heard that any man opened the eyes of one that was born blind" (John 9:32). This miracle took place in Jerusalem, where, John records, Jesus had gone for the Feast of Tabernacles (John 7:2). In the intertestamental period, the Jewish feast of *Sukkôt,* or Tabernacles, had acquired many customs in addition to those required by the law of Moses (Exodus 23:16; Leviticus 23:33–43). Some of these customs included the lighting of great lamps in the courts of the temple each evening during the seven days of the feast and the drawing of water from the Pool of Siloam, which was carried in procession up to the temple, where it was poured upon the altars.[19] Both of these elements, light and water, are featured in John's account of the healing of the man born blind.

No doubt drawing on the image of light so prevalent during the celebration of the Feast of Tabernacles, Jesus declared, "I am the light of the world: he that followeth me shall not walk in darkness, but shall have the light of life" (John 8:12). When Jesus met the man born blind, he declared to his disciples, "*I must work the works of him that sent me,* while it is day: the night cometh, when no man can work. As long as I am in the world, *I am the light of the world*" (John 9:4–5; emphasis added). That this story happens

*This model of Jerusalem shows the Pool of Siloam, enclosed by colonnades, at the south end of the City of David.*

on the Sabbath connects Jesus' reference to working to the Creation, just as it did with the earlier healing at the Pool of Bethesda, when Jesus had healed a man on the Sabbath and similarly made a reference to how "my Father worketh hitherto, and I work" (John 5:17). These references to working again set Jesus' healing ministry into the context of repairing the work of the Creation, which has become marred by the Fall. Jesus' repeated reference to his being the Light of the World ties this miracle more closely to himself, because the man born blind had lived his entire life without any light until he met Jesus.

The description of the method Jesus used for restoring this man's sight is unusual for John, who records that he made mud or paste (Greek, *pēlos;* KJV, "clay") with his saliva, placed it on the man's eyes, and then directed him to go wash at the Pool of Siloam (John 9:6–7). Like Matthew and Luke,

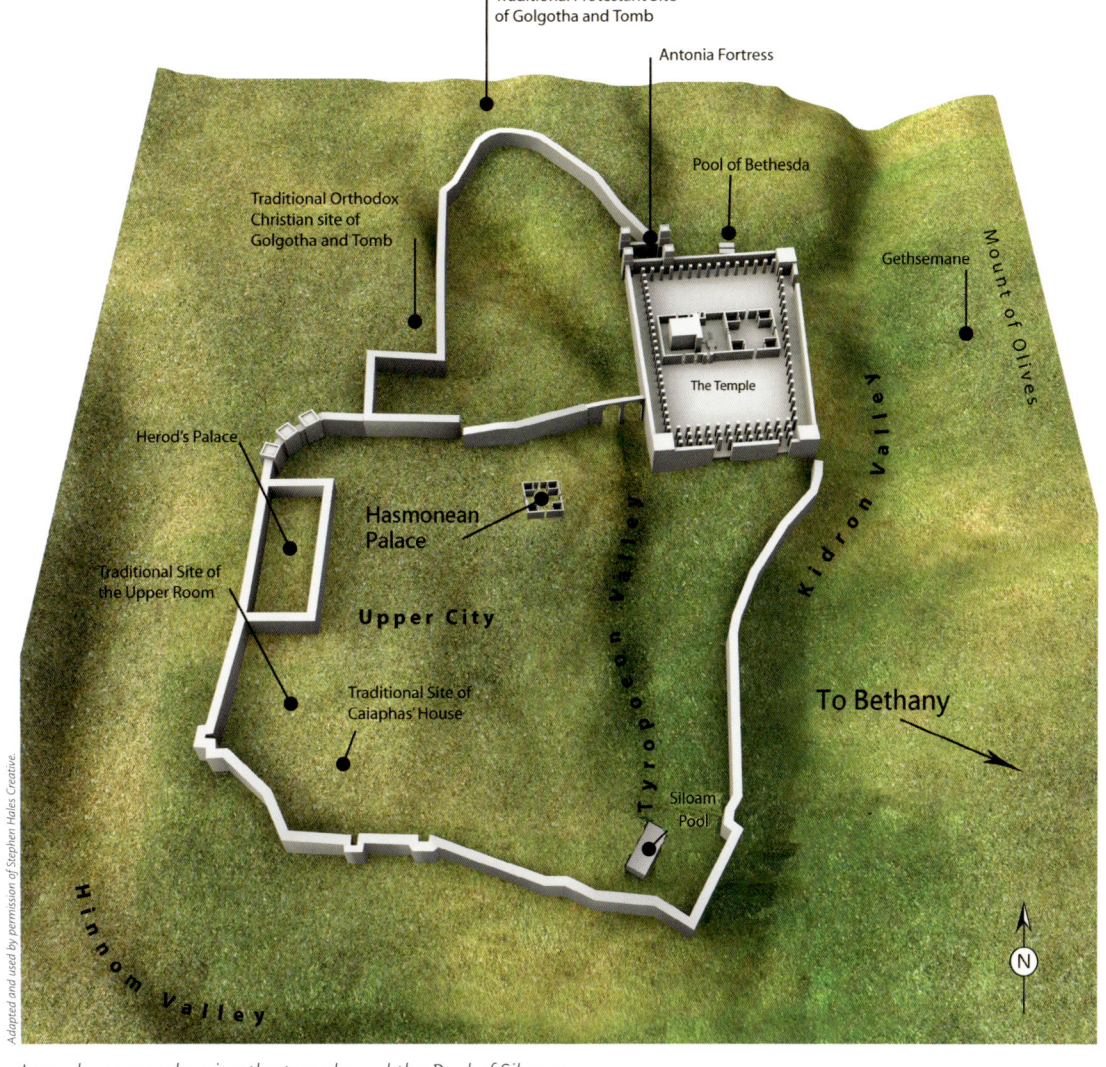

*Jerusalem map showing the temple and the Pool of Siloam.*

John usually omits the details of how Jesus actually performed his miracles, preferring to portray them as simple acts of power with little reference to actions he performed, steps he took, or words he said. But in this instance, Jesus not only uses saliva as an agent, as Mark records that he had done with the deaf-mute man and then the blind man at Bethsaida (Mark 7:33; 8:23) but uses it to make "clay" to anoint the man's eyes. Making this paste could have been taken as a violation of the Sabbath's prohibition against work, illustrating again that the importance of Jesus' healing ministry outweighed such

Jesus Opens the Eyes of a Man Born Blind, by Duccio di Buoninsegna.

The Blind Man Washes in the Pool of Siloam, by James Tissot.

Steps leading down into the remains of the partially excavated Pool of Siloam.

restrictions.[20] Washing away this mud has often been interpreted as representing how the man's blindness was "washed away."[21]

But the symbolism that we saw in John's account of the miracle at Cana, where water represented both spirit and divinity, together with this story's connection with the Creation narrative, may also help explain the symbolism of Jesus' action here. Just as the Lord God created Adam from the dust of the ground and placed "the breath of life [Hebrew, *nišmaṯ ḥayyîm*]" into him to make him "a living soul" (Genesis 2:7), so here Jesus took some of his saliva—a type of water, which can represent spirit in John's Gospel[22]—and mixed it with the dust of the ground. Man started out in a more perfect state, but since the Fall has become susceptible to all types of mortal frailties, including, in this case, blindness. Significantly, Jesus sent the man to wash in the Pool of Siloam (Hebrew, *šiloaḥ*), the pool used in the rituals of the Feast of Tabernacles. The name *šiloaḥ* means "sent," perhaps reflective that Jesus had been sent to redeem fallen man. One could, perhaps, even extend baptismal imagery to this act, seeing such "washing" as the means by which the benefits of Christ's Atonement are applied to all.

As washing in Siloam connects the healing of the blind man with the imagery of water in the Feast of Tabernacles, that feast's connection with light and Jesus' own claim to be the Light of the World suggests the imagery of regaining sight. After the man was healed, a controversy arose with the Pharisees, who questioned the man and then his parents about how his healing had come about. The Pharisees could not accept the man's story, because in their minds, Jesus' actions on the Sabbath disqualified him from being a man of God (John 9:16). Three times they revealed their ignorance, not understanding how this miracle could have taken place (John 9:16, 24, 29).[23] In their argument with Jesus, he made clear that their ignorance was a sign that they were, in fact, blinder than the blind man had been. After Jesus proclaimed that he had come "that they which see not might see; and that they which see might be made blind," the Pharisees asked whether they were blind, to which

> ### "Amazing Grace"
>
> The first verse of the beloved classic Christian hymn "Amazing Grace" attests to the power of Jesus to restore sight, both physical and spiritual, exclaiming: "I once was lost, but now am found, / *Was blind, but now I see.*"[24] Indeed, the life story of this hymn's author is a powerful illustration of the Lord's ability to help sinners see the error of their ways and come to a knowledge of his goodness and redemption. John Newton (1725–1807) lived the first part of his life as a dissolute sailor and then as captain of a British slave ship. On March 10, 1748, Newton's reading Thomas à Kempis's *Imitation of Christ* during a frightening storm while at sea began the process of his conversion.
>
> Becoming a Christian and leaving his inhumane profession, he later was ordained an Anglican minister. Throughout his ministry he worked for the abolition of slavery in the British Empire, and Parliament finally did so the year of his death.[25] Just as Newton came to see the error of his previous life and a new life was revealed to him, so can the grace of God open all our eyes and fit us for Christ's service.

Jesus responded, "If ye were blind, ye should have no sin: but now ye say, We see; therefore your sin remaineth" (John 9:39–41).

Likewise, when we refuse to see and accept Christ for who he is, we are blind to the forgiveness and salvation he offers us. In contrast, when we come to him and are obedient to his simple command to wash, he becomes our light.

## Seeing and Following Jesus

Jesus' last journey to Jerusalem drew to a close as he left Jericho and began the final ascent to Jerusalem. There he encountered and healed a blind man begging by the side of the road (Mark 10:46–52; Matthew 20:29–34; Luke 18:35–43). Neither Matthew nor Luke names the man; in fact, Matthew tells of two blind beggars on the road out of Jericho, which is probably another example of Matthean doubling. Mark, however, names him Bartimaeus, which is the patronymic *bar Tim'ai*, the Aramaic form of "son of Timaeus." Other than Luke's summary of women helped and healed by Jesus (Luke 8:1–3), the only beneficiaries of miracles whose names are recorded are Bartimaeus and Lazarus. The daughter of Jairus is identified by her father's name, and the name of the man whose ear is healed in Luke is known only by cross-referencing the story with the account in John. In this case, however, the name might also have been figurative, since it could have come from the Aramaic *tamea*, meaning "uncleanness." The name Bartimaeus might thus have meant something like "son of defilement," reflecting the rejection of the blind beggar by the larger society.[26] Regardless, the lack of precise naming in all the other miracle stories has allowed them to serve as types rather than restricting them

CAUSING THE BLIND TO SEE AND THE DEAF TO HEAR   101

The Healing of Two Blind Men from Jericho, *Byzantine School (sixth century).*

to precise, single experiences, but something about this particular man led Mark to preserve either his actual name or a figurative description.[27]

In all three synoptic Gospels, the blind man (or men, in Matthew's account) called upon Jesus as "son of David," even though this title is rare in Mark and Luke. This title is generally seen as messianic because of God's promise to David that his seed would reign forever (2 Samuel 7:12–16). Interestingly, by the first century A.D., Solomon, the only one in the Old Testament actually called "son of David," had come to be seen as a great healer and exorcist.[28] Although many Jews of Jesus' time might have been expecting a military deliverer as messiah, perhaps this blind beggar, having heard of Jesus' reputation as a healer and miracle worker in Galilee, was expressing his faith in Jesus' being a different kind of son of David. As those around him tried to silence him, Bartimaeus continued to cry, "Thou Son of David, have mercy on me" (Mark 10:48). When he was taken to Jesus and the Lord asked what he wanted, he answered directly, "*Lord* [Greek, *rabbouni*], that I might receive my sight" (Mark 10:51; emphasis added).

Christ Healing the Blind Man of Jericho, *Italian School (seventeenth century)*.

Though the King James Version renders the word simply as "lord," *rabbouni* actually means "my lord." Its use here is noteworthy because its only other use is by Mary Magdalene when she encountered the risen Lord (John 20:16).[29] The impression is that Bartimaeus did not just call upon Jesus for healing—he was calling on him as his master and Savior. Jesus responded by saying, "Go thy way; thy faith *hath made thee whole* [Greek, *sesōken se*]. And immediately he received his sight, and *followed* [Greek, *ēkolouthei*] Jesus *in the way*" (Mark 10:52; emphasis added).

Bartimaeus' faith had not just brought about his healing but saved him (*sesōken se*). Further, all three synoptic Gospels agree that after he regained his sight, he followed Jesus, the evangelists using forms of the Greek verb *akoloutheō* that is commonly used for disciples following their master. Mark adds that he "followed Jesus in the way," perhaps implying that he became a Christian, since in the first decades Christ's Church was known as "the way." In fact, Mark's detail that Bartimaeus had immediately cast aside his garment, perhaps meaning the cloak he had spread to gather alms, compares him favorably with the rich young man who was hesitant to give up all that he had to follow Jesus in discipleship (Mark 10:17–22).[30]

Following Jesus "in the way" in this instance literally meant to walk with him on the road up to Jerusalem, where Jesus was about to begin his Passion Week. The story of Bartimaeus concludes the section of the Gospel of Mark that treats the road to Jerusalem—and the blindness of the disciples. Whereas the healing of the blind man at Bethsaida in stages had represented how Peter and the other disciples started with an incomplete vision of who Jesus was and what he had come to do, the account of Bartimaeus shows that a full understanding of what it meant that Jesus was the Son of David included understanding that he had come to bring mercy and healing. As our spiritual eyes are more fully opened to this truth, and as we follow Jesus on his road to Gethsemane, Golgotha, and the empty tomb, we more fully appreciate the symbolism of opening eyes and ears to the truth of the gospel message of salvation.

# 5
# Raising the Dead
## *He That Believeth on Me Shall Never Die*

*And when he thus had spoken, he cried with a loud voice, Lazarus, come forth. And he that was dead came forth.*

—John 11:43–44

Perhaps no miracle is as momentous as one that involves the raising of the dead. Whether it happens to us or to those whom we love, death represents the greatest possible loss. For those without a firm conception of an afterlife, it can appear to be an absolute, often dreadful, end to existence. Even for those with a conviction that life continues after death, it can nonetheless be shrouded in uncertainty and even, at times, with fear. At the very least, it represents an unwelcome separation from those whom we love for a period of time. Only when death brings with it an end to extreme suffering, difficulty, or loneliness is it usually welcome. As a result, raising the dead represents the greatest of hopes, and its accomplishment results in pronounced joy.

Two Old Testament prophets, Elijah and Elisha, had each raised the son of a devastated mother (1 Kings 17:17–24; 2 Kings 4:32–37). Jesus, however, raised not one but at least three people from the dead, each from a very different social background and life situation. As with all of Jesus' miracles, these examples of his restoring individuals to life also involve great symbolism. Each person raised was returned to mortal life and would eventually die from other causes, whether old age, later illness, or accident. Yet each case also foreshadowed Jesus' own coming resurrection, which conquered death permanently by inseparably reuniting the spirit with an immortal body. Resurrection is thereby a miracle that will come to all of us on account of Jesus' victory over death, a miracle that is also combined with the greatest of healings, because it will also overcome all mortal disabilities, infirmities, and other challenges (2 Nephi 9:11–13; Alma 11:42–45; 40:21–23). Nevertheless, during his ministry Jesus taught, "I am come that they might have life, and that they might have it more abundantly" (John 10:10), referring to this life in mortality, not just the life to come. Thus, in addition to

### Raising the Dead

- Raising the son of the widow of Nain (Luke 7:11–17)

- Raising the daughter of Jairus (Mark 5:21–24, 35–43; parallels Matthew 9:18–19, 23–26; Luke 8:40–42, 49–56)

- Raising Lazarus (John 11:1–46)

Jesus also reports on his raising of the dead to the disciples of John the Baptist in Matthew 11:2–6 (parallel Luke 7:18–23).

*Opposite:* The Raising of Lazarus, *by Carl Bloch. Courtesy of Intellectual Reserve, Inc.*

the clear and vital symbolism about the eventual resurrection, the examples of Jesus' raising the dead, particularly in the case of Lazarus, also represent how those who believe in Jesus are raised to a higher, more spiritual life even while here on earth. By overcoming spiritual death for us, Jesus bridged the chasm that lies between fallen men and women and God.

## Raising the Son of the Widow of Nain

Of the four Gospel writers, only Luke tells the story of the widow of Nain, whose son Jesus revived even as his body was being taken to its burial (Luke 7:11–17). Placed in the Gospel after the account of the healing of the centurion's son and before the calming of the storm, this story may have been the first instance of Jesus' raising someone from the dead (see Appendix A). From Luke we learn that Jesus approached the city of Nain in Galilee, accompanied by a large following of disciples and others. The site of ancient Nain is now occupied by the Arab village of Na'in some four miles southeast of Nazareth. The town has a beautiful view of the Jezreel Valley, which might have given it its name, *na`în*, meaning "lovely" or "charming."[1]

At the gate of this town Jesus met the funeral procession of the young man, described as "the only son [Greek, *monogenēs huios*] of his mother, and *she was a widow*" (Luke 7:12; emphasis added). Moved with compassion, Jesus told the bereft mother not to weep, touched the funeral bier, and called upon the widow's son, saying, "Young man, I say unto thee, *Arise* [Greek, *egerthēti*]" (Luke 7:14; emphasis added). Immediately the young man sat up alive and began to speak.

Of the three recorded instances of Jesus' raising the dead, this story has the most in common with the Old Testament stories of Elijah and Elisha. Elijah raised the son of the woman of Zarephath, who, as in this story, was also a widow. Elisha revived the only son of the Shunamite woman, whose home, Shunem, was probably at the site of the modern Arab village of Sulam, less than two miles southwest of Nain.[2] Yet while Jesus' miracle at Nain might have been anticipated by these earlier Old Testament stories, there were significant differences. Jesus does not seem to have known the widow at Nain before he raised her son from the dead, and he helped her without any request or expression of faith on her part. Elijah and Elisha, on the other hand, had been guests of the women whom they helped, and both mothers had begged the prophets to help their sons, who were resuscitated privately in their own houses. Jesus, on the other hand, performed the miracle at Nain in public before much of the town. One other difference is that

*This small but beautiful church at Nain commemorates the raising of the widow's son.*

the Shunamite woman, whose son's conception had been a miracle itself, was not only married but also quite wealthy.³

The emphasis on the widowhood of the woman at Nain, however, underscores her desperate plight: both her husband and her son were dead. The Greek term used for the young man when Jesus calls upon him to arise is *neaniske*. Though this word means "youth," it can refer to any man until about the age of forty,⁴ making it possible that he had been a young adult and his widowed mother's only source of support. His death was thus not only a devastating personal loss for her but may also have represented an economic catastrophe. In Luke's account, she neither speaks nor acts at any point in the story; she is, according to one scholar, "a nameless, silent object of pity."⁵ As a result, the miracle is portrayed as a pure act of kindheartedness on the part of Jesus, illustrating his interest in and concern for women, the poor, and the marginalized.⁶

Jesus stopped the procession of the funeral cortege by touching the bier, an act that would have incurred ritual defilement according to strict interpretation of the law. As usual for Jesus, such considerations were not important in view of his healing ministry and his desire to help those who were suffering. Just as Jesus frequently healed people by raising them from their sick beds, so Jesus here commanded the young man to "arise," using a form of the same verb, *egeirō*, that is also used in connection with resurrection. Thus, while this man's resuscitation was only a return to mortal life,

*Nain, where Jesus raised the widow's son, lies within sight of Mount Tabor and is just over the hill from Shunem, where the prophet Elisha also raised a woman's son.*

it nevertheless serves as anticipation of Jesus' own permanent conquest of death. This connection is underscored by Luke's emphasis that the young man was the widow's only son (Greek, *monogenēs huios*), even as Christ is the Only Begotten (Greek, *monogenēs*) of the Father (John 1:18).[7] Though Mary had other children with Joseph (Mark 6:3; Matthew 13:55), Joseph is not mentioned again as being alive after the stories of Jesus' birth and boyhood. As a result, there is also a certain parallelism between the widow of Nain and Mary, a widow who was soon to witness the death of her own beloved son.

After the young man arose, Jesus "delivered him to his mother" (Luke 7:15), even as Elijah had delivered the child of the widow of Zarephath back to her, saying, "See, thy son liveth" (1 Kings 17:23). At Nain the crowd reacted with both fear and awe, giving glory to God and exclaiming, "A great prophet is risen up among us" and "God hath visited his people" (Luke 7:16). Given Nain's proximity to Old Testament Shunem, the multitude may well have had Elisha in mind. Yet the public wonder and expressions of praise must have paled in comparison to the heartfelt relief and overwhelming joy of the mother, which is not recorded.

Jesus Raising a Young Man from the Dead in a City Called Nain, by William Brassey Hole.

The miracle of Jesus' raising the widow's son was only the first of others he would perform, each of which looked forward to a much greater, everlasting restoration of life. That ultimate miracle will restore all of our loved ones to us, with a promise of our never being separated again if we are true and faithful.

## Raising the Daughter of Jairus

The loss of a child is terrible not only to the lonely or the poor but to every parent. Regardless of one's standing in life, the prospect of a parent needing to bury a child is one that tears at the heart,

> ## Views of Death and the Afterlife in the Ancient World
>
> For the earliest Hebrews, death may have been considered a relocation from this world to another in which one was "gathered unto his people," presumably one's parents and other ancestors who had already died (Genesis 25:8, 17; 35:29; 49:33). Whatever better understanding the early patriarchs and later prophets had of the afterlife, however, appears to have been lost to the Israelites generally, who seem to have had an unclear idea of the nature of life after death. Unlike the Egyptians or Mesopotamians, who had elaborate, detailed conceptions of the afterlife, the world of the dead is not well described in the surviving texts of the Hebrew Bible. It was imagined to be a place separate from *YHWH*, known as Sheol, or "the pit," which was the lowest part of the underworld, in contrast to the highest heaven. Uncertainty resulted in apprehension and fear of death, which was welcome only after a long and happy life and when one left a large, prosperous posterity behind.[8] Possible references to resurrection—such as Job 14:14; Isaiah 26:19; Ezekiel 37:12; or Daniel 12:1–3—do not seem to have been clearly understood or were interpreted metaphorically.[9]
>
> The situation was somewhat similar in traditional Greek mythology, which imagined Hades, or the underworld, as a gloomy, sad place where the dead existed as mere shades, which were pale reflections of people with only echoes of their personalities. With the rise of philosophy, however, the Greek view began to change. Socrates is reported to have believed that the soul was immortal and that death was a separation of the eternal from the mortal body, a separation that was welcome for the virtuous. Some, including Plato, even believed that the soul existed prior to birth.[10]
>
> In the intertestamental period, many Jews began to hold more developed views of the afterlife, including punishment for sins, rewards for righteousness, and even a resurrection of the body, though some, like the Sadducees, denied a resurrection.[11] Continuing uncertainty about the nature of the afterlife no doubt contributed to fear of death and grief over the loss of loved ones, but growing belief in the immortality of the soul, the prospect of judgment, and the hope of a resurrection no doubt prepared many for the good news Jesus preached.

representing death at its worst. The story of Jairus, recorded in all three of the synoptic Gospels, embodies this very situation (Mark 5:21–24, 35–43; Matthew 9:18–19, 23–26; Luke 8:40–42, 49–56). Significantly, Jairus is one of only three persons, Bartimaeus and Lazarus being the other two, whose names are directly connected to any of the Gospel miracle stories.[12] Mark gives what is not only the earliest but also the fullest, most detailed account of Jairus' request and the ensuing resuscitation of his daughter. A leader of the synagogue and apparently wealthy, Jairus met Jesus as he returned, probably to Capernaum, after having cast out the legion of devils on the other side of the Sea of Galilee. Seeing Jesus, Jarius disregarded his social status and, in front of the large crowd that was present, fell down at Jesus' feet,[13] begging Him to go to his home to help his young daughter (Greek, *thygatrion;* KJV, "little daughter"),[14] who was gravely ill and at the point of death. Indeed, Jairus expressed clear faith in Jesus, asking that Jesus lay hands on her "that she may be healed [Greek, *sōthē*]; and she shall live" (Mark 5:23). *Sōthē* is yet another form of *sōzō,* the Greek verb meaning "to save."

As they hurried through the crowds to Jairus' home, the woman with a persistent hemorrhage reached out and touched Jesus and was immediately healed (Greek, *sesōken,* "saved") because of her faith. Although the sequence of events may well have happened this way, the interweaving of these two stories illustrates that the serious illness of the woman and the fatal illness of the girl are both results of the same mortality that they, and we, share. Jesus pronounced that the woman's faith had saved her even as Jairus had begged Jesus to save his daughter, and this theme of healing as salvation ties the stories closely together. Further, the woman had suffered from her hemorrhage for twelve years (Mark 5:25; Luke 8:43), and Jairus' daughter is later described as being twelve years old (Mark 5:42; Luke 8:42). In other words, the whole time Jairus' daughter had been alive, this woman had suffered from her infirmity. Indeed, as these two stories are interwoven with each other, so are they part of a larger section of Mark's narrative that focuses on Jesus' power: first his calming of the storm (Mark 4:35–41), then his casting out of the legion of devils (Mark 5:1–20), and the twin stories of his healing the woman and raising the girl.

## "Death Shall Not Destroy My Comfort"

The stirring American folk song "Death Shall Not Destroy My Comfort" speaks tellingly of the power of Christ to deliver us from the fear of death and take us safely to heaven, where those who love Jesus wait to receive us. The lyrics as we have them now are an amalgamation of verses from different hymnals dating to the 1830s, but their combination has produced a contemplative, moving hope for a peaceful passing through the veil of death.[15] The repeated refrain, "Oh, hallelujah, how I love my Savior!" expresses beautifully the feelings that Jesus engenders in believers.

Death shall not destroy my comfort,
Christ shall guide me thro' the gloom;
Down He'll send some heavenly convoy,
To convey my spirit home.

Jordan's stream shall ne'er o'erflow me,
While my Savior's by my side;
Canaan, Canaan lies before me!
Rise and cross the swelling tide.

Oh, hallelujah! How I love my Savior!
Oh, hallelujah! That I do;
Oh, hallelujah! How I love my Savior!
Mourners, you may love Him too.

See the happy spirits waiting,
On the banks beyond the stream.
Sweet responses still repeating,
"Jesus! Jesus!" is their theme.[16]

The tune to which these lyrics is most often set comes from William C. Hauser's 1878 compilation of shape-note music entitled *Olive Leaf.*[17] The arrangement of this hymn most familiar to Latter-day Saints is the stirring 1998 arrangement by Mack Wilberg, which has been beautifully performed and recorded by both the Brigham Young University Men's Chorus and the Mormon Tabernacle Choir.[18]

As important as this healing was for the woman, to Jairus it no doubt represented a dangerous delay. After they left the woman, and while Jairus and Jesus were still on the way, word came from Jairus' house that his daughter had died. Jesus immediately comforted the bereft father, saying, "Be not afraid [Greek, *mē phobou*], only believe" (Mark 5:36). The form of the verb for "be not afraid" here is present imperative, which means "do not continue being afraid." Jairus had no doubt been frightfully worried from the moment he learned his daughter had become deathly ill. Now his worst fears had been realized, yet Jesus enjoined him to believe.

According to Mark and Luke, the apostles Peter, James, and John were witnesses of the miracle that took place next. Jesus arrived at the house to find it in an uproar of grief. Mocked by many present when he compared the girl's death to sleep,[19] Jesus sent everyone out of the girl's room except his three close disciples, Jairus, and his wife. Mark records, "He took the damsel by the hand, and said unto her, Talitha cumi; which is, being interpreted, Damsel, I say unto thee, *arise* [Greek, *egeire*]"

The Daughter of Jairus, by Carl Bloch.

(Mark 5:41; emphasis added). Although Mark's account records Jesus' actual words in Aramaic,[20] his translation into Greek connects this miracle with the raising of the son of the widow of Nain and with many other healing miracles by once again using a form of the verb *egeirō,* meaning "to raise/to arise." Matthew's Gospel markedly prunes the interwoven stories of Jairus' daughter and the woman with the hemorrhage, reducing them from twenty-two verses to eight. In doing so, Matthew's account telescopes events and leaves out some characters to focus squarely on Jesus and his exercise of power. For instance, Matthew's account omits the name of Jairus, and when the synagogue official first approaches Jesus to make his request, his daughter has already died. This may well have resulted from Matthew's abbreviating, because according to Mark, news of the girl's death reaches them while they are still on the way. But it allows the father to express even greater faith in Jesus' power when he exclaims, "Come and lay thy hand upon her, and she shall live" (Matthew 9:18). Likewise, Matthew leaves out Peter, James, and John as witnesses, focusing solely on Jesus, who entered the girl's room alone and raised her without even needing to say anything.[21]

Luke's account follows Mark's story more closely, leaving out some details but following the same basic order and involving the same characters. Two additions, however, tie Luke's account of the raising of Jairus' daughter more closely to the story of Jesus raising the son of the widow of Nain, to other miracles of Jesus, and to the broader mission of the Savior. First, Luke adds the detail that Jairus' daughter was his only child (Greek, *monogenēs*), using the same word that he uses to describe the widow's son and which John uses to describe Jesus as the Only Begotten. Second, when Jesus responded to the messengers who arrived to tell Jairus that his daughter had died, he again reaffirmed the salvation motif, saying, "Fear not: believe only, and she *shall be made whole* [Greek, *sōthēsetai*]" (Luke 8:50; emphasis added). Once again the Greek original is a form of the verb *sōzō,* meaning "to save." Here again this raising of a dead child is not just an example of resuscitation; it is, in fact, a symbol of how Jesus saves us from death but also from much more.[22]

## The Raising of Lazarus

The raising of Lazarus is the seventh, and arguably the greatest, of the miraculous signs in John (John 11:1–46). As a *sēmeion* (Greek, "sign"), this miracle reveals even more about Jesus than it does about the resuscitation of Lazarus and his restoration to his family. Of the three accounts of Jesus raising the dead, the story of Lazarus is the longest and most developed, partly because it is prefaced by Jesus' compassionate interaction with Lazarus' sisters, Martha and Mary, and because it includes his own powerful pronouncement of how he is the resurrection and the life. Even before those passages, however, John sets up the story by describing how Jesus delayed his going to Lazarus when he first heard that his friend was sick, ensuring that Lazarus would die before he got there. This delay provided him an opportunity to show God's power in the midst of sorrow and loss (John 11:1–16).

Lazarus and his sisters lived in Bethany, a village on the eastern side of the Mount of Olives traditionally associated with the Arab town of al-Eizariya, which preserves the name of Lazarus and is

Courtesy of Eric Huntsman.

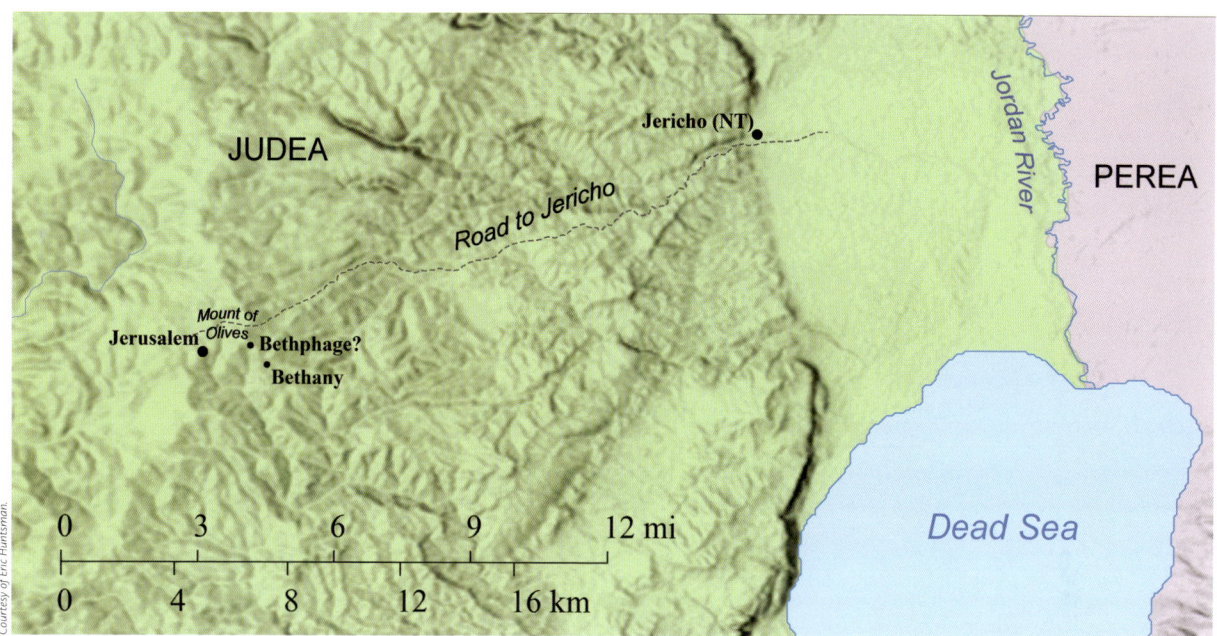

This map of Judea shows Jericho, where Jesus healed blind Bartimaeus, and Bethany, where Jesus raised Lazarus from the dead.

Courtesy of Eric Huntsman.

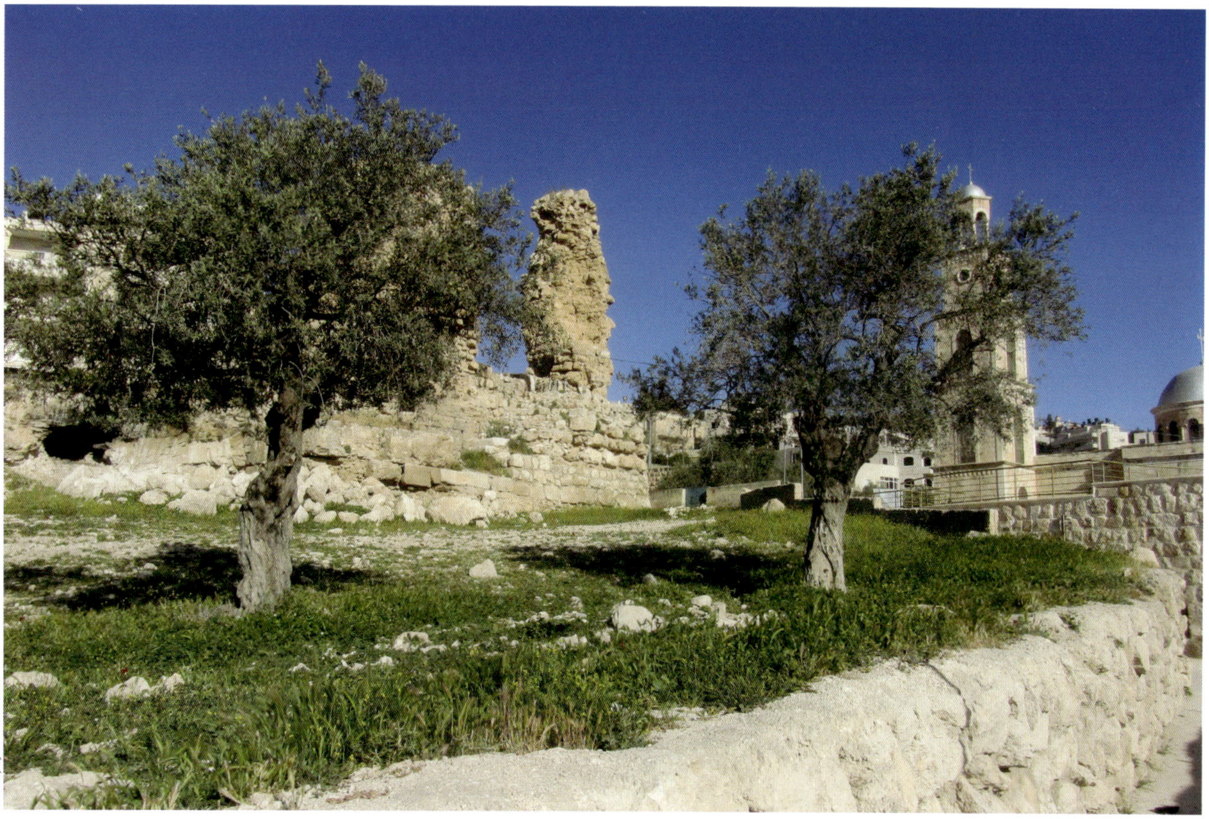

Ruins of a Byzantine church and a modern Greek Orthodox church atop the hill above al-Eizariya, the modern Arab town on the site of the New Testament town of Bethany.

*Inside the Franciscan church at Bethany a mural over the altar proclaims that Jesus is the Resurrection and the Life.*

less than two miles from Jerusalem.[23] The original town name, Bethany, might come from *bêt 'anya*, which is Hebrew for either "house of the poor" or "house of misery."[24] As a result, the New Testament town might have been associated with an almshouse meant to care for the poor and the sick close to but out of sight of Jerusalem.[25] Nevertheless, there are indications that Lazarus and his sisters might have been relatively prosperous. They hosted Jesus and his disciples regularly in their home (Luke 10:38–39; John 11:3; 12:1–8), they owned a substantial cave-tomb (John 11:38), and at Lazarus' death, Martha and Mary were visited by "the Jews" (John 11:19, 31, 45), a term which in John usually refers to members of the leadership in nearby Jerusalem. Socially and economically, therefore, Lazarus and his family seem to have been located somewhere between the poor widow of Nain and Jairus, the ruler of a synagogue. But a more definite difference between this story of raising the dead and the others is that when Jesus arrived in Bethany, he found that Lazarus had been in the tomb for four days (John 11:17). In contrast, the daughter of Jairus had just died in her own room, and the son of the widow of Nain was on his way to be buried. According to beliefs of the time, the spirit of the dead lingered in or near the tomb for up to three days, so the four days mentioned here indicated that Lazarus was definitely, irrevocably dead.[26]

When Martha heard that Jesus was near, she went out to meet him, leaving Mary in their home. Martha's subsequent interchange with Jesus reveals considerable faith and a good understanding of the gospel, which contrasts with the impression conveyed by the story in Luke of her busily preparing a meal while her sister Mary took the time to sit and learn at Jesus' feet (Luke 10:38–42).[27] For example, when Martha complained that Lazarus would not have died if Jesus had been there earlier, she immediately went on to testify, "But I know, that even now, whatsoever thou wilt ask of God, God will give it thee" (John 11:22). Then, after Jesus reminded her that her brother would rise again, she confessed her faith that he would rise in the resurrection at the last day.

Jesus' proclamation that he is the Resurrection and the Life, which follows this exchange, anticipated more than just the miracle that he was about to perform in raising Lazarus from the dead. It also looked forward to the glorious resurrection that his own conquest of death would make possible: "He that believeth in me, though he were dead, yet shall he live" (John 11:25). Lazarus, a disciple who had died, would soon live again. Yet all who believe in Jesus will also live again, and more than that, they will live forever. But when Jesus taught Martha that those who believed in him would live again, he was not just referring to the general resurrection. All who die will be restored to their bodies. In his

Raising of Lazarus, by J. Kirk Richards.

A sign in Hebrew, Arabic, and English marks the traditional site of Lazarus' tomb in al-Eizariya.

A first-century tomb in Bethphage is much like the tombs that would have held the bodies of Lazarus and Jesus.

discourse on the divine Son soon after the healing of the man at the Pool of Bethesda (John 5:17–47), Jesus had taught that all would come forth from their graves, "they that have done good, *unto the resurrection of life;* and they that have done evil, unto the resurrection of damnation" (John 5:29; emphasis added). Thus when Jesus referred to believers living again, he could have meant that they would rise in "the resurrection of life," receiving glorified, immortal bodies and eternal life, usually defined as the kind of life that God and Christ have.[28]

Bearing in mind this understanding of eternal life, however, we see that the next verse presents something of a conundrum: "And whosoever liveth and believeth in me shall never die" (John 11:26). Lazarus had believed in Jesus, yet he had died, as countless of believers in Christ have died since. Clearly when Jesus spoke of believers never dying, he must have been referring to more than just physical death. Indeed, in the Gospel of John, "life" is defined very broadly as the kind of spiritual life that one enjoys, whether in this life or the next, when one has been reborn in Jesus and enjoys his spirit.[29] Death, then, represents living without God's Spirit, which death is lastingly overcome by believers through their faith in Jesus even before the general resurrection. In other words, even if we temporarily die in regard to our physical bodies, those of us who are alive in Christ never die spiritually.

Martha immediately confessed her acceptance of these principles, bearing a profound testimony that mirrors the apostolic testimony borne earlier by Peter after the discourse on the Bread of Life (John 6:69): "Yea, Lord: I believe that thou art the Christ, the Son of God, which should come into the world" (John 11:27).[30] Conversely, Martha's sister, Mary, was too inconsolable in grief to engage in such theological discussions. When she came out to meet Jesus, "she fell down at his feet, saying unto him, Lord, if thou hadst been here, my brother had not died" (John 11:32). John then records that Jesus was deeply moved, groaned, and wept along with Mary, leading those who observed the scene to comment on how much he loved Lazarus (John 11:34–38). Jesus' "mourning with those who mourn"

## When Death Comes

Although there are attested cases of the dead being raised in the modern era,[31] the raising of the dead remains one of the rarest kinds of miracles today. For almost all of us, our own deaths and those of our loved ones will not be overcome until the Resurrection. As a result, the most meaningful miracles when death comes are those that involve an easy passing, relief from suffering, longed-for reunions with those who have gone before, and the sweet comfort that comes from the Holy Ghost in the face of loss.

The Lord understands the real pain of human loss. Recognizing the strength of our relationships, he commanded, "Thou shalt live together in love, insomuch that thou shalt weep for the loss of them that die" (D&C 42:45). During such times of grief we can and should turn to him for comfort. My maternal grandmother often spoke of how the devastating loss of her beloved husband was cushioned by the overwhelming power of the Spirit, which she described as enveloping her like a thick, warm gray blanket as she mourned alone in the hospital. In addition, the Lord expects us to comfort others, which we must do sensitively and with the Spirit. Frequently our attempts at expressing sympathy fail, sincere but oft-repeated platitudes fall flat, or words escape us entirely. Jesus' own example before the raising of Lazarus, therefore, stands as an important example of how to comfort people. When Martha responded to her grief with faith and hope, Jesus responded with testimony and the teaching of doctrine. But when Mary wept, Jesus did not speak. He simply wept with her.

After several long battles with cancer, my father was told by his doctors that his last month would be agonizing and difficult, but in my final blessing to him, I was impressed to promise him that while it was not permitted for him to live longer than his body could sustain life, it was nonetheless his blessing and his privilege to call upon his Father in Heaven when he was ready to go and then pass easily. Three nights later he died quietly in his sleep. That may not be the case for everyone, and many are called upon to endure pain until the very end. But we are assured that at least from a spiritual perspective, death *can* be easy for believers: "It shall come to pass that those that die in me shall not taste of death, *for it shall be sweet unto them*" (D&C 42:46; emphasis added).

on this occasion, even when he knew full well that he was about to raise Lazarus from the grave, witnesses powerfully how much he loves his disciples and feels their pains.

The miracle that followed when Jesus called Lazarus forth from his grave was more strongly connected to his own coming resurrection than either the story of the son of the widow of Nain or of Jairus' daughter. Upon their deaths, both Lazarus and Jesus were laid in rock tombs sealed with stones. While that was not in itself unusual, John's specific reference to taking away the stone from the opening of each tomb connects these episodes (John 11:41; 20:1). Lazarus' coming forth from the tomb therefore symbolizes Jesus' resurrection, but there are also differences. Lazarus was called out of his tomb, whereas Jesus, at least in John's account, came forth from the sepulcher on his own. As he had taught earlier in his discourse on the Good Shepherd (John 10:1–18), "Therefore doth my Father love me, because I lay down my life, that I might take it again. No man taketh it from me, but I lay it down of myself. I have power to lay it down, and *I have power to take it again*" (John 10:17–18; emphasis added). Likewise, both Lazarus and Jesus were buried with their bodies wrapped in grave clothes and their faces covered by a facecloth (Greek, *soudarion;* KJV, "napkin"), but the disposition of those grave goods after their coming forth from their tombs was different. Lazarus came forth still dressed in the grave clothes and facecloth (John 11:44), whereas Jesus came forth from the tomb on his own, after having previously removed the facecloth and his grave clothes and placing them separately in the tomb (John 20:7). The implication is that Lazarus, having been restored to mortal life, will need his grave clothes again, whereas Jesus, having risen from the tomb once and for all, has no more need of them.[32]

## Conquering Death, Granting Life

The positions of these three stories in the narratives of the Gospels reveals important truths about Jesus. Luke places the story of the raising of the son of the widow of Nain immediately before Jesus' report to the disciples of John the Baptist that they had witnessed "the blind see, the lame walk, the lepers are cleansed, the deaf hear, *the dead are raised,* to the poor the gospel is preached," all of which were signs that Jesus was the One for whom they had been waiting (Luke 7:22; emphasis added; Matthew 11:5). Although that saying of Jesus is only loosely based upon such passages in the Hebrew Bible as Isaiah 35:5–6 and 42:7, it nonetheless clearly reflects an important messianic expectation at his time. Further, the great Old Testament prophet Isaiah had certainly foreseen and celebrated how God would finally defeat the power of death (Isaiah 25:8; 26:19); thus, Jesus' miracles, especially his power over death, demonstrated that he was in fact *the* Messiah. Luke followed Mark's lead in placing the raising of the daughter of Jairus at the

*The Garden Tomb north of the Old City of Jerusalem is a peaceful spot where pilgrims may picture in their minds what the scene might have been like at Jesus' resurrection on the first Easter morning.*

culmination of a series of miracles (Luke 8:22–56; compare Mark 4:35–5:43). Jesus' power over the storm and sea, the legion of devils, the illness of the woman with the hemorrhage, and then even death illustrates vividly his control of the elements, spiritual forces, sickness, and finally life itself. But, most powerfully, the account in the Gospel of John of the raising of Lazarus occurs immediately before Jesus' Passion Week (John 12:1–19:42), showing that just as he had restored Lazarus to life, so he would overcome death for himself and thereby conquer death for all of us.

In all three stories of Jesus' raising people from the dead, he not only restored life to those who had lost it but healed them of whatever diseases or illnesses had brought about their deaths, pointing to the great restoration that will occur for all of us in the resurrection, when mortal infirmities, disabilities, and other challenges are overcome. Jesus also showed great compassion for those who had lost loved ones, erasing grief and giving joy to a desolate widow who had lost a son, to shattered parents mourning their daughter, and to anguished sisters who had buried their beloved brother. Nevertheless, these reunions anticipate only a fraction of joy that will greet the reunions that will accompany the resurrection (see 1 Thessalonians 4:13–18).

In addition to all this, the stories of Jesus raising the dead are also about his granting us life in a spiritual sense. Those who are separated from God because of the Fall and their own sins suffer from a form of spiritual death even while they are alive physically (Alma 42:9; D&C 29:41–44). Thus Jesus' raising individuals from the dead during his ministry may be taken as a type of his power to come into people's lives and free them from spiritual death when they are born again spiritually (John 3:3–5; Romans 6:4; Mosiah 5:7; Alma 5:14). This kind of Spirit-filled life in Christ helps explain sayings of Jesus in the Gospel of John in which believers are described as enjoying everlasting or eternal life even *while in this life* (see, for example, John 3:36; 5:24; 6:47; 10:28). Still, as rich and abundant as this Spirit-filled life can be, it is only a foretaste of that eternal life that Christ will grant after the resurrection, which is the greatest of the gifts of God (1 Nephi 15:36; D&C 14:7).

## Conclusion
# THE GREATEST MIRACLES OF ALL

*Lo, he cometh unto his own, that salvation might come unto the children of men
even through faith on his name; and even after all this they shall consider him a man,
and say that he hath a devil, and shall scourge him, and shall crucify him. And he shall arise
the third day from the dead; and behold, he standeth to judge the world; and behold, all
these things are done that a righteous judgment might come upon the children of men.*

—Mosiah 3:9–10

In a stinging rebuke Jesus condemned three of the cities where he had performed most of his miracles: "Woe unto thee, Chorazin! woe unto thee, Bethsaida! for if the mighty works [Greek, *dynameis*], which were done in you, had been done in Tyre and Sidon, they would have repented long ago in sackcloth and ashes. But I say unto you, It shall be more tolerable for Tyre and Sidon at the day of judgment, than for you. And thou, Capernaum, which art exalted unto heaven, shalt be brought down to hell: for if the mighty works [again, Greek, *dynameis*], which have been done in thee, had been done in Sodom, it would have remained until this day. But I say unto you, That it shall be more tolerable for the land of Sodom in the day of judgment, than for thee" (Matthew 11:21–24; parallel Luke 10:13–15). In this passage, the evangelists describe the mighty works of Jesus by using the Greek word commonly used to mean "miracles." Matthew and Luke thereby underscore a vital point: As powerful as miracles may be and no matter how much they might bless the lives of their recipients, they do not bring about salvation if people do not allow those miracles to bring them to Christ.

As the Lord explained to Joseph Smith, we should seek for spiritual gifts, including miracles, "always remembering for what they are given" (D&C 46:8). Although Jesus in his compassion certainly alleviated suffering, healed illness, and assuaged grief, the symbolism involved in these miracles suggests that they have greater, lasting meaning that is intended to bring people, then and now, more fully to him.

The story of the woman caught in adultery (John 8:1–11) stands in marked contrast to the responses of the people of Bethsaida, Chorazin, and Capernaum. In the account as it has come down to us,[1] Jesus performed no mighty work as such for the woman, but he accomplished perhaps an even greater feat by saving the woman from the angry, judgmental mob as he taught a lasting principle, "He that is without sin among you, let him first cast a stone at her" (John 8:7). He then put her on the

*Opposite:* Christ Consolator, *by Carl Bloch.*
*Courtesy of Statens Museum for Kunst, Copenhagen.*

Jesus and the Sinner Woman, by Vasily Polenov.

path to repentance: "When Jesus had lifted up himself, and saw none but the woman, he said unto her, Woman, where are those thine accusers? hath no man condemned thee? She said, No man, Lord. And Jesus said unto her, Neither do I condemn thee: go, and sin no more" (John 8:10–11). Though nothing is known about the woman's subsequent actions, her encounter with Jesus may well have worked a mighty change in her that was even greater than the changing of water into wine by leading her to forgiveness, sanctification, and eventual eternal life.

Tellingly, Jesus' direction to the woman that she should "go, and sin no more" reveals that his compassion did not minimize the significance of her sin nor absolve her of responsibility. Yet while mercy cannot rob justice, "mercy claimeth all which is her own" (Alma 42:24). Jesus' compassion in this instance is the same as his response in so many other stories of his miracles, illustrating how the higher laws of love and mercy transcended the demands of strict legalism and ritual observance. Yet as the Word made flesh, this very Jesus was the same *YHWH*, the Great I Am, who had given the law

> ### "Come unto Him"
>
> Daniel Carter based the beautiful song "Come unto Him," which is at once calming and stirring, on the text of Matthew 11:28–30. Working long hours at a factory to put himself through school had exhausted him, but on a hot summer evening in 1978, reading this passage in Matthew inspired him. The family with whom he was living had just bought a new piano that was placed in the room where he was staying. Quietly playing it as he composed, he worked through the night until he had produced this moving testament to miracles of rest, forgiveness, and eternal love that we find when we come to Christ.[2]
>
> Come unto Him.
> All ye who labor and are weary.
> Come unto Him.
>
> Forsake thy sins,
> Take His yoke upon you,
> And learn of Him.
>
> Come and find rest in Him
> All ye who are heavy laden.
> Come all ye laboring souls
> And ye shall rest in His eternal love.
>
> Come unto him.[3]

(3 Nephi 15:5), some of whose requirements he seemed at times to violate as he reached out in love and power to help those who were suffering and in need. Perhaps the resolution of this seeming tension can be found in looking at the miracles Jesus performed, which, as we have observed, Elder James E. Talmage maintained were not performed in violation of natural law but through the exercise of even higher laws.[4] Indeed, the higher law of love allows mercy to satisfy justice because Jesus himself has paid its demands through his own sacrifice (Alma 34:15–16; 42:13–15). The example of Jesus' love may be particularly important for us in instances when its manifestation superseded not so much legal requirements but rather gender and racial stereotypes, social conventions, self-righteousness, and contemporary expectations, calling us to do likewise as we reach out to individuals in need.[5]

What manner of man, then, is this Jesus? His miracles help us answer that question.[6] His power over the elements helps us understand his divine identity as the great Jehovah, who created heaven and earth and seeks to sustain us, feeding us spiritually even as he provides for our temporal needs. His great acts of healing remind us that he came to heal our hearts and souls as well as our physical bodies, forgiving our sins and strengthening us to do good and enabling us to endure in faith. Casting out devils reveals his great ability to banish from our lives Satan and his influence in all of its forms, even as He works to overcome the effects of the Fall that Satan helped bring about. Restoring sight and hearing reflects Jesus' ability to open our spiritual eyes and ears, helping us learn to recognize truth, especially the truth about himself and his mission. Only then can we hear his voice, enabling us to follow him and preach his word more clearly. Finally, raising the dead points our minds forward to the universal resurrection when Christ will fully and completely defeat death and erase the sorrow of loss.

Christ in Gethsemane, *by Heinrich Hofmann.*

But it also represents his ability to reverse spiritual death, giving us a more abundant spiritual existence in this life and holding out to us the promise of eternal life in the world to come.

Indeed, the greatest miracles of all are those that arise from the atoning suffering and death of Jesus Christ and his gracious intervention in our lives. While miracles like those the Gospels witness that Jesus performed during his ministry can and do happen today, the greater miracles are those that are available to all who will leave behind their sins and burdens and come unto Christ in faith: a change of heart, forgiveness of sin, the healing of the soul, and that strengthening and enabling power that comes from his Atonement. Crowning these miracles are the resurrection, which will come to us all, and the precious gift of eternal life to those who are true and faithful until the end.

# Appendix A
# Miracles in the Gospels

*Whithersoever he entered, into villages, or cities, or country, they laid the sick
in the streets, and besought him that they might touch if it were but the border
of his garment: and as many as touched him were made whole.*

—Mark 6:56

Considerable scholarship in the study and explication of Jesus' miracles continues to unfold, and understanding some of it can help our appreciation of both the power of the Gospel narratives and the importance of the evidence that these texts provide for Jesus' miracle working. This scholarship includes analysis of the literary forms represented by the narratives, summaries, and reports of the miracles in the Gospels. Equally important is how scholarship can help us appreciate the approach of each Gospel author to the miracles, revealing how his particular emphases may have affected his reporting of the mighty deeds of Jesus. While believers accept the Gospel accounts as authoritative and truthful, it is also interesting how biblical scholarship has demonstrated that many of the miracles can, in fact, be largely corroborated as historical by objective historical method.

## Miracle Stories, Summaries, and Reports

The study of miracle accounts in the Gospels often falls under the rubric of form criticism, a scholarly method that examines the structure and characteristics of short, self-contained blocks of text known as pericopes. These pericopes can be seen simply as the rough equivalent of paragraphs, and as such they are helpful in producing outlines of the Gospels that reveal their structure. Form criticism also observes that pericopes can be classified and grouped by the different genres or kinds of writing that they represent. These genres sometimes provide clues to the history and transmission of material found in the Bible. The Gospels, for instance, include both narrative pericopes, which simply relate or tell a story, often in third person, and blocks of discourse, which include the sayings of Jesus and the words of others in the first or second person. Examples of discourse include aphorisms, or short pithy sayings; parables, or comparative stories; dialogues and controversy stories; and longer sermons, such as the Sermon on the Mount. Although the most straightforward kind of narrative is historical narrative, in which the author describes an event, narratives can, of course, include the words of a story's characters when they are subsumed as parts of a larger episode being related by the author, as in a

---

*Opposite:* Christ's Miracles of Healing, *illuminated manuscript from the Bible Moralisee, Paris, ca. 1240, French School. Courtesy of Bridgeman Art Library. Used by permission.*

pronouncement or a commissioning story.[1] Miracle stories often consist of this type of mixed narrative and discourse,[2] and with at least thirty-six examples in the Gospels, stories about the miraculous deeds of Jesus are one of the most common narrative forms (see accompanying list, "The Miracles of Jesus").[3]

Early form criticism developed partially as an attempt to discover the history of oral traditions behind the earliest acknowledged sources for the Gospels, and some early form critics maintained that many Gospel pericopes were preexisting units that the evangelists artfully incorporated into their larger Gospel narratives. Some proponents of this position have gone to considerable lengths to demonstrate how this material was shaped, and perhaps even created, by the first generation of Christians before any of it was incorporated into the written Gospels.[4] Without necessarily accepting the extremes of such form criticism,[5] we can nonetheless benefit from being familiar with some of its more secure observations about the types of writing represented by different pericopes and how they are structured.

For instance, the thirty-six clear miracle stories generally have three sections, or parts. First, a person in need or an individual with a problem is presented to Jesus. Second, Jesus resolves the problem with a word of power or sometimes through an action. Interestingly, the details of how the miracle itself occurred are never narrated: the miracle as an event is beyond human understanding and cannot be fully described.[6] Third and finally, there is a response, ranging from awe, amazement, and gratitude to expressions of faith, though sometimes the recipient continues in disbelief.[7] Through these stories, the evangelists reveal something about the identity of Jesus—his miraculous acts usually allude to his past role as Creator, witnessing that he was, in fact, God made flesh, or pointing to his coming atoning death and resurrection and the eternal blessings that would flow from them.

Besides being an effective storytelling and teaching method, the consistency and relative inflexibility of the miracle story form suggests that these stories were part of a preexisting tradition, probably oral, before the composition of the Gospels. This stability and consistency in form are important because just as the teachings and sayings of Jesus were preserved in the preaching of the apostles before the Gospels were written, so Jesus' deeds also were an important part of the early Christian tradition, no doubt because of what they revealed about him.

Studying the miracle stories as a type of writing also reveals some interesting observations that might not be noticed if each miracle was considered separately. For instance, an interesting feature of the form of miracle stories is that except for Jesus and his main disciples, the recipient of a miracle or those who are interceding for him or her are often left unnamed—Jairus, Bartimaeus, and Lazarus are the only clear exceptions.[8] Likewise, the details of an illness and the exact location where a miracle occurred are often left deliberately vague. In addition, many of the miracle stories are presented as encounters between Jesus and those asking for miracles, revealing important things about the character of each person in the process. Jesus, for instance, consistently demonstrates *philanthrōpia,* or "loving concern," for all he meets; *praotēs,* perhaps best translated as "gentle self-restraint" as he responds to those who act inappropriately or fail to meet expectations; and *epieikeia,* a quality that reflects both "sweetness" and "understanding."[9] Similarly, the behavior of those seeking or receiving miracles show

# The Miracles of Jesus

Producing a secure chronology of the ministry of Jesus is fraught with difficulties, but I have nonetheless attempted in the charts that follow to arrange the miracles of Jesus in approximate sequential order. The following chart lists thirty-six discrete miracle stories, most of which follow the usual pattern established by form criticism: a three-part narrative sometimes mixed with dialogue or another genre of writing.

| Miracle | Main Reference | Parallels | Type |
|---|---|---|---|
| Water to wine | John 2:1–11 | | Nature, Epiphany |
| Royal official's son | John 4:46–54 | compare Matthew 8:5–13; Luke 7:1–10 | Healing |
| Astonishing catch of fish | Luke 5:1–11 | compare John 21:6–11 | Nature, Provision |
| Capernaum demonic | Mark 1:21–28 | Luke 4:33–37 | Exorcism |
| Peter's mother-in-law | Mark 1:29–31 | Matthew 8:14–15; Luke 4:38–39 | Healing |
| Cleansing a leper | Mark 1:40–45 | Matthew 8:1–4; Luke 5:12–15 | Healing |
| Paralytic forgiven and healed | Mark 2:1–12 | Matthew 9:1–8; Luke 5:17–26 | Healing |
| Centurion's servant | Matthew 8:5–13 | Luke 7:1–10; compare John 4:46–54 | Healing |
| Man at the Pool of Bethesda | John 5:5–16 | | Healing, Epiphany |
| Man with withered hand | Mark 3:1–6 | Matthew 12:9–14; Luke 6:6–11 | Healing |
| Raising the son of the widow of Nain | Luke 7:11–17 | | Raising the dead |
| Calming the stormy sea | Mark 4:35–41 | Matthew 8:23–27; Luke 8:22–25 | Nature, Epiphany |
| Gadarene demonic | Mark 5:1–20 | Matthew 8:28–34; Luke 8:26–39 | Exorcism |
| Woman with the hemorrhage | Mark 5:25–34 | Matthew 9:20–22; Luke 8:43–48 | Healing |
| Raising the daughter of Jairus | Mark 5:21–24, 35–43 | Matthew 9:18–19, 23–26; Luke 8:40–42, 49–56 | Raising the dead |
| Two blind men | Matthew 9:27–31 | | Restoring sight and hearing |
| Mute demonic | Matthew 9:32–34 | | Healing, Exorcism |
| Blind and mute demonic | Matthew 12:22–23 | Luke 11:14 | Healing, Exorcism |
| Feeding of the five thousand | Mark 6:32–44; John 6:1–15 | Matthew 14:13–21; Luke 9:12–17 | Nature, Provision, Epiphany |
| Walking on water | Mark 6:45–52; John 6:16–21 | Matthew 14:22–33 | Nature, Epiphany |

| Miracle | Main Reference | Parallels | Type |
|---|---|---|---|
| Daughter of the Syrophoenician woman | Mark 7:24–30 | Matthew 15:21–28 | Exorcism |
| Deaf-mute | Mark 7:31–37 | | Restoring sight and hearing |
| Feeding of four thousand | Mark 8:1–9 | Matthew 15:32–39 | Nature, Provision |
| Blind man at Bethsaida | Mark 8:22–26 | | Restoring sight and hearing |
| Transfiguration | Mark 9:2–9 | Matthew 17:1–9; Luke 9:28–36 | Nature, Epiphany |
| Demonic or epileptic boy | Mark 9:14–29 | Matthew 17:14–21; Luke 9:37–43 | Exorcism, Healing |
| Fish with a coin in its mouth | Matthew 17:24–27 | | Nature, Provision |
| Man born blind | John 9:1–12 | | Restoring sight and hearing |
| Bent woman | Luke 13:10–17 | | Healing, Exorcism language |
| Man with dropsy | Luke 14:1–6 | | Healing |
| Ten lepers | Luke 17:11–19 | | Healing |
| Blind Bartimaeus | Mark 10:46–52 | Matthew 20:29–34; Luke 18:35–43 | Restoring sight and hearing |
| Raising of Lazarus | John 11:1–46 | | Raising the dead |
| Fig tree without fruit | Mark 11:12–14, 20–26 | Matthew 21:18–22; compare Luke 13:6–9 | Nature, Cursing, Parabolic |
| Ear of the servant of the high priest | Luke 22:50–51 | | Healing |
| Astonishing catch of 153 fish | John 21:4–14 | compare Luke 5:3–10 | Nature, Provision, Epiphany |

Three other possible miracles of Jesus do not have the usual miracle story form; in these instances, the evangelists simply described a miraculous action of Jesus, such as passing unseen through a hostile crowd (Luke 4:28–30; John 8:59) or causing his opponents to fall over by simply announcing "I am he" (John 18:6).

| Miracle | Main Reference | Type |
|---|---|---|
| Passing through mob in Nazareth unseen | Luke 4:28–30 | Unusual personal power |
| Passing through mob at temple unseen | John 8:59 | Unusual personal power |
| Words of Jesus causes arresting mob to fall backwards | John 18:6 | Unusual personal power |

that some had faith, some did not, some were timid, some were desperate, and others were demanding—in short, they represent the character and behavior of all of us. Such observations about the function of miracle stories suggests that for the early Christians who preserved and transmitted them, the historical individuals and the original situations were not what was important. Instead, they served as types, or paradigms, of all who come to Christ. Even more important than the miracles themselves is what they say about the identity of Jesus, his character, and the wider salvation that he came to bring.[10]

A second way in which the evangelists describe the miracles of Jesus can be found in another distinct literary form, the summary. The first example of this form in the synoptic Gospels occurs at the end of an account of a busy day of preaching and healing in Capernaum, a day which may have been intended as a paradigm of the work of Jesus. Mark concludes his description of this paradigmatic day with this summary: "And at even, when the sun did set, they brought unto him all that were diseased, and them that were possessed with devils. And all the city was gathered together at the door. And he healed many that were sick of divers diseases, and cast out many devils; and suffered not the devils to speak, because they knew him" (Mark 1:32–34). Such summaries tend to describe groups, not individuals, and types of miracles performed, not particular cases.

Thirteen such summaries appear in the four Gospels, but the greatest number in a single Gospel, ten, occurs in the Gospel of Matthew, which regularly uses summaries at the beginning or end of sections of his text or at pivotal transition points. Matthew's summaries direct the focus of attention to Jesus, not to the sick persons or the crowds, and often pair Jesus' miracle working with his preaching and teaching, though miraculous deeds take less priority than the power of the word (see, for example, Matthew 4:23–25; 9:35–38).[11] Perhaps the most powerful such summary is the Matthean restatement of the Marcan summary of the paradigmatic day at Capernaum, which is made theologically more meaningful by Matthew's linking it with a formula quotation from Isaiah 53:4: "When the even was come, they brought unto him many that were possessed with devils: and he cast out the spirits with his word, and healed all that were sick: *That it might be fulfilled which was spoken by Esaias the prophet, saying, Himself took our infirmities, and bare our sicknesses*" (Matthew 8:16–17; emphasis added).

## Summaries of Jesus' Miracle Working

| Miracle | Main Reference | Parallels | Type |
|---|---|---|---|
| Miracles at Passover | John 2:23 | | Summary |
| Crowds healed and devils cast out | Matthew 4:23–25 | | Healing, Exorcism |
| Healing many at sundown | Mark 1:32–34 | Matthew 8:16–17; Luke 4:40–41 | Healing, Exorcism |
| Crowds healed and devils cast out | Mark 3:7–12 | Matthew 12:15–16 (15–21); Luke 6:17–19 | Healing, Exorcism |

| Miracle | Main Reference | Parallels | Type |
|---|---|---|---|
| Mary Magdalene and other women | Luke 8:2 | | Healing, Exorcism |
| Healed a few sick in Nazareth | Mark 6:2, 5 | Matthew 13:54, 58 | Healing |
| Crowds healed | Matthew 9:35 (35–38) | | Healing |
| Heals before feeding the five thousand | Matthew 14:13–14; John 6:2 | compare Luke 9:10–11 | Healing |
| Many at Gennesaret | Mark 6:53–56 | Matthew 14:34–36 | Healing |
| Many healed and restored | Matthew 15:29–31 | | Healing, Restoring sight and hearing |
| Many healed beyond Jordan | Matthew 19:1–2 | | Healing |
| Blind and lame in the temple | Matthew 21:14 | | Healing, Restoring sight |
| Signs in the presence of disciples | John 20:30–31 | | Summary |

One other form warrants mention, that of the report. On six occasions, the synoptic Gospels preserve pericopes of discourses in which other people report the kinds of miracles that Jesus has performed. On one occasion, scribes from Jerusalem accuse Jesus of casting out devils by means of Beelzebub, thereby providing evidence that they had either seen or heard of Jesus performing such exorcisms (Mark 3:22; Matthew 9:32–34); this charge is repeated on a later occasion (Matthew 12:22–37; Luke 11:14–26). At another time the crowds on the Mount of Olives praise God "for all the mighty works [*dynameōn*] that they had seen" (Luke 19:37). But perhaps the most significant report of a miracle comes from the lips of Jesus himself when he instructs some disciples of John the Baptist, "Go and shew John again those things which ye do hear and see: The blind receive their sight, and the lame walk, the lepers are cleansed, and the deaf hear, the dead are raised up, and the poor have the gospel preached to them" (Matthew 11:4–6; Luke 7:18–22). All but one of these reports appear in Matthew and Luke, the writers of which often seem to share a common source for material they preserve that is not found in Mark. Because both form and source critics suggest that the sayings of Jesus were preserved and circulated separately from stories about the deeds of Jesus, these miracle reports are particularly important in corroborating the types of miracles that Jesus performed.[12]

## Reports of Jesus' Miracle Working

| Miracle | Main Reference | Parallels | Type |
|---|---|---|---|
| Casting out of devils | Mark 3:22 | Matthew 9:34; compare Matthew 12:24–30; Luke 11:15–26 | Report of exorcism |
| Works done in Capernaum | Luke 4:23 | | Report of "what was done" |
| Report to disciples of John the Baptist | Matthew 11:2–6 | Luke 7:18–23; compare John 10:41 | Report of healing, restoring sight, exorcism, raising the dead |
| Woes on Chorazin, Bethsaida, and Capernaum | Matthew 11:20–24 | Luke 10:12–15 | Report of mighty works |
| Casting out of devils | Matthew 12:24–30 | Luke 11:15–26 | Report of exorcism |
| Crowds praise Jesus for the mighty works they have seen | Luke 19:37 | | Report of mighty works |

Although his is not a direct report, Luke as narrator observes that Herod was glad to see Jesus "because he had heard many things of him; and he hoped to have seen some miracle [*sēmeion*] done by him" (Luke 23:8).

## Miracles and the Evangelists

Although many students of the scriptures commonly harmonize the Gospels when studying the ministry and mission of Jesus, harmonizing the texts can obscure the unique emphases, themes, and artistry of the individual evangelists.[13] Unlike form and source criticism, which are primarily concerned with the origins of material in the Gospels, examining the final form of the text to understand how the author used and artfully arranged this material is an important part of the critical tool known as narrative criticism. As part of this approach, understanding the particular styles and the distinct approach of the authors to the figure of Jesus helps explain their depiction of his miracles. Thus a brief review of the evangelists and the main characteristics of their respective texts helps explain why some miracles are recorded in only one of the Gospels and why miracles that do appear in more than one Gospel vary as they do in their parallels.

Though it appears second in the New Testament canon, many scholars believe that the Gospel of Mark was, in fact, the first written. This possibility is strengthened by the fact that the accounts of Matthew and Luke largely follow the outline of Mark, and there are clear examples where these other Gospels have taken an episode or account from Mark and then adapted or changed it. By tradition, the author of the Gospel of Mark is considered to be John Mark, a missionary companion of Paul who later served as the interpreter and assistant of Peter, who may have been the principal source for most of Mark's information about deeds and teachings of Jesus.[14] This authority from Peter, whether directly from the chief apostle or implied by Mark's association with him, helps explain why Matthew's Gospel often follows the Marcan account, even though the author of Matthew, traditionally assumed to have been the apostle Matthew, was presumably an eyewitness to many of the events of Jesus' ministry.[15] Perhaps because Mark is the earliest written of the Gospels, when that Gospel presents miracle stories as encounters between Jesus and individuals, it seems to best preserve the earliest function of these stories as illustrations not only of Jesus' power but also of his character and that of those who sought his help.[16]

Mark records nineteen miracle stories, four summaries, and one report, which together make up a full third of his Gospel. Because Mark is the shortest of the Gospels, it thus has the highest proportion of miracles, even though the other synoptic Gospels record a slightly larger number. Mark's narrative moves very quickly and generally preserves only short sayings of Jesus, but it is nonetheless very descriptive of the actions of Jesus, particularly of his miracles. As a result, in Mark the account of a miracle is often twice as long as the story of the same miracle in Matthew or even Luke. More so than Matthew or Luke, Mark is willing to describe Jesus' words or actions when performing a miracle, despite the possibility that some actions, such as using saliva or pronouncing certain words, could have been confused with contemporary magical practices. Marcan christology portrays Jesus as the strong, though still rather human, representative of the kingdom of God who has come to overthrow the kingdom of Satan. That characterization is particularly apparent in the first part of Mark's Gospel, which perhaps explains why the first miracle he chose to relate is the casting out of the demon in Capernaum (Mark 1:21–28). In short, miracles take precedence over teachings in the first half of Mark, though in that Gospel's Passion narrative the presentation of Jesus as the powerless suffering servant of God results in no miracle other than the cursing of the fig tree (Mark 11:12–14, 20–21).[17]

Matthew, on the other hand, emphasizes the teachings of Jesus over his deeds. Matthew's Gospel contains twenty-one discrete miracle stories, ten summaries, and four reports. Matthew tends to shorten or abridge descriptions of miracles while expanding any discourse associated with them. Although this Gospel contains a summary of Jesus' miracle working in Matthew 4:23–25, the first miracle story is delayed until Matthew 8:2–4, after the Sermon on the Mount (Matthew 5–7). At that point Matthew collocates a series of miracles in ten episodes in Matthew 8–9, perhaps to strengthen his portrayal of Jesus as the New Moses: just as Jesus improved upon Moses' giving of the law with His Sermon on the Mount, likewise He matches the ten plagues of Moses in Egypt with the performance of ten miracles. But for Matthew, Jesus' fulfillment and expansion of the law of Moses comes before miracle working, and in the Matthean summaries, preaching and teaching take precedence over healing (see again Matthew 4:23–25; 9:35–38).[18] Matthew omits some miracles found in Mark, because, perhaps, they did not quite fit his christology, or Mark's description of them was too magical or easily confused with the miracle-working activity of others in the period (Mark 7:31–37; 8:22–26).[19] Also in line with Matthew's emphasis in his christology is his refraining from using encounters in miracle stories to reveal aspects of the character of petitioners. Instead, in Matthew's account, those asking for help do so respectfully and more often with expressions of faith. Above all, the miracles are solidly about Jesus' identity and power.[20]

In contrast to Mark, who emphasizes deeds, including miracles, and Matthew, who stresses the teachings of Jesus, Luke carefully balances the miracles and messages of Jesus in his Gospel.[21] Luke's Gospel includes twenty-one secure miracle stories, not all the same as Matthew's, as well as four summaries, four reports, and one implied report. Not surprisingly, given his traditional identification as the "beloved physician" of Colossians 4:14, Luke evidences particular interest in healings, adding more detail to some healing stories and preserving accounts of three healings not found in the other Gospels (Luke 13:10–17; 14:1–6; 17:11–19). Despite his presumed medical background, Luke is prone to portray healings in the same terms as exorcisms: Jesus rebukes illnesses and casts them out even as he casts out demons, perhaps suggesting that Luke understands that physical infirmities are more than just sicknesses—they are, in fact, a consequence of the Fall, and overcoming the effects of mortality is as much a defeat of Satan as is driving out his minions.[22]

Other characteristics of Luke's Gospel, such as its interest in women and highlighting of the compassion of Jesus even in times of distress, may explain the inclusion of the story of the raising of the son of the widow of Nain (Luke 7:11–17) and the healing of the ear of the high priest's servant at the time of Jesus' arrest (Luke 22:50–51). In line with Luke's christology, the miracles focus on the importance of Jesus, often omitting details about others involved to keep the focus squarely on the Lord.[23] For Luke, the miracles of Jesus identify him as a loving, compassionate, and healing Savior, both for individuals in their need and for all mankind through the salvation he offers.[24] Perhaps more than in the other Gospels, Luke also aligns miracles with faith, whether the faith that precedes the miracle or the faith that its performance engenders.[25]

As is so often the case, the Gospel of John stands apart from the synoptic Gospels. As noted above, John consistently uses the terms *sēmeion,* "sign," or *ergon,* "work," for the miracles of Jesus rather than the usual synoptic term *dynamis,* meaning "powerful deed."[26] In the case of both terms, this usage seems to be a result of John's high christology, meaning that miracles are not just blessings for individual recipients but above all are signs that signify or point to something about Jesus. Likewise, just as the Father worked in

### Seven Signs in the Gospel of John

1. Water into wine (2:1–11)
2. Healing of the nobleman's son (4:46–54)
3. Healing of the lame man at the Pool of Bethesda (5:1–18)
4. Feeding of the five thousand (6:1–15)
5. Walking on water (6:16–21)
6. Healing of the man born blind (9:1–41)
7. Raising of Lazarus (11:1–57)

creation, so Jesus works in the act of re-creation, whether it be through miracles of healing and restoration or the still greater miracle of overcoming sin and death. John makes these christological points by selecting the miracles he chooses to relate: In the first half of his Gospel, John features only seven signs, but they so inform and shape the text that the section composed of John 2–11 is often known as the Book of Signs. John includes one final miracle in John 21:4–14, the astonishing catch of 153 fish.

In addition to these eight miracle stories, John includes two references to the power of the clearly divine Jesus: he passes unseen through a hostile mob in the temple (John 8:59) and causes those in the arresting party to fall over backwards by the simple but powerful words "I am he," which illustrated his true identity as the divine "I Am," or *YHWH* (John 18:6). John also includes two summaries mentioning other signs (*sēmeia*) of Jesus. Interestingly, in all these accounts of miracles, John includes no exorcisms, perhaps because for him the real and final defeat of Satan was accomplished on the cross and not through individual contests with Satan or his demons.[27]

## The "Historicity" of the Miracles

Beginning most notably with David Hume (1711–1776), rationalist authors and thinkers discounted the possibility of miracles, thereby questioning the historicity of the miracle stories contained in the Bible.[28] Thomas Jefferson (1743–1826), Hume's younger contemporary, similarly rejected both the divine identity of Jesus and the reality of his miracles. Although not a biblical scholar or critic himself, nonetheless as an Enlightenment thinker he produced his own edition of the Gospels that excised references to either, thus reducing Jesus to the status of a great moral teacher.[29] Subsequently, two prominent specialists in biblical studies, David Friedrich Strauss (1808–1874) and Rudolf Bultmann (1884–1976), discounted or seriously called into question the historical reliability of the Gospels' testimonies of Jesus' miracles. One of the main points made by such critics as these is that the accounts of miracles in the Gospel texts are largely the creation of the earliest generations of Christians, who they believed interpreted, embellished, or even invented some of the acts of Jesus to reflect their own theological understanding or beliefs.[30]

Nevertheless, some scholars have used the tools of historical criticism to demonstrate the historical probability that Jesus performed acts that his contemporaries saw as miraculous. These efforts are academic rather than being tied to belief or faith, but they are important because they provide objective support to the historicity of Jesus' miracles. In seeking to evaluate historicity, it is important to distinguish between whether something actually happened, which is an objective truth regardless of whether we believe it or can prove it, and whether it can be demonstrated by historical methods to be probable. Only the latter is meant in this discussion of an account's historicity.

Such biblical critics, using the tools of historical criticism, employ several criteria to evaluate the evidence of the New Testament Gospels. One criterion is multiple attestation of sources. Because the Gospels were written surprisingly late (perhaps between A.D. 60 and 90 and thus thirty to sixty years after the events they record), when more than one of the sources presumably used by the evangelists describes a miracle, this multiple attestation strengthens historical probability because the sources were closer to the events than the final texts were. As a result, such attestation of sources gives a greater weight of evidence than more than one Gospel attesting a particular miracle. Such multiple attestation occurs when one of Mark's sources, for instance, the preaching of Peter, and a source common to Matthew and Luke all attest the same miracle.

Another, similar criterion is multiple attestation of forms. Because many form critics maintain that accounts of the deeds and sayings of Jesus may have been preserved, circulated, and transmitted independently, a miracle report in which Jesus or another person claims that He performed exorcisms supports the discrete stories that Jesus cast out demons. For form critics, this is a particularly strong criterion, since they maintain that the forms they have identified are even older, and hence closer to Jesus, than the immediate sources the evangelists used when writing their Gospels.[31]

Because some of these scholars hold that the evangelists exercised considerable liberty—even creativity—when writing their Gospels, a third criterion used is that of coherence, whereby an act is demonstrably in harmony with other acts and teachings of the historical Jesus. Two further criteria include dissimilarity, in which a particular deed is out of character with the Gospel's portrayal of Jesus and hence not likely to have been the creation of the evangelist, and even embarrassment, meaning that an act of Jesus, such as using saliva to heal, was hard to understand or too similar to contemporary pagan practices and hence not likely to have been made up by early Christians.[32]

Of course, believers who accept the Gospels as reliable witnesses do not need such proofs to accept the miracles of Jesus as real. Especially for those who hold that the authors of Matthew and John were, in fact, the apostles of those names, these two evangelists were themselves the eyewitnesses and sources of much of their own material, even if they did draw upon other sources when they finally wrote their Gospels decades later. Nevertheless, the work of some critical scholars who use such historical criteria demonstrates that the historical Jesus was, in fact, renowned as a healer and an exorcist. This historical probability accords with and supports the testimony of faith that Jesus worked miracles.

On the other hand, these methods produce less convincing evidence that Jesus was able to control the elements and work what we call miracles of nature and provision.[33] This historical skepticism reveals a fatal deficit in such an overly secular approach, because these miracles are the very ones that most clearly demonstrate the divine identity of Jesus as Creator and Redeemer. Instead, accepting the miracle stories in faith and seeing their greater symbolism best accomplishes the purpose expressed by John when he wrote, "And many other signs truly did Jesus in the presence of his disciples, which are not written in this book: But these are written, that ye might believe that Jesus is the Christ, the Son of God; and that believing ye might have life through his name" (John 20:30–31). As a result, for us the testimony of the Gospels provides the deepest and most faith-inspiring witnesses of the reality of Jesus' miracles and their symbolism.

# Appendix B
# Our Galilee Miracle

*Jesus said unto him, If thou canst believe, all things are possible to him that believeth. And straightway the father of the child cried out, and said with tears, Lord, I believe; help thou mine unbelief.*

—Mark 9:23–24

Beginning in August of 2011, my wife, Elaine, our children, Rachel and Samuel, and I lived in the Holy Land for a year while I taught at the Brigham Young University–Jerusalem Center. Experiencing that land and being able to teach the Bible in many of the very places where its events took place was a dream come true for me. For my family, though, it was not always as easy: they needed to adjust to living, shopping, and going to school in very different surroundings. And differences are particularly hard for our son, Samuel. Being on the autism spectrum, Samuel has always found change extremely difficult, so we knew that living in a different apartment rather than in our home, going to a different school, and being surrounded by different people, hearing different languages, and even eating different foods would be terrifying for him.

We worked hard to prepare him, spending months beforehand looking at pictures, talking about Jerusalem, and discussing what would be different but also what would be the same that year. Miraculously, things went much better than we expected. Yes, things were hard and he certainly missed home, but right away he would say and do touching things, such as when we were driving from the airport to the BYU–Jerusalem Center and he asked us when we were going to meet Jesus. As we settled into routines, he grew more comfortable, and the rest of us had special experiences tracing the life and ministry of the Savior.

But that was the very part that Samuel did not seem to be getting. Field trips with the college students were too long, too loud, and too confusing for him to handle with his sensory processing disorder (SPD), a condition that often accompanies autism. The Old City was too crowded, smelled too different, and was too scary for him to visit until the very last weekend we were in Jerusalem. Samuel had a few choice experiences with us, such as a family visit to Gethsemane and a wonderful Christmas Eve singing Christmas carols at Shepherds Field as we looked over at Bethlehem. But as our year went on, I had a growing feeling of sadness and disappointment as I realized that my son was not, by and large, able to understand and appreciate what the rest of us were experiencing in the Holy Land.

One of the highlights of each semester was an extended visit to Galilee, the land where Jesus spent

*Opposite: The Sea of Galilee from the chapel at Tiberias.*
*Courtesy of Eric Huntsman.*

*Boats such as this one can often be seen on the Sea of Galilee.*

so much of his ministry, where he taught, and where he worked so many of his miracles. My family went with me for part of each of these Galilee rotations, but on my third and last trip with the students in July 2012, my wife and children were with me for the entire ten days, and I was anxious for them to experience what I believe is one of the best parts of the rotation, a boat ride on the Sea of Galilee.

I could not see how that could happen for Samuel, however. The boat ride was to be followed by a field trip on a bus with all the students for the rest of the day. That was too many people and much too long a trip for Samuel to endure. Elaine insisted, however, thinking that not only would it be fun for our son but he might learn something meaningful from it as well. So she arranged for the wife of one of the other faculty members to meet us on the opposite side of the Sea of Galilee to drive Elaine and Samuel back to where the family was staying. All that remained was to convince Samuel to go. The night before, in fact, he began to express hesitation about being out on the sea in a boat.

"Are there sharks in the Sea of Galilee, Dad? What if the boat sinks?" he worried.

The next morning we took him to the dock, arriving before all the students to minimize his confusion and fear. He hesitated to get on the boat at first, but after he had made up his mind, he charged down the gangplank, being the first to board. When the boat started to cruise towards the middle of the lake and the sea breeze picked up, he went to the front of the boat and leaned out over the water. I went up to the prow, partly to be with him but mostly to make sure he did not fall into the water.

With one arm around him, I asked him whether he knew what Jesus had done here on the Sea of Galilee. I told him that at least twice Jesus had helped his friends when they were on a boat and a big storm scared them. And then I said that on one of those times, Jesus actually walked across the water to help the disciples. Then ensued a conversation between the two of us that I will always remember.[1]

"How did Jesus walk on water, Dad?"

"Well, Jesus can do anything, Samuel."

"How?"

Our precious Samuel, thinking hard, on a boat on the Sea of Galilee.

Answering Samuel's questions while on the Sea of Galilee.

"He is the Son of God, so he can do anything that Heavenly Father can do, and he uses that power to help us, just like he helped his friends long ago."

From this simple but actually quite profound exchange we began to experience our Galilee miracle. There on the very sea on and around which Jesus had worked so many miracles, Samuel asked me a stream of questions about Jesus, about God, about blessings, about life and death—so many that I could hardly keep up with them. But somehow I was able to give him a more or less satisfactory answer to each.

One of the features of Samuel's autism explains why this conversation was such a miracle. As functional as Samuel is in many other ways, he is heavily affected in the area of verbal communication. True, he has gone from speaking and understanding very little when he was four or five years old to being able now to understand most of what is said to him, and he can express himself adequately enough—at least when he chooses to. But he does not easily grasp abstract concepts and rarely asks how, why, and what kinds of questions. Furthermore, conversations rarely go beyond three or four exchanges. But here was a conversation consisting of more than twenty questions, each of them deep.

"How is Jesus the Son of God, Dad?"

"Well, son, do you remember what we talk about at Christmas each year, how Mary had the baby Jesus? His father was God."

"How did that happen, Dad?"

Try to answer that one for a nine year old! "It was a miracle, Samuel. But it really happened."

"Why does Jesus bless us?"

"Because he loves us, just like Heavenly Father does, and he wants to help us."

"Where did Jesus get his power, Dad? How much of it does he have?"

"Jesus has the same power that God does, Samuel. It is the same power by which the world was created, so he can do anything to help us."

"But how did God create the world?"

"Well, buddy, you know how you like to make things out of play dough? In kind of the same way, God takes dust and gas and stars and space itself and makes stuff out of it."

"Thousands of people have died, Dad."

"I know, pal. But that's why we like Easter so much."

"But if all those people come alive again, where will they all live?"

Perhaps we are so overwhelmed with the idea of the resurrection that we do not think much about the practicalities of it.

Finally Samuel said, "I know I am asking a lot of questions, Dad. But I just need to know stuff."

He just needed to know stuff. And so did I. I needed to know that inside my little boy was an inquisitive mind and a sensitive spirit. That God was aware of him and of me. And that he could bring us together for that moment.

And for just a moment it was. In an instant, the miracle was over. Water sprayed up and a bird or something flew over, distracting Samuel. The spell was broken, he suddenly stopped talking, and then he was just a cute but autistic boy again, staring absently at the water as the boat cruised along.

*I am amazed at God's love and mercy for my son and for each of us.*

*Sunset over the Sea of Galilee.*

Elaine came up to us. As I turned to her, the immensity of what had happened hit me. For fifteen minutes or so, Samuel's autism had been effectively suspended, allowing him to ask me questions and me to teach him as I had so longed to do. When I realized that, I could not speak. Finally, through sudden tears, I blurted out, "I have just had the most miraculous experience of my time in the Holy Land. We have been praying and praying that Samuel would have experiences here that would help him understand and know the Lord, and one just happened." I could hardly talk.

Less than ten minutes later, the captain cut the engine so we could have quiet for our traditional devotional out on the Sea of Galilee. Together with my students, I read the account in Mark 4:35–41 of Jesus' calming the storm, and we sang "Master, the Tempest Is Raging."[2] Then we read in Matthew 14:22–33 about Jesus and Peter walking on the water, and we sang again. But most of all I testified of the miracle that had just happened to my son and of the miracles that can happen to each of us.

# Notes

### Introduction: A Ministry of Miracles

1. Several New Testament authorities consider some miracles to be different accounts of the same events. Three possible, or implied, miraculous acts are not included in this number.
2. *Moses* (not including the miracles God performed in front of Moses at his call): rod changed into a serpent (Exodus 7:10–12); waters become blood (Exodus 7:19–25); frogs (Exodus 8:2–15); lice (Exodus 8:16–19); flies (Exodus 8:20–32); cattle smitten (Exodus 9:1–7); boils (Exodus 9:8–12); thunder and hail (Exodus 9:22–35); locusts (Exodus 10:4–20); darkness (Exodus 10:21–27); death of the firstborn (Exodus 11:4–10; 12:29–30); Red Sea divided (Exodus 14:21–31); healing of the waters of Marah (Exodus 15:23–25); manna received from heaven (Exodus 16:14–35); quail (Exodus 16:3); Moses' face shines (Exodus 34:29-35); water from the rock (Exodus 17:5, 7); Nadab and Abihu devoured by fire (Leviticus 10:1–2); people consumed by fire at Taberah (Numbers 11:1–3); Miriam stricken with leprosy (Numbers 12:10-15); earth swallows Korah and his company (Numbers 16:32–34); 250 persons consumed by fire at Kadesh (Numbers 16:35–45); plague begun and then stayed at Kadesh (Numbers 16:46–50); Aaron's rod buds (Numbers 17:8); water from the rock, smitten twice by Moses (Numbers 20:7–11); brazen serpent (Numbers 21:8–9).
*Joshua*: waters of Jordan divided (Joshua 3:14–17); destruction of the walls of Jericho (Joshua 6:6–20); Israel's enemies destroyed in hailstorm (Joshua 10:11); sun and moon stayed (Joshua 10:12–14).
*Elijah*: drought upon Israel (1 Kings 17:1–18:46; James 5:17–18); fed by ravens (1 Kings 17:6); meal and oil multiplied (1 Kings 17:14); child restored to life (1 Kings 17:22); sacrifice consumed by fire (1 Kings 18:38); rain sent to end drought (1 Kings 18:41–46); captain and fifty men slain by fire (2 Kings 1:10–12); waters of Jordan divided (2 Kings 2:8); carried into heaven (2 Kings 2:11).
*Elisha*: waters of Jordan divided (2 Kings 2:14); waters of Jericho healed (2 Kings 2:19–22); mocking children torn by bears (2 Kings 2:23–24); water supplied for Jehoshaphat and his armies (2 Kings 3:16–20); widow's oil multiplied (2 King 4:1–7); Shunamite woman conceives (2 Kings 4:16–17); Shunamite woman's child raised to life (2 Kings 4:32–37); pottage rendered harmless (2 Kings 4:38–41); one hundred persons fed with twenty loaves (2 Kings 4:42–44); Naaman's leprosy healed (2 Kings 5:1–14); Gehazi struck with leprosy (2 Kings 5:27); iron axe caused to float (2 Kings 6:4–7); Syrians blinded and trapped (2 Kings 6:8–23); dead man revived by the bones of Elisha (2 Kings 13:21).
3. "Miraculum" and "Miror," *Oxford Latin Dictionary,* 1115.
4. "Miracle," *New Oxford American Dictionary,* 1089; see also Twelftree, *Jesus the Miracle Worker,* 26–27, 348–50.
5. Josephus, *Antiquities of the Jews,* 18.3.3 (§ 63).
6. Franz Annen, "Thauma," *Exegetical Dictionary,* 2:134; Bauer, "Thauma," *Greek-English Lexicon,* 444.
7. Gerhardsson, *Mighty Acts of Jesus,* 15; Franz Annen, "Thaumastos, thaumasios," *Exegetical Dictionary,* 2:135–36; Bauer, "Thaumasios," *Greek-English Lexicon,* 445.
8. Gerhardsson, *Mighty Acts of Jesus,* 12–15.
9. Brown, "Gospel Miracles," 180–81; Gerhardsson, *Mighty Acts of Jesus,* 16; Morris, *Gospel according to John,* 607–13; Twelftree, *Jesus the Miracle Worker,* 224–28.
10. Note in particular the well-known opposition of

David Hume to the possibility of miracles: "A miracle is a violation of the laws of nature. . . . There must, therefore, be a uniform experience against every miraculous event, otherwise the event would not merit that appellation. And as a uniform experience amounts to a proof, there is here a direct and full proof from the nature of the fact, against the existence of any miracle" (*Human Understanding,* 150–51). See the discussions of this tendency in Kellenberger, "Miracles," 145–53; Meier, *Marginal Jew,* 2:512–15; and Keener, *Miracles,* 107–70.

11. Talmage, *Jesus the Christ,* 148–49; Matthews, *Miracles of Jesus,* 1, 11–15; Howick, *Miracles of Jesus the Messiah,* 10–13. Speaking of miracles generally and the miracles of Jesus in particular, the *Encyclopedia of Mormonism* explains: "A miracle is a beneficial event brought about through divine power that mortals do not understand and of themselves cannot duplicate. . . . Just as a shepherd tends his flocks, watches over them, and uses his power to help them, so Jesus Christ used his power and knowledge to help others when he was on earth" (Paul C. Hedengren, "Miracles," 908).

12. After Jesus drove out an evil spirit from a man in the synagogue at Capernaum, all present were astonished (Mark 1:27, *ethambēthēsan;* KJV, "were amazed"). Likewise, Luke records that the miraculous catch of fish that accompanied Jesus' call of Simon Peter from his boat caused "astonishment" (Greek, *thambos*) to fall upon him and all those who were with him (Luke 5:9). Most frequently, however, forms of the verb *thaumazō,* meaning "wonder" or "marvel," describe the reactions of crowds present when Jesus performed a mighty deed (Mark 5:20; Matthew 8:27; 9:33; 15:31; 21:20; Luke 8:25; 11:14; see also John 5:20; 7:21).

13. Brown, "Gospel Miracles," 170–72; Gerhardsson, *Mighty Acts of Jesus,* 16–17; Johannes Friedrich, "Dynamis," *Exegetical Dictionary,* 1:356–58; Bauer, "Dynamis," *Greek-English Lexicon,* 262–63.

14. Addison Everett, cited in O. B. Huntington, "Words and Incidents of the Prophet Joseph's Life," *Young Woman's Journal* 2, no. 2 (November 1890): 76.

15. See the first paragraph of "The Living Christ: The Testimony of the Apostles," The Church of Jesus Christ of Latter-day Saints, April 2000; available online at lds.org. Biblical scholars have pointed out the difference between the uses of *Elohim* in the first Creation account of Genesis 1:1–2:4 and *YHWH,* or "Jehovah," in the second, Genesis 2:5–25. Although subsequent editors and scribes of the Hebrew Bible may not have fully understood the difference between these important divine name-titles, the Latter-day Saints' understanding that the Father directed the Creation through the agency of his Son helps explain the appearance of both in the tradition. For the history of Latter-day Saint uses of the terms *Elohim* and *Jehovah,* see Davis and Hoskisson, "Usage of the Title Elohim," 115–24.

16. Temperley, *Haydn,* 19–20, 26–31, 35–36, 39.
17. Osbek, *101 Hymn Stories,* 100–101.
18. Davidson, *Our Latter-day Hymns,* 128–29.
19. See the detailed discussion of these Infancy narratives in Hunstman, *Good Tidings of Great Joy,* 19–115.
20. See Huntsman, *God So Loved the World,* especially 49–119.
21. See Huntsman, *God So Loved the World,* 116–17.
22. See Huntsman, *Good Tidings of Great Joy,* 121–25.

## Chapter 1: Power over the Elements

1. Horst Balz, "phobeomai" and "phobos," *Exegetical Dictionary,* 3:430, 433.
2. Meier, *Marginal Jew,* 2:874–80, 967–70; Twelftree, *Jesus the Miracle Worker,* 314.
3. *Ta idia* is often taken to mean "his own place" or "his own home," partially by analogy to John 19:27, where the beloved disciple takes the mother of Jesus *eis ta idia,* or "to his own home." See Brown, *Gospel according to John,* 10; Bruce, *Gospel of John,* 37–38; Morris, *Gospel according to John,* 85–86. But because *ta idia* is the subject of "receive" and is parallel to the following *hoi idioi,* it seems as likely that "his own things" (meaning his creation) received him, whereas "his own men" (that is, his people) did not.
4. Brown, *Gospel according to John,* 103: "Then John tells us what the sign accomplished: through it Jesus revealed his glory and his disciples believed on him. Thus, the first sign had the same purpose as all the subsequent signs will have, namely, *revelation about the person of Jesus.*" This story is recorded only by John, but some of its elements, such as a wedding feast (Mark 2:19; Matthew 22:1–14; 25:1–13; Luke 12:36) and the importance of new wine (Luke 5:37–39), appear in the other Gospels. See Morris, *Gospel according to John,* 155.
5. Brown, *Gospel according to John,* 98; Walker, *In the Steps of Jesus,* 37.
6. Morris, *Gospel of John;* 160–61; Twelftree, *Jesus the Miracle Worker,* 191–92.

7. Mary's concern about the success of the wedding feast might indicate that one of her own family might have been involved (see, for instance, McConkie, *Doctrinal New Testament Commentary,* 1:135). While several early Latter-day Saint authorities speculated about the possible role of Jesus himself (see, for example, Orson Hyde, *Journal of Discourses,* 2:82 [October 6, 1854]; B. H. Roberts, *Defense of the Faith and the Saints,* 2.272), the narrative in John stresses that Jesus was *invited* (Greek, *eklēthē;* KJV, "called"), presumably as a guest. Other suggestions for the groom have been made, including John himself, who does not name himself anywhere in the text. Perhaps the most intriguing possibility is Nathanael. Newly called as a disciple immediately before this episode (John 1:45–51), Nathanael is the only character explicitly described as being from Cana (John 21:2).
8. Brown, *Gospel according to John,* 103–10; Bruce, *Gospel of John,* 68–72; Morris, *Gospel according to John,* 153–64; Huntsman, "Word Was Made Flesh," 55–56.
9. Talmage, *Jesus the Christ,* 146–49; McConkie, *Mortal Messiah,* 1:453–54.
10. Talmage, *Jesus the Christ,* 147–48.
11. See Huntsman, "Lamb of God," 51–52, and "Word Was Made Flesh," 56–57.
12. Theissen, *Miracle Stories of the Early Christian Tradition,* 94–99.
13. Achtemeier, "Person and Deed," 170–75; Harrington, *Gospel of Matthew,* 123.
14. Twelftree, *Jesus the Miracle Worker,* 112–14, 155–56.
15. Meier, *Marginal Jew,* 2:925–28.
16. Achtemeier, "Person and Deed," 176.
17. Theissen, *Miracle Stories of the Early Christian Tradition,* 99–101.
18. Meier, *Marginal Jew,* 2:931–32; Twelftree, *Jesus the Miracle Worker,* 70–71.
19. Witherington, *Gospel of Mark,* 31, 34–36.
20. Marcus, *Mark 1–8,* 336–37.
21. Twelftree, *Jesus the Miracle Worker,* 112–13.
22. The absence of an account by Luke of Jesus' walking on the water is the beginning of the so-called "Great Omission" of Luke, in which he omits all of the material from Mark 6:45–8:26. If Luke knew of this miracle and other stories from Mark that he passed over, it may be that he felt that the earlier calming of the storm was sufficient to illustrate Jesus' power over nature; Luke likewise omits recording the feeding of the four thousand after giving an account of Jesus' feeding of the five thousand.
23. While Meier, *Marginal Jew,* 2:919–24, acknowledges this double attestation, he remains doubtful about the episode's historicity because he feels that it is not in harmony with the overall picture of the historical Jesus. See, however, the arguments of Twelftree, *Jesus the Miracle Worker,* 320–22, who responds to Meier's objections and makes a strong case for the story's historical claims.
24. Davidson, *Our Latter-day Hymns,* 147–48.
25. "Master, the Tempest Is Raging," *Hymns,* no. 105; or "Peace, Be Still," *Murray's Songs for Sunday Schools,* 10.
26. Brown, *Gospel according to John,* 533–38; Marcus, *Mark 1–8,* 427.
27. Marcus, *Mark 1–8,* 426.
28. Theissen, *Miracle Stories of the Early Christian Tradition,* 103–6.
29. Murphy-O'Connor, *Holy Land,* 250–55; Knight, *Holy Land,* 250–52.
30. Meier, *Marginal Jew,* 2:903–4.
31. Matthew 5:21 notes that there were women and children in addition to five thousand men who ate of the bread Jesus provided.
32. The complicated relationships among these four accounts, apparently based on the two different traditions found in the Marcan and Johannine sources, and the connection of this Marcan account with the later Matthean and Marcan feeding of the four thousand have been much studied. See, for instance, Barnett, "Feeding of the Multitude in Mark 6/John 6," 273–89; Meier, *Marginal Jew,* 2:950–59; and Marcus, *Mark 1–8,* 491–97.
33. Murphy-O'Connor, *Holy Land,* 314–17.
34. Marcus, *Mark 1–8,* 407.
35. Huntsman, "Bread of Life Sermon," 92–103.
36. Marcus, *Mark 1–8,* 487–90; Twelftree, *Jesus the Miracle Worker,* 81–82. At the very least, seven is the number of completeness or fulness, which supports the idea of the gospel going to all people and the potential of all people to be gathered into Christ's fold.
37. Theissen, *Miracle Stories of the Early Christian Tradition,* 106, calls this miracle a rule miracle, because it is a miracle that settles a point and serves to establish and strengthen a point of procedure. Nonetheless, since Jesus here in fact provides Peter with something that he needed but did not have, to my mind the miracle falls within the general category of a miracle of provision, or gift miracle.

38. Stackhouse, "Hymnody and Politics," 45–47.
39. Watts, *Psalms of David Imitated,* 27.
40. Wilberg, "My Shepherd Will Supply My Need," in *Consider the Lilies,* 6.
41. Twelftree, *Jesus the Miracle Worker,* 137.
42. Meier, *Marginal Jew,* 2:880–84; Twelftree, *Jesus the Miracle Worker,* 137–38.
43. Murphy-O'Connor, *Holy Land,* 412–15; Knight, *Holy Land,* 239–40.
44. Walker, *In the Steps of Jesus,* 96–97; Knight, *Holy Land,* 266–67.
45. One other standard interpretation of this passage holds that the coming of the kingdom in glory was realized at Pentecost, when eleven of Jesus' original twelve apostles witnessed the Church empowered by the Spirit (Acts 2:1–4).
46. The King James Version's regular use of *Elias* for the Greek form of Elijah led the Prophet Joseph Smith to consider and teach about the role of Elias, both as an individual prophet of that name and also as a prophetic role. Because the role of an Elias is that of a forerunner, the Joseph Smith Translation of Mark 9:3 emends the King James Version of Mark 9:4 to read "And there appeared unto them Elias with Moses, *or in other words, John the Baptist and Moses.*" Although there are several possible explanations for this change, which is not repeated in the Matthean or Lucan accounts of the Transfiguration in the Joseph Smith Translation, the Latter-day Saint Bible Dictionary suggests, "The curious wording of JST, Mark 9:3 does not imply that the Elias at the Transfiguration was John the Baptist, but that in addition to Elijah the prophet, John the Baptist was present." See also Holzapfel, "Transfiguration," 66.
47. Holzapfel, "Transfiguration," 51–53.
48. Smith, *Teachings of the Prophet Joseph Smith,* 158; or *History, 1838–1856,* vol. C-1, p. 546.
49. Smith, *Doctrines of Salvation,* 2:165.
50. Holzapfel, "The Transfiguration," 57–58.
51. Twelftree, *Jesus the Miracle Worker,* 95, 335.
52. Meier, *Marginal Jew,* 2:895–96.
53. Twelftree, *Jesus the Miracle Worker,* 91; Huntsman, *God So Loved the World,* 17–19.
54. Murphy-O'Connor, *Holy Land,* 318–19; Walker, *In the Steps of Jesus,* 78.
55. Because of these similarities, some scholars believe that the two miracles are in fact one and the same, perhaps with Luke retrojecting to the beginning of Jesus' ministry a miraculous event that was attributed originally to the risen Lord. See Meier, *Marginal Jew,* 2:896–907; Twelftree, *Jesus the Miracle Worker,* 149, 217–18.
56. Huntsman, *God So Loved the World,* 68–69.
57. For ancient attempts to explain the precise number allegorically, see the discussion of Augustine and Jerome's proposals in Twelftree, *Jesus the Miracle Worker,* 218–19.

## Chapter 2: Healing the Sick

1. Meier, *Marginal Jew,* 2:969–70; Twelftree, *Jesus the Miracle Worker,* 253–57, 298.
2. Meier, *Marginal Jew,* 2:628–30, 646–47.
3. The narrative of John is, of course, difficult to harmonize with the basic storyline told by Mark, which is largely followed by Matthew and Luke. As a result, it is possible that many of the miracles the synoptic Gospels tell of the early Galilean ministry had already been performed and were well known throughout the area. John himself notes that many in Jerusalem had begun to believe in Jesus "when they saw the miracles (*sēmeia*) which he did" (John 2:23; compare 3:2).
4. Twelftree, *Jesus the Miracle Worker,* 198–99.
5. Meier, *Marginal Jew,* 2:718–26.
6. See Cotter, *Christ of the Miracle Stories,* 109–19, for a survey of the continuing discussion of the centurion's status.
7. Morgan, *Then Sings My Soul,* 167.
8. Morgan, *Then Sings My Soul,* 166; or "Sometimes I feel discouraged (Balm in Gilead)," *Folk Songs of the American Negro (No. 1),* 31.
9. Some of these problems include the absence of the participle for "kneeling" (*gonypetōn*) in many early manuscripts and whether Jesus' response originated in his being "moved with compassion" (*splanchnistheis*) or "out of anger" (*orgistheis*). See Metzger, *Textual Commentary,* 65, and the discussions of Twelftree, *Jesus the Miracle Worker,* 62, and Cotter, *Christ of the Miracle Stories,* 31–32, 38.
10. Cotter, *Christ of the Miracle Stories,* 29, 33–37.
11. Demaitre, *Leprosy in Premodern Medicine,* 234–35.
12. Walter Radl, "*sōzō,*" *Exegetical Dictionary,* 3:320.
13. Meier, *Marginal Jew,* 2:703.
14. Hulse, "Nature of Biblical 'Leprosy,'" 87–88, 92–100, 103–4; Meier, *Marginal Jew,* 2:699–700; Demaitre, *Leprosy in Premodern Medicine,* 83–84; Cotter, *Christ of the Miracle Stories,* 23–30.
15. "DNA of Jesus-Era Shrouded Man in Jerusalem," *Science Daily,* December 16, 2009.

16. David P. Wright and Richard N. Jones, "Leprosy," *Anchor Bible Dictionary*, 4:281.
17. See Matthew 8:17; Luke 5:15; 8:2; 13:11–12; John 5:5. For the root sense of "weakness," see Gerhard Schneider, "astheneia," *Exegetical Dictionary*, 1:170.
18. Bednar, "In the Strength of the Lord," 76–78.
19. Twelftree, *Jesus the Miracle Worker*, 64.
20. See Cotter, *Christ of the Miracle Stories*, 91–101, for a discussion of the obstacles, both social and physical, that the friends of the paralytic actually needed to overcome to get him to Jesus.
21. Madsen, "Medicine and Healing in the Time of Jesus," 116–17; Howard Clark Kee, "Medicine and Healing," *Anchor Bible Dictionary*, 4:659–60; Pilch, *Healing in the New Testament*, 62–63.
22. Madsen, "Medicine and Healing in the Time of Jesus," 117–18; J. T. Vallance, "Medicine," *Oxford Classical Dictionary*, 946–48; Nutton, *Ancient Medicine*, 53–71, 77–86.
23. Madsen, "Medicine and Healing in the Time of Jesus," 119–23.
24. Pilch, *Healing in the New Testament*, 13–14.
25. Murphy-O'Connor, *Holy Land*, 29–33; Knight, *Holy Land*, 105–6.
26. Metzger, *Textual Commentary*, 179.
27. Packer, "Moving of the Water," 9.
28. See Hamilton, *Book of Genesis, Chapters 1–17*, 115.
29. Morris, *Gospel according to John*, 268n17; Twelftree, *Jesus the Miracle Worker*, 201.
30. Jacob Kremer, "egeirō," *Exegetical Dictionary*, 1:372–76; Twelftree, *Jesus the Miracle Worker*, 202–3.
31. Witherington, *Women and the Genesis of Christianity*, 65, 86–87, 118–20, 201–2; Reid, *Choosing the Better Part*, 2–4, who nonetheless warns of the ambiguous portrayal of women in Luke.
32. Witherington, *Women and the Genesis of Christianity*, 76.
33. Reid, *Choosing the Better Part*, 101–2.
34. Reid, *Choosing the Better Part*, 138–39.
35. Jeffrey R. Holland, "Like a Broken Vessel," *Ensign*, November 2013, 41–42.
36. "Lord, I Would Follow Thee," *Hymns*, no. 220; emphasis added; copyright Emma Lou Thayne; used by permission.
37. Meier, *Marginal Jew*, 2:709.
38. Reid, *Choosing the Better Part*, 164.
39. Gerhard Schneider, "apolyō," *Exegetical Dictionary*, 1:140.
40. Witherington, *Women and the Genesis of Christianity*, 79; Reid, *Choosing the Better Part*, 165–68.
41. Meier, *Marginal Jew*, 2:682–83.
42. Witherington, *Women and the Genesis of Christianity*, 87.
43. Twelftree, *Jesus the Miracle Worker*, 164. See also Marshall, *Gospel of Luke*, 837.

## Chapter 3: Casting Out Devils

1. See Bauer, "exorkizō, exorkistēs," *Greek-English Lexicon*, 351; Ingo Broer, "exorkizō, exorkistēs," *Exegetical Dictionary*, 2:9; Twelftree, *In the Name of Jesus*, 25n2.
2. Meier, *Marginal Jew*, 2:405, 457n19; Keener, *Miracles*, 2:793–819, 852–56.
3. Twelftree, *In the Name of Jesus*, 105–6; Keener, *Miracles*, 2:820–25, 837–43.
4. *History of the Church*, 1:82–83; or Davidson et al., *Histories*, 1:382–86.
5. Twelftree, *Jesus the Miracle Worker*, 177; *In the Name of Jesus*, 108, 118–19, 127–28; Keener, *Miracles*, 2:785.
6. Brown, "Gospel Miracles," 172.
7. Twelftree, *In the Name of Jesus*, 196.
8. Brown, "Gospel Miracles," 172–73; Twelftree, *Jesus the Miracle Worker*, 176; *In the Name of Jesus*, 132; Pilch, *Healing in the New Testament*, 104–6.
9. Twelftree, *In the Name of Jesus*, 184–97.
10. Alexander B. Morrison, "Myths about Mental Illness," *Ensign*, October 2005, 29–30, 33.
11. Marcus, *Mark 1–8*, 175.
12. Heinz Geisen, "epitimaō," *Exegetical Dictionary*, 2:42–43; Horsley, *Hearing the Whole Story*, 137–38, notes that *epitimaō* seems to be used for the Hebrew *ga'ar*, which in the Dead Sea scrolls is used to mean "destroy, root out, vanquish."
13. Horz Balz, "phimoō," *Exegetical Dictionary*, 3:428; see also Twelftree, *Jesus the Miracle Worker*, 285.
14. Knight, *Holy Land*, 256–57. Magdala's name in Greek, *Tarichae*, means "pickled fish," which suggests that this town may have been a center of fish processing, where fish caught in the Sea of Galilee were dried, salted, or pickled.
15. Reid, *Choosing the Better Part*, 125–26, esp. n. 5.
16. Witherington, *Women and the Genesis of Christianity*, 111–12.
17. Meier, *Marginal Jew*, 2:405.
18. Joanne K. Kuemmerlin-McLean, "Demons: Old Testament," *Anchor Bible Dictionary*, 2:138–40.
19. Duane F. Watson, "Devil," *Anchor Bible Dictionary*, 2:183–84.

20. H. S. Versnel, "daimōn," *Oxford Classical Dictionary*, 426; Keener, *Miracles*, 2:769–76.
21. David George Reese, "Demons: New Testament," *Anchor Bible Dictionary*, 2:140–41.
22. Reid, *Choosing the Better Part*, 126.
23. Although the version of Mark 5:1 used by the King James translators reads "Gadara," better, earlier manuscripts have "Gerasa," although at thirty-seven miles from the Sea of Galilee, this name is the least likely. Many manuscripts of Matthew 8:28 read "Gadara"; others have "Gerasa" or an otherwise unknown "Gergesa." Most reliable manuscripts of Luke 8:28 read "Gergesa," though "Gadara" is also attested, as is "Gerasa." Whenever "Gergesa" appears in manuscripts of any of these Gospels, it is most likely a scribal correction based not on textual considerations but on the opinion of Origen, who first postulated the existence of the town Gergesa. See Metzger, *Textual Commentary*, 18–19, 72, 121.
24. Meier, *Marginal Jew*, 2:651–52; Witherington, *Gospel of Mark*, 179–80.
25. Murphy-O'Connor, *Holy Land*, 354–55; Walker, *In the Steps of Jesus*, 81.
26. Meier, *Marginal Jew*, 2:652.
27. Witherington, *Gospel of Mark*, 178.
28. Nolland, *Gospel of Matthew*, 375.
29. *Joseph Smith's New Translation of the Bible*, 254 (Matthew 8:11–30).
30. Horsley, *Hearing the Whole Story*, 140–41, 144–48; "Jesus and Empire," 86.
31. Russell M. Nelson, "Addiction or Freedom," *Ensign*, November 1988, 6.
32. See the suggestions for professional help in Benjamin R. Erwin, "Overcoming Addiction through the Atonement," *Ensign*, September 2012, 65–68.
33. M. Russell Ballard, "O That Cunning Plan of the Evil One," *Ensign*, November 2012, 110.
34. Marshall, *Gospel of Luke*, 336; Witherington, *Gospel of Mark*, 182.
35. Marshall, *Gospel of Luke*, 339.
36. Twelftree, *In the Name of Jesus*, 157, 159–60.
37. The sole attestation of this miracle here and its similarity to the next story has led some to question whether Matthew has, in fact, created this story to complete his cycle of ten miracles in three blocks. See Meier, *Marginal Jew*, 2:657.
38. See Hans Hübner, "kōphos," *Exegetical Dictionary*, 1:333.
39. Davidson, *Our Latter-day Hymns*, 170–72.
40. "Where Can I Turn for Peace," *Hymns*, no. 129; copyright Emma Lou Thayne; used by permission; emphasis added.
41. "Where Can I Turn for Peace," *This Is the Christ*, 7, and back cover.
42. Twelftree, *Jesus the Miracle Worker*, 121, 160.
43. The use of "finger" in Luke 11:20 seems to be a reference to Pharaoh's magicians acknowledging that Moses acted with the "finger" of God (Exodus 8:19), God's stretching out his "hand" against the Egyptians (Exodus 3:20) and writing the Ten Commandments with his "finger" (Exodus 31:18; Deuteronomy 9:10). See Meier, *Marginal Jew*, 2:415–17; Twelftree, *Jesus the Miracle Worker*, 160.
44. Bruce, *Hard Sayings of Jesus*, 110–11; Witherington, *Women and the Genesis of Christianity*, 74.
45. Cotter, *Christ of the Miracle Stories*, 152–54.
46. Richard G. Scott, "To Heal the Shattering Consequences of Abuse," *Ensign*, May 2008, 41–42.
47. Twelftree, *Jesus the Miracle Worker*, 79–80; France, *Gospel of Mark*, 298.
48. Witherington, *Gospel of Mark*, 232.
49. Witherington, *Women and the Genesis of Christianity*, 75–76.
50. Bauer, "selēniazomai," *Greek-English Lexicon*, 919.
51. Jacob Kremer, "anastasis, anistēmi," and "egeirō," *Exegetical Dictionary*, 1:372–76.

## Chapter 4: Causing the Blind to See and the Deaf to Hear

1. Witherington, *Gospel of Mark*, 239.
2. Perhaps the most famous was the healing of a blind man in Egypt by future emperor Vespasian. See Tacitus, *Annals*, 4.81.
3. In both this case and the instance of the Syrians who were temporarily blinded so they could be led into Samaria, only to have their eyes opened again in the midst of the enemy city, the text is clear that it was the Lord who shut and opened their eyes.
4. Twelftree, *Jesus the Miracle Worker*, 299. While the Masoretic Hebrew text of Isaiah 61:1, which was the basis of the King James Version translation, makes no reference to giving sight to the blind, the Greek Septuagint version of this Isaiah passage explicitly reads "*kai typhlois anablepsin*," which is translated as "recovery of sight to the blind." An eschatological Dead Sea Scroll text may refer to this passage as well when it renders what in the English translation

of Isaiah is "opening of the prison" with "release from darkness" (4Q521, Messianic Apocalypse).
5. Twelftree, *Jesus the Miracle Worker*, 120.
6. Twelftree, *Jesus the Miracle Worker*, 120.
7. Max Sussman, "Sickness and Disease: Diseases of the Eyes and Ears," *Anchor Bible Dictionary*, 6:12.
8. Aune, "Magic in Early Christianity," 1537–38.
9. Meier, *Marginal Jew*, 712–14; Twelftree, *Jesus the Miracle Worker*, 322–23.
10. Witherington, *Gospel of Mark*, 234.
11. Twelftree, *Jesus the Miracle Worker*, 81; Witherington, *Gospel of Mark*, 233–34.
12. *Babylonian Talmud, Nedarim* 64b. See Max Sussman, "Sickness and Disease: Diseases of the Eyes and Ears," *Anchor Bible Dictionary*, 6:12; Twelftree, *Jesus the Miracle Worker*, 83–84, 299; Cotter, *Christ of the Miracle Stories*, 56–57.
13. Cotter, *Christ of the Miracle Stories*, 58–59.
14. Meier, *Marginal Jew*, 2:692–93; Murphy-O'Connor, *Holy Land*, 237–39.
15. Witherington, *Gospel of Mark*, 239.
16. Cotter, *Christ of the Miracle Stories*, 45.
17. First prediction of the Passion: Mark 8:31–33; Matthew 16:21–23; Luke 9:22. Second prediction: Mark 9:20–32; Matthew 17:22–23; Luke 9:43–45. Third prediction: Mark 10:32–34; Matthew 20:17–19; Luke 18:31–34.
18. Meier, *Marginal Jew*, 2:691–92; Twelftree, *Jesus the Miracle Worker*, 84–85.
19. Brown, *Gospel according to John*, 326–27.
20. Twelftree, *Jesus the Miracle Worker*, 212.
21. Meier, *Marginal Jew*, 2:697.
22. See Huntsman, "Word Was Made Flesh," 54–55, 57–59, 63–65.
23. Twelftree, *Jesus the Miracle Worker*, 213.
24. "Hymn 209 (Amazing Grace)," *Choice Selection*, 170; emphasis added.
25. Osbeck, *101 Hymn Stories*, 28–30.
26. Cotter, *Christ of the Miracle Stories*, 47.
27. Bauckham, *Jesus and the Eyewitnesses*, 39–55, has asserted that most, if not all, of the named figures in the Gospels, especially in Mark, may have been sources for the evangelists or at least figures who were well known in early Christian circles. If correct, his assertion is particularly true when it comes to named figures in the miracles, since the miracles may have been instrumental in their subsequent conversion.
28. Josephus, *Antiquities of the Jews*, 8.2.5 (§45–49). See also the discussion in Meier, *Marginal Jew*, 2:688–90.

For that view, as well as several contrary ones, see Cotter, *Christ of the Miracle Stories*, 62–63.
29. Witherington, *Gospel of Mark*, 291.
30. Witherington, *Gospel of Mark*, 292–93; for some contrary suggestions, see Cotter, *Christ of the Miracle Stories*, 67–71, who in the end settles on seeing it as Bartimaeus' rejecting social niceties in his eagerness to follow Jesus.

## Chapter 5: Raising the Dead

1. Knight, *Holy Land*, 225–26.
2. Knight, *Holy Land*, 226–27.
3. Meier, *Marginal Jew*, 2:792–93.
4. Rolf Dabelstein, "neaniskos," *Exegetical Dictionary*, 2:459.
5. Reid, *Choosing the Better Part*, 104.
6. Witherington, *Women and the Genesis of Christianity*, 85.
7. Some important manuscripts of John 1:18 actually read "only begotten god" (Greek, *monogenēs theos*) instead of "only begotten Son," though the adjective that is translated "only begotten" here is the same in both cases. See Metzger, *Textual Commentary*, 169–70.
8. Kent Harold Richards, "Death, Old Testament," *Anchor Bible Dictionary*, 2:108–10.
9. Robert Martin-Achard, "Resurrection, Old Testament," *Anchor Bible Dictionary*, 5:680–84.
10. Albert Henrichs, "Hades," and Christopher C. Rowe, "Soul," *Oxford Classical Dictionary*, 661–62, 1428.
11. George W. E. Nickelsburg, "Resurrection, Early Judaism and Christianity," *Anchor Bible Dictionary*, 5:684–88.
12. Meier, *Marginal Jew*, 2:628–30; Twelftree, *Jesus the Miracle Worker*, 306. Mary Magdalene, Joanna, and Susanna are mentioned in a miracle summary in Luke 8:2–3. As we have noted, although the Gospel of John names Malchus as the servant of the high priest whose ear is cut off in the Garden of Gethsemane (John 18:12), no name is given in the Gospel of Luke, the only Gospel that records how Jesus healed the man's ear.
13. Twelftree, *Jesus the Miracle Worker*, 73.
14. Gerhard Schneider, "thygatrion," *Exegetical Dictionary*, 2:159. The diminutive in Greek can also carry the meaning of "dear daughter."
15. Howard, "Program Notes," *Come, Thou Fount of Every Blessing*, 5.
16. "Hymn no. 57 (Death Shall Not Destroy My Comfort)," *New and Most Complete Collection*, 79, with

the added refrain written for and performed by the Mormon Tabernacle Choir in "Death Shall Not Destroy My Comfort," in *Come, Thou Fount of Every Blessing*; see "Program Notes," *Come, Thou Fount of Every Blessing*, p. 5.
17. Hauser, "At the Stream," *Olive Leaf*, no. 231.
18. Wilberg, *Death Shall Not Destroy My Comfort*.
19. Whether Jesus compared the girl's death to sleep using a common metaphor for death or whether he was referring to how believers in the resurrection ought to view death is much discussed. See, for example, Witherington, *Gospel of Mark*, 189–90.
20. Meier, *Marginal Jew*, 2:785–86; Witherington, *Gospel of Mark*, 190. For the original Aramaic *talitha koum*, see Metzger, *Textual Commentary*, 74–75.
21. Twelftree, *Jesus the Miracle Worker*, 118–19. Matthew also seems hesitant to record any special words that Jesus spoke when performing miracles, perhaps to avoid having them seem anything like magical incantations.
22. Twelftree, *Jesus the Miracle Worker*, 157.
23. Murphy-O'Connor, *Holy Land*, 152–54.
24. Capper, "Bethany, near the Mount of Olives," 955–57.
25. Note "house of Simon the Leper" in Mark 14:3–9 and Matthew 26:6–13. See Capper, "John, Qumran and Virtuoso Religion," 108–9.
26. Brown, *Gospel according to John*, 424n17; Morris, *Gospel according to John*, 485nn40–41.
27. Brown, *Gospel according to John*, 433–34; Strathearn, "Mary, Martha, and Lazarus," 158–61.
28. Catherine Corman Parry, "Eternal Life," *Encyclopedia of Mormonism*, 464.
29. See Brown, *Gospel according to John*, 425n26; Meier, *Marginal Jew*, 2:811. This concept is known as realized eschatology. Eschatology is the study of the end, and future eschatology, as usually presented in Mark and Matthew, usually portrays such end-time events as Jesus' conquest of evil, the resurrection, and the judgment as lying in the future. John and sometimes Luke, however, often present realized eschatology, when the effects of those future events can be experienced and enjoyed by believers now.
30. Witherington, *Women and the Genesis of Christianity*, 106–7; Meier, *Marginal Jew*, 2:812; Strathearn, "Mary, Martha, and Lazarus," 168–69.
31. See, for instance, the stories of Wilford Woodruff's raising his wife Phoebe in 1838, early in the Restoration (Cowley, *Wilford Woodruff*, 96–98), and Lorenzo Snow's raising a young girl named Ella Jensen (Snow, "Raised from the Dead," 885–86). For other modern accounts, see Keener, *Miracles*, 543–79.
32. Brown, *Gospel according to John*, 427n44; Strathearn, "Mary, Martha, and Lazarus," 171–72.

## Conclusion: The Greatest Miracles of All

1. This passage presents some textual difficulties, the greatest of which is that it is absent from some of the oldest and best manuscripts of John (Metzger, *Textual Commentary*, 187–89). Nevertheless, noted biblical scholars (for instance, Brown, *Gospel according to John*, 335–36, and Morris, *Gospel according to John*, 778–79) have noted that the passage seems to be ancient and may be genuine, perhaps having been displaced from its original context (say, from an original position in the Gospel of Luke) and representing a scribal attempt to restore a lost text, or arising from a strong oral tradition. For careful, recent Latter-day Saint treatments of this issue, see Wayment, "Woman Taken in Adultery," 372–97, and Blumell, "Text-Critical Comparison," 107–13.
2. Carter, "Story of How It Came to Be."
3. Carter, "Come unto Him"; copyright © 1984 by Jackman Music Corporation, all rights reserved. Used by permission.
4. Talmage, *Jesus the Christ*, 148–49.
5. Cotter, *Christ of the Miracle Stories*, 9, observes: "The portrait of Jesus in the miracle-story encounters calls for the abandonment of judgment, rejection, reproof, or denial on any grounds, and calls the followers to look beneath the externals to the desperate need, the anxiety, the shame, the abuse, and the social rejection that explain the externals. It calls on the followers to feel compassion, understanding, and more."
6. See also the summation in Howick, *Miracles of Jesus the Messiah*, 215–16.

## Appendix A: Miracles in the Gospels

1. Bailey and Vander Broek, *Literary Forms in the New Testament*, 12–14, 98–112, 114–21, 137–46.
2. Betz, "Early Christian Miracle Story," 71, notes that a feature of miracle stories is "that they are sometimes 'disturbed' by other literary genres. Frequently, dialogues are inserted in which theological themes are discussed. Or the miracle story can be narrated in such a way that it 'flips' into the genre of a 'call narrative' or 'conversion story.' Such 'disturbances' may

even push the miracle story to the point where it loses its character and changes into another literary genre."
3. The tabulations and totals presented here and in the tables accompanying the text are my own. I note the observation of Meier, *Marginal Jew*, 2:618, who writes, "It is difficult to give precise statistics on how many separate miracle stories there are in the Gospels, since scholars do not always agree on which pericope should be counted as a separate story and which pericope is just a literary parallel or a variant of a story present in another Gospel." Compare my tables and lists with those of Aune, "Magic in Early Christianity," 1523–24.
4. McKnight, *What Is Form Criticism?* 13–37.
5. An important recent critique on some extreme form criticism is Bauckham, *Jesus and the Eyewitnesses*, 15–34, 202–4. Bauckham differentiates carefully between oral tradition, which is anonymous, usually spans many generations, and is often fluid, and oral history, which is more immediate, includes eyewitnesses, and is more reliable in preserving material in its original form.
6. Betz, "Early Christian Miracle Story," 70.
7. Bailey and Vander Broek, *Literary Forms in the New Testament*, 137–43; McKnight, *What Is Form Criticism?* 22, 31–32.
8. Meier, *Marginal Jew*, 2:628–30. The high priest's servant whose ear is restored can be identified as Malchus only by cross-referencing Luke 22:50–51 with John 18:10.
9. Cotter, *Christ of the Miracle Stories*, 5–13, 254–57.
10. Meier, *Marginal Jew*, 2:628–30, 646–47.
11. Gerhardsson, *Mighty Acts of Jesus*, 20–24.
12. Meier, *Marginal Jew*, 2:619–22, 832–37.
13. See Strathearn and Judd, "Distinctive Testimonies of the Four Gospels," 60–61; Huntsman, *God So Loved the World*, 125–26.
14. See the testimony of the early Christian authorities Papias and Clement of Alexandria in Eusebius, *Church History*, 3.39.15–16; 6.14.6–7; and Irenaeus, *Against Heresies*, 3.1.1; Strathearn and Judd, "Distinctive Testimonies of the Four Gospels," 61–62.
15. See Huntsman, "Petrine *Kērygma* and the Gospel according to Mark," in Judd, Huntsman, and Hopkin, *Ministry of Peter* (forthcoming).
16. Cotter, *Christ of the Miracle Stories*, 3, 6–7.
17. See Twelftree's detailed discussion in *Jesus the Miracle Worker*, 57–58, 92–101.
18. Twelftree, *Jesus the Miracle Worker*, 102–6, 140–43.
19. Aune, "Magic in Early Christianity," 1537–38.
20. Cotter, *Christ of the Miracle Stories*, 7–8.
21. Achtemeier, "Lukan Perspective on the Miracles of Jesus," 156; Twelftree, *Jesus the Miracle Worker*, 167, 178–81; Achtemeier, *Jesus and the Miracle Tradition*, 15–17.
22. Twelftree, *Jesus the Miracle Worker*, 175–78; Achtemeier, *Jesus and the Miracle Tradition*, 25.
23. Achtemeier, *Jesus and the Miracle Tradition*, 17–18.
24. Twelftree, *Jesus the Miracle Worker*, 181–83, 187.
25. Achtemeier, "Lukan Perspective on the Miracles of Jesus," 159–61; Twelftree, *Jesus the Miracle Worker*, 183–86; Achtemeier, *Jesus and the Miracle Tradition*, 19–22.
26. Brown, "Gospel Miracles," 180–81; Gerhardsson, *Mighty Acts of Jesus*, 16; Morris, *Gospel according to John*, 607–13; Twelftree, *Jesus the Miracle Worker*, 224–28.
27. Twelftree, *Jesus the Miracle Worker*, 222–24.
28. Hume, *Human Understanding*, 146–72; Kellenberger, "Miracles," 145–53; Meier, *Marginal Jew*, 2:512–15; Keener, *Miracles*, 107–70.
29. Jefferson, *Life and Morals of Jesus of Nazareth*.
30. Twelftree, *Jesus the Miracle Worker*, 32–37.
31. Meier, *Marginal Jew*, 2:619–23; Twelftree, *Jesus the Miracle Worker*, 251; Evans *Fabricating Jesus*, 140.
32. Meier, *Marginal Jew*, 2:623–28; Twelftree, *Jesus the Miracle Worker*, 252; Evans, *Fabricating Jesus*, 140–41.
33. Meier, *Marginal Jew*, 2:874–80, 967–70.

### Appendix B: Our Galilee Miracle

1. See "Our Galilee Miracle," *Huntsmans in the Holy Land*, July 17, 2012, available at http://huntsmansintheholyland.blogspot.com/. Accessed January 15, 2014.
2. *Hymns*, no. 105.

# Sources

Achtemeier, Paul J. *Jesus and the Miracle Tradition.* Eugene, Ore.: Cascade Books, 2008.

———. "The Lukan Perspective on the Miracles of Jesus: A Preliminary Sketch." In *Perspectives on Luke–Acts,* edited by Charles H. Talbert, 156–67. Perspectives in Religious Studies: Special Studies Series 5. Edinburgh: T. & T. Clark, 1978.

———. "Person and Deed: Jesus and the Storm-Tossed Sea." *Interpretation* 16 (1962): 169–76.

*The Anchor Bible Dictionary.* Edited by David Noel Freedman et al. 6 vols. New York: Doubleday, 1992.

Aune, David E. "Magic in Early Christianity. In Principat. Part II, vol. 23, book 2, of *Aufstieg und Niedergand der römischen Welt,* edited by Hildegard Temporini and Wolfgang Haase, 1504–1556. New York: Walter de Gruyter, 1983.

*Babylonian Talmud.* Edited by Isidore Epstein. 36 vols. London: Soncino Press, 1935–52. Reprint, 1970.

Bailey, James L., and Lyle D. Vander Broek. *Literary Forms in the New Testament: A Handbook.* Louisville, Ky.: Westminster/John Knox Press, 1992.

Ballard, M. Russell. "O That Cunning Plan of the Evil One." *Ensign,* November 2010, 108–10.

Barnett, P. W. "The Feeding of the Multitude in Mark 6/John 6." In *The Miracles of Jesus,* vol. 6 of Gospel Perspectives, edited by David Wenham and Craig Blomberg, 273–94. Sheffield, England: JSOT, 1986.

Bauckham, Richard. *Jesus and the Eyewitnesses: The Gospels as Eyewitness Testimony.* Grand Rapids, Mich.: Eerdmans, 2006.

Bauer, Walter. *A Greek-English Lexicon of the New Testament and Other Early Christian Literature.* Edited by Frederick William Danker. Translated by William F. Arndt, F. Wilbur Gingrich, and F. W. Danker. 3d ed. Chicago: University of Chicago, 2000.

Bednar, David A. "In the Strength of the Lord." *Ensign,* November 2004, 76–78.

Betz, Hans Dieter. "The Early Christian Miracle Story: Some Observations on the Form Critical Problem." *Semeia* 11 (1978): 69–81.

Blumell, Lincoln H. "A Text-Critical Comparison of the King James New Testament with Certain Modern Translations." *Studies in the Bible and Antiquity* 3 (2011): 67–126.

Brown, Raymond E. *The Gospel according to John.* The Anchor Bible 29. Garden City, N.Y.: Doubleday, 1966–70.

———. "The Gospel Miracles." Chap. 10 in *New Testament Essays.* 3d ed. New York: Paulist, 1982.

Bruce, F. F. *The Gospel of John.* Grand Rapids, Mich.: Eerdmans, 1983.

———. *The Hard Sayings of Jesus.* Downers Grove, Ill.: InterVarsity, 1983.

Capper, Brian J. "Bethany, near the Mount of Olives." In vol. 1 of *The Encyclopedia of the Bible and Its Reception,* edited by Lindsay Jones, 955–57. 2d ed. Detroit: Macmillan, 2005.

———. "John, Qumran, and Virtuoso Religion." In *John, Qumran, and the Dead Sea Scrolls: Sixty Years of Discovery and Debate,* edited by Mary L. Coloe and Tom Thatcher, 93–116. Atlanta, Ga.: Society of Biblical Literature, 2011.

Carter, Daniel. "Come unto Him." Orem, Utah: Jackman Music, 1984.

———. "The Music of Daniel Carter: Come unto Him; The Story of How It Came to Be." *HubPages.* Available at http://danielcarter.hubpages.com/hub/Come-unto-Him-Music-Video-by-Daniel-Carter.

*A Choice Selection of Psalms, Hymns and Spiritual Songs for the Use of Christians.* Edited by John Mackenzie. Woodstock, Vt.: David Watson, 1819.

*Come, Thou Fount of Every Blessing: American Folk Hymns & Spirituals.* Salt Lake City: Mormon Tabernacle Choir, 2009. Audio CD.

*Consider the Lilies.* Salt Lake City: Mormon Tabernacle Choir, 2003. Audio CD.

Cotter, Wendy J. *The Christ of the Miracle Stories: Portrait through Encounter.* Grand Rapids, Mich.: Baker Academic, 2010.

Cowley, Matthias F. *Wilford Woodruff: History of His Life and Labors As Recorded in His Daily Journals.* Salt Lake City: Deseret News, 1909.

Davidson, Karen Lynn. *Our Latter-day Hymns: The Stories and the Messages.* Rev. ed. Salt Lake City: Deseret Book, 2009.

Davidson, Karen Lynn, David J. Whittaker, Mark Ashurst-McGee, and Richard L. Jensen. *Histories, Volume 1: Joseph Smith Histories, 1832–1844.* Vol. 1 of Histories series of *The Joseph Smith Papers*, edited by Dean C. Jessee, Ronald K. Esplin, Richard Lyman Bushman. Salt Lake City: Church Historian's Press, 2012.

Davis, Ryan Conrad, and Paul Y. Hoskisson. "Usage of the Title Elohim." *Religious Educator* 14, no. 1 (2013): 109–27.

Demaitre, Luke. *Leprosy in Premodern Medicine: A Malady of the Whole Body.* Baltimore, Md.: Johns Hopkins University Press, 2007.

"DNA of Jesus-Era Shrouded Man in Jerusalem Reveals Earliest Case of Leprosy." *Science Daily.* Last modified December 16, 2009. http://www.sciencedaily.com/releases/2009/12/091216103558.htm.

*Encyclopedia of Mormonism.* Edited by Daniel H. Ludlow et al. 4 vols. New York: Macmillan, 1992.

Erwin, Benjamin R. "Overcoming Addiction through the Atonement." *Ensign,* September 2012, 65–68.

Eusebius. *The Church History: A New Translation with Commentary.* Translated by Paul L. Maier. Grand Rapids, Mich.: Kregel, 1999.

Evans, Craig A. *Fabricating Jesus: How Modern Scholars Distort the Gospels.* Downers Grove, Ill.: Intervarsity Press, 2006.

*Exegetical Dictionary of the New Testament.* Edited by Horst Balz and Gerhard Schneider. 3 vols. Grand Rapids, Mich.: Eerdmans, 1990–93.

*Folk Songs of the American Negro (No. 1).* Edited by Frederick J. Work. Nashville: Work Bros. & Hart, 1907.

France, R. T. *The Gospel of Mark.* The New International Greek Commentary. Grand Rapids, Mich.: Eerdmans, 2002.

Gerhardsson, Birger. *The Mighty Acts of Jesus according to Matthew.* Lund, Sweden: LiberLäromedel/Gleerup, 1979.

Hamilton, Victor P. *The Book of Genesis, Chapters 1–17.* The New International Commentary on the Old Testament. Grand Rapids, Mich.: Eerdmans, 1990.

Hauser, William. *Olive Leaf: A Collection of Beautiful Tunes, New and Old; the Whole of One or More Hymns Accompanying Each Tune. . . .* Wadley, Ga.: William Hauser and Benjamin Turner, 1878.

Harrington, Daniel J. *The Gospel of Matthew.* Sacra Pagina 1. Collegeville, Minn.: Liturgical Press, 1991.

Harrod, John J., comp. *The New and Most Complete Collection of Camp, Social, and Prayer Meeting Hymns and Spiritual Songs Now in Use.* Baltimore, Md.: J. J. Harrod, 1830.

*History, 1838–1856.* volume C-1 (2 November 1838–31 July 1842). The Joseph Smith Papers. Available online at http://josephsmithpapers.org/paperSummary/history-1838-1856-volume-c-1-2-november-1838-31-july-1842?p=546.

*History of The Church of Jesus Christ of Latter-day Saints.* Edited by B. H. Roberts. 7 vols. 2d ed. rev. Salt Lake City: The Church of Jesus Christ of Latter-day Saints, 1932–51.

Holland, Jeffrey R. "Like a Broken Vessel." *Ensign,* November 2013, 40–42.

Holzapfel, Richard Neitzel. "The Transfiguration." In *From the Transfiguration to the Triumphal Entry,* 43–73. Salt Lake City: Deseret Book, 2006.

Holzapfel, Richard Neitzel, and Thomas A. Wayment, eds. *From the Transfiguration to the Triumphal Entry.* Vol. 2 of The Life and Teachings of Jesus Christ. Salt Lake City: Deseret Book, 2003–2006.

Horsley, Richard A. *Hearing the Whole Story: The Politics of Plot in Mark's Gospel.* Louisville, Ky.: Westminster John Knox Press, 2001.

———. "Jesus and Empire." In *In the Shadow of Empire: Reclaiming the Bible As a History of Faithful Resistance,* 75–96, edited by Richard A. Horsley. Louisville, Ky.: Westminster John Knox Press, 2008.

Howard, Luke. "Program Notes." *Come, Thou Fount of Every Blessing.* Audio CD. Salt Lake City: Mormon Tabernacle Choir, 2009.

Howick, E. Keith. *The Miracles of Jesus the Messiah.* St. George, Utah: WindRiver, 2003.

Hulse, E. V. "The Nature of Biblical 'Leprosy' and the Use of Alternative Medical Terms in Modern Translations of the Bible." *Palestine Exploration Quarterly* 107, no. 2 (1 July 1975): 87–105.

Hume, David. *An Enquiry concerning Human Understanding.* Edited by Lorne Falkenstein. Peterborough, Ont.: Broadview, 2011.

Huntington, O. B. "Words and Incidents of the Prophet Joseph's Life." *Young Woman's Journal* 2, no. 2 (November 1890): 75–77.

Huntsman, Eric D. "'And the Word Was Made Flesh': A Latter-day Saint Exegesis of the Blood and Water Imagery in the Gospel of John." *Studies in the Bible and Antiquity* 1 (2009): 51–65.

———. "The Bread of Life Sermon." In *Celebrating Easter,* 87–112, edited by Thomas A. Wayment and Keith J. Wilson. Provo, Utah: BYU Religious Studies Center, 2007.

———. *God So Loved the World: The Final Days of the Savior's Life.* Salt Lake City: Deseret Book, 2011.

———. *Good Tidings of Great Joy: An Advent Celebration of the Savior's Birth.* Salt Lake City: Deseret Book, 2011.

———. "The Lamb of God: Unique Aspects of the Passion Narrative in John." In *Behold the Lamb of God: An Easter Celebration,* 49–70, edited by Richard Neitzel Holzapfel, Frank F. Judd Jr., and Thomas A. Wayment. Provo, Utah: BYU Religious Studies Center, 2008.

———. *Huntsmans in the Holy Land* (blog). http://huntsmansintheholyland.blogspot.com/.

*Hymns of The Church of Jesus Christ of Latter-day Saints.* Salt Lake City: The Church of Jesus Christ of Latter-day Saints, 1985.

Irenaeus. *Against Heresies.* In *Apostolic Fathers, Justin Martyr, Irenaeus,* vol. 1 of *Ante-Nicene Fathers: The Writings of the Fathers Down to A.D. 325.* 10 vols. Edited by Alexander Roberts and James Donaldson. Revised by A. Cleveland Coxe. Peabody, Mass.: Hendrickson, 1994.

Jefferson, Thomas. *The Life and Morals of Jesus of Nazareth: Extracted Textually from the Gospels in Greek, Latin, French, and English.* Washington, D.C.: Government Printing Office, 1904.

*Joseph Smith's New Translation of the Bible: Original Manuscripts.* Edited by Scott H. Faulring, Kent P. Jackson, and Robert J. Matthews. Provo, Utah: BYU Religious Studies Center, 2004.

Josephus. *Antiquities of the Jews.* In *The New Complete Works of Josephus.* Edited by Paul L. Maier. Translated by William Whiston. Rev. ed. Grand Rapids, Mich.: Kregel, 1999.

*Journal of Discourses.* 26 vols. London: Latter-day Saints' Book Depot, 1854–86.

Judd, Frank F., Jr., Eric D. Huntsman, and Shon D. Hopkin. *The Ministry of Peter, the Chief Apostle,* pages forthcoming. Provo, UT: Religious Studies Center and Salt Lake City: Deseret Book, 2014.

Keener, Craig S. *Miracles: The Credibility of the New Testament Accounts.* 2 vols. Grand Rapids, Mich.: Baker Academic, 2011.

Kellenberger, J. "Miracles." *International Journal for the Philosophy of Religion* 10, no. 3 (1979): 145–62.

Knight, George W. *The Holy Land: An Illustrated Guide to Its Geography, Culture, and Holy Sites.* Uhrichsville, Ohio: Barbour, 2011.

*The Living Christ: The Testimony of the Apostles.* Salt Lake City: The Church of Jesus Christ of Latter-day Saints, 2000.

Madsen, Ann N. "'Wilt Thou Be Made Whole?' Medicine and Healing in the Time of Jesus." In *The Lord of the Gospels: The 1990 Sperry Symposium on the New Testament,* edited by Bruce A. Van Orden and Brent L. Top, 113–28. Salt Lake City: Deseret Book, 1991.

Marcus, Joel. *Mark 1–8.* The Anchor Bible 27. Garden City, N.Y.: Doubleday, 2000.

Marshall, I. Howard. *The Gospel of Luke: A Commentary on the Greek Text.* The New International Greek Testament Commentary. Grand Rapids, Mich.: Eerdmans, 1978.

Matthews, Robert J. *The Miracles of Jesus.* Provo, Utah: Brigham Young University Press, 1969.

McConkie, Bruce R. *Doctrinal New Testament Commentary.* 3 vols. Salt Lake City: Bookcraft, 1965–73.

———. *The Mortal Messiah: From Bethlehem to Calvary.* 4 vols. Salt Lake City: Deseret Book, 1979–81.

McKnight, Edgar V. *What Is Form Criticism?* Eugene, Ore.: Wipf & Stock, 1997.

Meier, John P. *Mentor, Message, and Miracles.* Vol. 2 of *A Marginal Jew: Rethinking the Historical Jesus.* New York: Doubleday, 1994.

Metzger, Bruce M. *A Textual Commentary on the Greek New Testament.* 2d ed. United Bible Societies, 1994.

Morgan, Robert J. *Then Sings My Soul.* Special edition. Nashville, Tenn.: Thomas Nelson, 2010.

Morris, Leon. *The Gospel according to John.* The New International Commentary on the New Testament. Rev. ed. Grand Rapids, Mich.: Eerdmans, 1995.

Morrison, Alexander B.. "Myths about Mental Illness." *Ensign,* October 2005, 31–35.

Murphy-O'Connor, Jerome. *The Holy Land: An Oxford Archaeological Guide from Earliest Times to 1700.* 5th ed. rev. Oxford: Oxford University Press, 2008.

*Murray's Songs for Sunday Schools and Gospel Meetings.* Edited by James R. Murray. Boston: White, Smith, 1876.

Nelson, Russell M. "Addiction or Freedom." *Ensign,* November 1988, 6–9.

*The New Oxford American Dictionary.* Edited by Frank Abate and Elizabeth J. Jewell. Oxford: Oxford University Press, 2001.

Nolland, John. *The Gospel of Matthew: A Commentary on the Greek Text.* The New International Greek Testament Commentary. Grand Rapids, Mich.: Eerdmans, 2005.

Nutton, Vivian. *Ancient Medicine.* 2d ed. London: Routledge, 2013.

Osbeck, Kenneth W. *101 Hymn Stories: The Inspiring True Stories behind 101 Favorite Hymns.* Grand Rapids, Mich.: Kregel, 2012.

*The Oxford Classical Dictionary.* Edited by Simon Hornblower and Antony Spawford. 3d ed. New York: Oxford University Press, 1996.

*Oxford Latin Dictionary.* Edited by P. G. W. Glare. Oxford: Clarendon Press, 1982.

Packer, Boyd K. "The Moving of the Water." *Ensign,* May 1991, 7–9.

Pilch, John J. *Healing in the New Testament: Insights from Medical and Mediterranean Anthropology.* Minneapolis, Minn.: Fortress, 2000.

Reid, Barbara E. *Choosing the Better Part? Women in the Gospel of Luke.* Collegeville, Minn.: Liturgical Press, 1996.

Roberts, B. H. *Defense of the Faith and the Saints.* 2 vols. Salt Lake City: Deseret News Press, 1907–12.

Scott, Richard G. "To Heal the Shattering Consequences of Abuse." *Ensign,* May 2008, 40–43.

Smith, Joseph. *Teachings of the Prophet Joseph Smith.* Selected by Joseph Fielding Smith. Salt Lake City: Deseret Book, 1976.

Smith, Joseph Fielding. *Doctrines of Salvation.* Compiled by Bruce R. McConkie. 3 vols. Salt Lake City: Bookcraft, 1954–56.

Snow, LeRoi C. "Raised from the Dead." *Improvement Era* 32, no. 11 (September 1929): 881–86.

Stackhouse, Rochelle A. "Hymnody and Politics: Isaac Watts's 'Our God, Our Help in Ages Past' and Timothy Dwight's 'I Love Thy Kingdom, Lord'." In *Wonderful Words of Life: Hymns in American Protestant History and Theology,* edited by Richard J. Mouw and Mark A. Noll. Grand Rapids, Mich.: Eerdmans, 2004.

Strathearn, Gaye. "Mary, Martha, and Lazarus." In *From the Transfiguration through the Triumphal Entry,* 152–75. Salt Lake City: Deseret Book, 2006.

Strathearn, Gaye, and Frank F. Judd. "The Distinctive Testimonies of the Four Gospels." *The Religious Educator* 8, no. 2 (2007): 59–85.

Tacitus. *The Complete Works of Tacitus.* Edited by Moses Hadas. New York: Random House, 1942. Translated by Alfred John Church and William Jackson Brodribb.

Talmage, James E. *Jesus the Christ: A Study of the Messiah and His Mission According to Holy Scriptures Both Ancient and Modern.* 1924. Reprint, Salt Lake City: Deseret Book, 1982.

Temperley, Nicholas. *Haydn: The Creation.* Cambridge: Cambridge University Press, 1991.

Theissen, Gerd. *The Miracle Stories of the Early Christian Tradition.* Edited by John Riches. Translated by Francis McDonagh. Philadelphia: Fortress, 1983.

*This Is the Christ.* Salt Lake City: Mormon Tabernacle Choir, 2011. Audio CD.

Twelftree, Graham H. *In the Name of Jesus: Exorcism among Early Christians.* Grand Rapids, Mich.: Baker Academic, 2007.

———. *Jesus the Miracle Worker: A Historical and Theological Study.* Downers Grove, Ill.: InterVarsity, 1999.

Walker, Peter. *In the Steps of Jesus: An Illustrated Guide to the Places of the Holy Land.* Grand Rapids, Mich.: Zondervan, 2006.

Watts, Isaac. *The Psalms of David, Imitated in the Language of the New Testament, and Applied to the Christian State and Worship.* London: J. Bruce, D. Burnet, R. Hopper, R. Pennington, and L. Martin, 1792.

Wayment, Thomas A. "The Woman Taken in Adultery and the History of the New Testament Canon." In *From the Transfiguration through the Triumphal Entry,* 372–97. Salt Lake City: Deseret Book, 2006.

Wilberg, Mack. *Death Shall Not Destroy My Comfort.* Oxford Church Music for Mixed Choir series. Oxford: Oxford Universty Press, 1998.

———. *My Shepherd Will Supply My Need.* Chapel Hill, N.C.: Hinshaw Music, 1995.

Witherington, Ben. *The Gospel of Mark: A Socio-Rhetorical Commentary.* Grand Rapids, Mich.: Eerdmans, 2001.

———. *Women and the Genesis of Christianity.* New York: Cambridge University Press, 1990.

# Index

*Page numbers in bold indicate paintings and photographs.*

Abinadi, 72
Abuse, 81
Abusers, as flesh-and-blood devils, 85
*Abyssos*, 76
*Accursed Fig Tree, The* (Tissot), **37**
Addiction, 75, 85
Adultery, woman caught in, 121–22
Afterlife, views on, in ancient world, 109
Ahura Mazda, 71
Aivazovsky, Ivan, **12**
*Akoloutheō* (also *ēkolouthēsan*), 89, 102
Al-Eizariya, 112–14
*All the City Was Gathered at His Door* (Tissot), **62**
"Amazing Grace," 100
American folk song, 31, 110
Anderson, Harry, **27**
Andrew, 27, 92
Angra Mainyu, 71
*Anistēmi* (*anestē*), 84
Anonymity: as feature of miracle stories, 18; of recipients of miracles, 42, 100–101; of lepers, 48; of paralytic, 49; of healed women, 56; of high priest's servant, 63; of widow of Nain, 107
*Apolyō* (*apolelysai*), 60
*Astheneia*, 49
Atonement: hope through, 7–8, 75; healing power of, 10, 11, 50, 51, 81; as act of re-organization or restoration, 20, 55; salvation through, 22; internalizing, 30; Transfiguration and, 36; strengthening and enabling power of, 50, 87, 125; Fall cured through, 51; liberation from Satan through, 67
Attestation of sources, 137
Authority, of Jesus Christ, 69
Autism spectrum disorder (ASD), 53, 84, 139, 141

Baker, Mary Ann, 23
Balm in Gilead, 45
Barley, 29
Bartimaeus, 100–103
Bauckham, Richard, 153n5
Beelzebub (*Ba'al Zəḇûḇ*), 79, 132
beggar, blind, 100–101
begging, 92
Benson, Ezra Taft, 6
Bethany (*Bêt 'anya*), 112–14
Bethphage, tomb in, **116**
Bethsaida, 27, 29–30, 92–95, 121
Bethsaida, healing of blind man at, 91–96
Betrayal, 81
Biblical criticism: source criticism, 2, 14, 22, 41, 128, 132–33, 147n32; narrative criticism, 127–28; form criticism, 127–31, 137; historical criticism, 136–37
Blind, healing: scriptural references to, 87; symbolism of, 87–88; healing of two blind men and deaf-mute, 88–91; healing of blind man in stages, 91–96; healing of man born blind, 96–100; healing of Bartimaeus, 100–103. *See also* Blindness
*Blind and Mute Man Possessed by Devils, The* (Tissot), **77**
*Blind Man Washes in the Pool of Siloam, The* (Tissot), **99**
Blindness: demonic possession resulting in, 76–79; spiritual, 87–88, 99–100; in ancient world, 92; symbolism of healing, in stages, 95–96, 103. *See also* Blind, healing
*Blind of Capernaum, The* (Tissot), **88**
Bloch, Carl: *Wedding at Cana*, **17**; *Healing the Blind Man*, **86**; *The Raising of Lazarus*, **104**; *The Daughter of Jairus*, **111**; *Christ Consolator*, **120**
Blood, symbolism of, 19. *See also* Hemorrhage, healing of woman with

Boat, Galilee, **20**
Boucher, François: *The Light of the World* (*Nativity*), **7**; *Saint Peter Attempts to Walk on Water*, **24**
"Bowels of mercy," 30
Bread: symbolism of, 15; miracles providing, 26; and feeding of five thousand, 29–30; and feeding of four thousand, 30
Bread of life discourse, 30
Brickey, Wayne, 84
Brigham Young University Men's Chorus, 110
Bultmann, Rudolf, 136
di Buoninsegna, Duccio, **98**

Caesarea Philippi, 33, 95
Cana, location of, 16. *See also* Wedding at Cana
Canaanites, 80
Capernaum: economy of, 26–27; monumental synagogue in, 68; devil cast out from man in, 68–69; condemnation of, 121
Carter, Daniel, 123
Centurion's servant, healing of, 44–45
Chemical dependency, 75
Children: healing of disabled, 53; devils cast out of, 79–84; death of, 108–9
Chora Church: *Resurrection* fresco in, **8**; mosaic depicting miracle at Cana in, **16**; *Jesus Healing the Deaf Man* mosaic, **89**
Chorazin, **93**, 94, 121
*Christ among the Lepers* (Richards), **47**
*Christ and the Canaanite Woman* (Drouais), **79**
*Christ Asleep During the Tempest* (Delacroix), **21**
*Christ at the Pool of Bethesda* (Murillo), **54**
*Christ Consolator* (Bloch), **120**

158

*Christ Healing the Blind Man of Jericho*, **102**
*Christ Heals the Centurion's Servant* (Ricci), **44**
Christians, earliest generations of, 128, 131, 136, 137
*Christ in Gethsemane* (Hofmann) **124**
*Christ Stilling the Tempest* (Tissot), **14**
*Christ Walking on the Sea* (Tissot), **22**
*Christ Walking on Water* (Aivazovsky), **12**
Chronic pain, 59
Chronology of miracles, 129–30
Church of the Primacy of St. Peter, **39**
Church of the Transfiguration, **33**
Clay, 97–99
Cleanliness, 46–49
Coherence, 137
*Come Follow Me* (Anderson), **27**
"Come unto Him," 123
Comfort, for grief, 117
Compassion: in feeding of four thousand and five thousand, 30; for grief, 116–17; for woman caught in adultery, 121–22
Copping, Harold: *The Miracle of the Loaves and Fishes*, **28**; *The Woman of Canaan*, **80**
Cosmologies, Near Eastern, 76
Cotter, Wendy J., 153n5
Cowdery, Oliver, 35
Creation: as miracle of Jesus Christ, 5–7; music inspired by, 6; and power over elements, 14–15; and Atonement, 20, 55; and miracles of provision, 25–32; healing and, 43; and healing of deaf, 91; and healing of man born blind, 96–97, 99
*Creation, The* (Haydn), 6
Cursing, 36–37

*Daimōn*, 71
Dalmanutha, 91
Daughter of Jairus, raising of, 108–12
*Daughter of Jairus, The* (Bloch), **111**
Dead, raising: scriptural references to, 105; symbolism of, 105–6; son of widow of Nain, 106–8; daughter of Jairus, 108–12; Lazarus, 112–18; significance of, 118–19. *See also* Resurrection
Deaf, healing: scriptural references to, 87; symbolism of, 87–88; healing of two blind men and deaf-mute, 88–91
Deafness, spiritual, 87–88
Death: and blessing for easy passing, 9–10, 117; attitudes regarding, 105; of children, 108–9; views on, in ancient world, 109; spiritual, 116, 119; miracles at time of, 117. *See also* Dead, raising
"Death Shall Not Destroy My Comfort," 110
Decapolis, 73, 90
Delacroix, Eugene, **21**
Demonic possession: represents effects of Fall, 66–67, 70–72; mental illness as, 67; addiction and, 75; resulting in muteness and blindness, 76–79; reality of, 84–85. *See also* Demons; Devil(s), casting out; Exorcism
Demons: views on, in ancient world, 71; power of, opposite that of Holy Ghost, 77. *See also* Demonic possession; Devil(s), casting out; Exorcism
Depression, 59, 67
*Desmos*, 90
Developmental challenges, 59, 63. *See also* Autism spectrum disorder (ASD)
Devil(s), casting out: scriptures referencing, 65; Gospel accounts of, 65–67; from man in Capernaum, 68–69; from Mary Magdalene, 69–72; from Gadarene demonic, 72–76; from children, 79–84; in Gospel of John, 136. *See also* Demonic possession; Demons; Exorcism
*Diakoneō* (*diēkonei*), 56
Didrachma, 32
Disabilities, care for those with, 53. *See also* Infirmities
Disciples: and calming of sea, 13, 19–25; and turning water into wine, 15–16; and catch of fish at Capernaum, 27–29; and feeding of five thousand, 29; and feeding of four thousand, 30; Transfiguration and, 32–36; and catch of 153 fish, 38–39; to speak by Holy Ghost, 77; and Syrophoenician woman, 82; spiritual understanding of, 88, 91–92, 95–96; Jesus' love for, 116–17. *See also* Discipleship
Discipleship: and restoration of sight to two blind men, 89; of Bartimaeus, 102–3
Discouragement, 53, 59, 66, 67, 78, 84
Discourse, 127–28
Dissimilarity, 137
Dissociative identity disorder, 67
Distance, healing from, 42–45, 46, 79–82
Divine Son, discourse on, 55, 116
Dogs, 76, 81–82

Dopamine, 75
*Doxazō* (*edoxazen*), 60
Dropsy, healing of man with, 60–61
Drouais, Jean-Germain, **79**
Dumbness, 79, 91
*Dynamis* (also *dynamin*, *dynameis*, *dynameōn*), 3, 5, 57, 121, 132, 135

Ear, healing of, of high priest's servant, 63, 152n12
Ears to hear, 87–88
Edema, 60
*Egeirō* (also *egeire*, *egeiren*), 55, 56, 84, 107, 111, 112
*Egō eimi*, 25
ʿ*Ehyeh ʾašer ʿehyeh*, 25
*Eis tēn abysson*, 76
*Ekballō* (*ekballōn*), 78
*Ēkolouthēsan*. *See also Akoloutheō* (also *ēkolouthēsan*)
Elements, power over: scriptural references to, 13; significance of, 13–15; water turned into wine, 15–19; calming of storm and walking on water, 19–25; catch of fish at Capernaum, 26–29; feeding of five thousand, 29–30; feeding of four thousand, 30; fish with coin in its mouth, 30–32; Transfiguration, 32–36; cursing of fig tree, 36–37; catch of 153 fish, 37–39
*Elephantiasis*, 48
Elias, 148n46
*Ēlias*, 34
Elijah: Transfiguration and, 34, 36; and raising of dead, 106–7, 108; miracles performed by, 145n2
Elisha: miracles performed by, 29, 145n2; and healing of Naaman, 46; spiritual eyes of servant of, opened, 87, 88; and raising of dead, 106–7
Embarrassment, 137
Emotional challenges, 59
Empty tomb, 18, 103
*Endoxon*, 3
Enlightenment, 2, 136
*Ephphatha*, 90
*Epieikeia*, 128
Epilepsy, 82
Epiphany, 20, 25, 32–33
*Epitimaō* (*epetimēsen*), 20, 57
*Ergon* (also *erga*), 3, 135
Eschatology, realized, 152n29
*Esōthē*, 76
*Esōzonto*, 63
Evangelical triangle, **93**, 94

## INDEX

Exorcism, 65–67, 79, 135. *See also* Demonic possession; Demons; Devil(s), casting out
*Exorkizō*, 65
Eyes to see, 87–88
Ezekiel, 88

Faith: required for miracles, 9; in rescue, 21–22; through trials, 23, 25; of woman with hemorrhage, 57–60; strengthened, 84; of Bartimaeus, 102. See also *Sōzō* (also *esōzonto, sōthēsetai, sōson, sesōken, sōthē*)
Fall: sickness as type of, 43–44, 53–54; demonic possession represents, 66–67, 70–72; blindness as result of, 92, 99; infirmities as consequence of, 135
Fallen state, weakness and, 49–50. *See also* Natural men and women, as subjects of Fall
Feast of Tabernacles, 96, 99
Fig tree, cursing of, 36–37
Finger of God, 79, 150n43
Fish: catching, at Capernaum, 26–27; and feeding of five thousand, 29–30; catch of one hundred fifty-three, 37–39
Fish with coin in its mouth, 30–32
Five thousand, feeding of, 29–30
Forgiveness: as miracle, 10; healing and, 42; of paralyzed man at Capernaum, 49–50; availability of, 63; of woman caught in adultery, 121–22
Forms, literary, 127–31, 137
Four thousand, feeding of, 30

Gadara, 72, 150n23
Gadarene demonic, 72–76
Galilee, 68, 139–43
Galilee, Sea of, **26, 93**; Jesus Christ calms and walks on, 19–25; and feeding of five thousand, 29–30; and catch of 153 fish, 36; and calling of Peter, 38; and casting out Legion, 72–76; traveling by, 92; author's miracle on, 140–43
Garden Tomb, **118**
Gentile(s): Eastern side of Galilee and, 30, 73–74; seven and seventy symbolizing, 30; centurion as, 44; in Luke, 76; Syrophoenician woman as, 79–82
Gerasa, 73, 150n23
Gergesa, 73, 150n23
Gethsemane, 36, 103
Gift miracles, 25–32

God of Miracles, 9
Golgotha, 103
Good Shepherd, discourse on, 117–18
Grace, 100
Grave clothes, 118
Greatest miracle(s): strengthening and enabling power of Atonement as, 1, 125; eternal life as, 9; resurrection as, 11, 125; change of heart as, 125; forgiveness as, 125; healing of soul as, 125
"Great Omission" of Luke, 147n22
Grief, 117

Hades, 109
Half-shekel temple tax, 32
Handel, George Frideric, 6
Handicapped, healing of disabled, 53
Hands, used in healing, 89, 90, 94–95, 97–98
Hansen's disease, 48
Harmonization, 133, 137
Haydn, Franz Joseph, 6
Healers, traditional, 51
*Healing* (Richards), **2**
*Healing of the Lepers at Capernaum* (Tissot), **46**
*Healing of the Officer's Son, The* (Tissot), **42**
*Healing of Two Blindmen from Jericho, The*, **101**
Healing(s): prayer for, 8–10; scriptural references to, 41; statistics on, 41; significance of, 41–42; of royal official's son, 42–45; of centurion's servant, 44–45; from leprosy, 45–49; of paralyzed man at Capernaum, 49–50; in ancient world, 51; of man at Pool of Bethesda, 52–55; of women, 55–60; of man with withered hand, 60; of man with dropsy, 60–61; of high priest's servant, 63, 152n12; from abuse and betrayal, 81; of possessed child, 82–84; of woman with hemorrhage, 110–11; in Gospel of Luke, 135. *See also* Blind, healing; Deaf, healing
*Healing the Blind Man* (Bloch), **86**
Hearing, restoration of. *See* Deaf, healing
Hebrew Bible: Jesus' creative role throughout, 5; miracles connect Jesus with Jehovah of, 19; God as provider in, 25; leprosy in, 48; health and sciences in, 51; restoration of hearing and sight in, 87; afterlife described in, 109; raising of dead in, 118; titles of Jesus Christ in, 146n15. *See also* Old Testament

*He Did No Miracles but He Healed Them* (Tissot), **42**
Hemorrhage, healing of woman with, 57–60, 110–11
Herod Antipas, 27, 32, 43, 44
Herodians, 68
High priest's servant, healing of, 63, 152n12
Hind, S. K., 6
Hippocrates, 51
Hippos, 73
Historical criticism, 136–37. *See also* Biblical criticism
Hofmann, Heinrich, **124**
*Hoi idioi*, 14–15, 146n3
Hole, William Brassey, **108**
Holland, Jeffrey R., 59
Holy Ghost: and ability to speak, 77; comfort through, 117
Homer, 92
Hope, through miracles, 7–8
House divided against itself, parable of, 79
"How Great Thou Art," 6
Hume, David, 136, 146n10
Huntsman, Dennis C., 8–10, 117
Huntsman, N. Elaine, 9–10, 139, 140
Huntsman, Rachel, 139
Huntsman, Samuel P., 9–10, 84, 139–43
*Hydrōpikos*, 60

*Iaomai* (*iasatō*), 82
*Iēsous*, 30
Illness. *See* Sickness
Incarnate Word, 7, 14, 18, 39, 43, 44, 52, 122, 128
Incarnation, 7, 19
Infancy narratives, 7
Infidelity, 81
Infirmities: healing of, at resurrection, 10, 63, 84; demonic possession resulting in, 76–79; as consequence of Fall, 135. *See also* Disabilities, care for those with
Innocents, suffering, 79–84
Intertestamental period, 71, 96, 109
*In the Villages the Sick Were Brought unto Him* (Tissot), **x**
*I Shall Be Whole* (Young), **58**
Israel: Jehovah's covenant relationship with, 18; miracle of manna feeding, 29–30; wandering of, 54; knowledge of, of afterlife, 109
"It is I," 25

Jacob, 67, 88
Jairus, 108–12
James, son of Zebedee: as witness of Transfiguration, 33–34; receives priesthood keys, 35–36; as witness of Jairus' daughter raised from dead, 111
Jefferson, Thomas, 136
Jehovah: incarnation of, 7; Israel's covenant relationship with, 18; miracles connect Jesus with, 19, 20; identification of, 25. *See also* Jesus Christ; YHWH
Jericho, 100, **113**
Jerusalem: triumphal entry into, 15, 36; Atonement in, 36, 96; destruction of, 37; model of, **96, 97**; final ascent to, 100, 103; author's experiences in, 139
*Jesus and the Sinner Woman* (Polenov), **122**
Jesus Christ: as Savior, 1; identity of, 1–2, 5, 7, 13–39, 43, 91–92, 95–96, 123, 128, 131, 135, 136, 137; work of, 3, 9, 55, 96–97, 121, 135; as Creator, 5–7; birth of, 7, 19; Passion of, 11, 96; salvific suffering, death, and resurrection of, 11, 36; as exorcist, 14, 65–85, 137; as healer, 14, 41–63, 137; triumphal entry of, 15; compassion of, 30, 116–17, 121–22; Transfiguration of, 32–36; battling Satan, 65–66, 68–69, 76; forty days in wilderness, 68; hard sayings of, 81; knowing identity and role of, 95–96; and mourning with those who mourn, 116–17; Resurrection of, 117–18; atoning suffering and death of, 125; unusual personal power of, 130, 135, 136. *See also* Atonement; Epiphany; Jehovah; Titles and roles of Jesus Christ; YHWH
*Jesus Healing the Deaf Man* (Chora Church), **89**
*Jesus Heals a Mute Possessed Man* (Tissot), **90**
*Jesus Heals the Crippled* (Kim), **40**
*Jesus Opens the Eyes of a Man Born Blind* (Buoninsegna), **98**
*Jesus Raising a Young Man from the Dead in a City Called Nain* (Hole), **108**
Jezreel Valley, 33, 106
Joanna, 56, 152n12
John, Gospel of: miracles as signs in, 3, 5, 7, 15–16, 43, 52, 91; miracles as works in, 3, 96; terminology in, 3, 5; power over elements described in, 15; wedding at Cana recorded in, 18; "I Am" statements in, 25, 136; concept of life in, 44; Atonement and healing as re-creation in, 55, 135–36; exorcisms lacking in, 66–67; first miracle in, 68; healing of man born blind in, 96–100; "the Jews" in, 114; high christology of, 135; characteristics of, 135–36; Book of Signs in, 136; selective in miracles portrayed, 136; harmonizing, with other Gospels, 148n3. *See also* Signs in John
John, son of Zebedee: as witness of Transfiguration, 33–34; receives priesthood keys, 35–36; as witness of Jairus' daughter raised from dead, 111
John Mark, 134
John the Baptist, report to disciples of, 9, 41, 47–48, 63, 91, 118, 132
Jonah, 21
Jordan River, 29, 92
Joseph, husband of Mary, 108
Joseph Smith Translation, 74, 148n46
Josephus, 3
Joshua: as Moses' successor, 29–30; miracles performed by, 145n2
Julias, 92, 93
Justice, 122–23

Kafr Kannā: Roman Catholic church in, **15**; as location of Cana, 16
Keys, given to Peter, James, and John, 35–36
Kfar Naḥûm, 26–27
Khirbet Qânâ, 16
Kim, Yongsung, **40**
Kirtland Temple, 35
Knight, Newell, 65
*Kōphos* (also *kōphon*), 77, 89
Kursi, 73
*Kynarion*, 81

Last Supper, 18, 30
Law and the Prophets, 34
Law of Moses, 16, 46, 48, 96, 134
Law(s), miracles and natural, 4, 18–19
Lazarus, raising of, 112–18
Legalism, 122
*Legio*, 74
Legion, 74–75
Legion of devils, cast out, 72–76
*Lepra*, 48
Leprosy, cleansing of, 45–49
Life: in Gospel of John, 44; abundant, in Jesus Christ, 105, 119; spiritual, 116, 119
Light, and healing of man born blind, 96–97, 99
*Light of the World, The* (Nativity) (Boucher), **7**
Literary forms: miracle story, 127–31; miracle summary, 131; miracle report, 132
Livia, 92
Loaves and fishes, 29–30
"Lord, I Would Follow Thee," 59
Love, 122–23
Luke, Gospel of: balances teachings and deeds, 3; infancy narrative of, 7; emphasizes role of faith in miracles, 46, 49; women in, 56, 57, 60, 61, 70, 100, 107, 135; gender pairs in, 61; inclusive approach to, 61–63; portrays Jesus as loving, compassionate, healing Savior, 63, 106, 107, 135; broad use of exorcism motif in, 66; demonic possession in, 66, 76; healings use language and imagery of demonic possession in, 66; first miracle in, 68; raising of son of widow of Nain in, 106; raising of Jairus' daughter in, 112; "beloved physician" traditional author of, 135; characteristics of, 135; "Great Omission" of, 147n22

Magdala, 70
Major depressive disorder (MDD), 59
Malchus, 63, 152n12
Man at Pool of Bethesda, healing of, 52–55
Manna, 29–30
*Man Possessed of a Devil in the Synagogue, The* (Tissot), **69**
*Man with the Withered Hand, The* (Tissot), **61**
Mark, Gospel of: priority of, 2, 133; first miracle in, 68; emphasizes deeds over teachings, 68–69; miracle stories longer in, 76, 82; as more descriptive of miracles, 89; healing of blind and deaf in, 89–90; "On the Road to Jerusalem" / "About the Blindness of the Disciples," 95–96; raising of Jairus' daughter in, 110–12; possible connection with Peter, 133–34; characteristics of, 134
Marriage, infidelity in, 81
Martha, 112–16
Mary, mother of Jesus: and miracle at Cana, 16, 18, 19; and widow of Nain, 108

Mary Magdalene, 69–72, 152n12
Mary of Bethany, 112–14, 116–17
Massacio, **32**
"Master, the Tempest Is Raging," 23
Matthew, Gospel of: infancy narrative of, 7; first miracle in, 68; Matthean doubling, 74, 100; demonic possession in, 76; exorcisms downplayed in, 76; Son of David title common in, 88–89; healing of blind and deaf in, 89; abbreviations of miracle accounts in, 112, 134; raising of Jairus' daughter in, 112; summaries in, 131; Gospel of Mark and, 134; Jesus as New Moses in, 134; eliminates or downplays magical aspects of miracles, 134–35; characteristics of, 135; emphasizes teachings over deeds, 135
Medicine, in ancient world, 51
Meier, John P., 153n3
Mental illness, 65, 67
Mercy, 122–23
Meredith, Joleen G., 78
Messiah, Jesus Christ as, 87, 88, 118
Messianic age, 49, 87, 91
Messianic banquet, 16, **39**
Messianic expectations, contemporary, 88–89, 101, 118
*Miracle of the Loaves and Fishes, The* (Copping), **28**
Miracles: possibility of, 2–4, 146n10; Greek words for, 3; lacking, 8–10; chronology of, 129–30; defined, 146n11; features of, 153nn2,3. *See also* Greatest miracle(s)
Miracle stories: foreshadow Jesus' salvific acts, 2; anonymity of characters in, 18; consistency and inflexibility of, 128; as encounters, 128; reveal divine identity, 128, 131, 136; tripartite form of, 128; as paradigms of those who come to Christ, 131; serve as types, 131; portray characteristics of Jesus, 134
*Miraculum*, 2
*Mirari*, 2
Missionary work, and catch of 153 fish, 38–39
*Mogilalos* (also *mogilalon*), 89–90, 91
*Monogenēs*, 106, 108, 112, 152n7
Mormon Tabernacle Choir, 78, 110, 152n16
Morrison, Alexander, 67
Moses, 29–30, 34, 36, 145n2
Mother-in-law, healing of Peter's, 56–57
Mount Hermon, 33
Mount of Olives, 132

Mount Tabor, **33**
Mud, 97–99
Multiple attestation: of sources, 136–37; of forms, 137
Murillo, Bartolomé Esteban, **54**
Muteness, 76–79, 91
"My Shepherd Will Supply My Need," 31

Naaman, 46
Nain (Na'in): church at, **106**; raising of son of widow of, 106–8; location of, **107**
Named figures, in miracle stories. *See* Anonymity
Narrative criticism, 127–28
Nathaniel, 147n7
Natural law(s), 4, 18–19
Natural men and women, as subjects of Fall, 72, 85, 106
Nazareth, **49**, 66, 130, 132
*Neaniskos* (*neaniske*), 107
Negro spiritual, 45
Nelson, Russell M., 75
Nephi, vision of, 10–11
Newton, John, 100
Nobleman's son, healing of, 42–45

Old Testament: use of *erga* in, 3; Jesus Christ as Jehovah of, 5, 19, 20, 25; covenant relationship with Israel in, 18; punitive miracles in, 36; leprosy in, 48; references to physicians and medicines in, 51; demons in, 71; witness requirement in, 74; Phoenicians in, 80; raising of dead in, 87, 105, 106; restoration of hearing and sight in, 87; Son of David in, 101. *See also* Hebrew Bible
Osteoporosis, 60

Packer, Boyd K., 53
*Pais*, 44
*Palsied Man Let Down through the Roof, The* (Tissot), **50**
Palsy, healing of man with, 8, 10, 49–50
Paradigmatic day, 56, 131
*Paradoxon*, 3
Paralyzed man, healing of, at Capernaum, 49–50
Passion, of Jesus Christ, 11, 96
Passion narratives, 134
Passion predictions, 96, 151n17
Passion Week, 63, 103, 119
Peace, desire for, 78
*Pēlos*, 97
Pericopes, 127–28, 132

Peter: walks on water, 25; and miracle of fish at Capernaum, 27–29; and miracle of fish with coin in its mouth, 32; as witness of Transfiguration, 33–34; receives priesthood keys, 35–36; and catch of 153 fish, 38–39; healing of mother-in-law of, 56–57; knowledge of, of Jesus' identity, 95–96; as witness of Jairus' daughter raised from dead, 111
Pharisees: and defilement of Gentiles, 80, 82; seek signs, 91–92; and healing of man born blind, 99–100
*Philanthrōpia*, 128
Philip, disciple, 92
Philip, tetrarch of northwestern territories, 27, 92
*Phimoō* (also *phimōthēti*), 69
*Phobeomai* (also *ephobēthēsan*), 13, 146n1
*Phobos* (also *phobou*, *phobon*), 13, 111
Phoenicians, 80
Pigs, 76
Pilate, 95
Plato, 109
*Pneuma*, 82
Polenov, Vasily: *The Raising of Jairus' Daughter*, **11**; *Jesus and the Sinner Woman*, **122**
Pool of Bethesda, healing of man at, 52–55, 56, 60, 97
Pool of Siloam, **96**, 97, 99
Poor: hear gospel, 9, 48, 53, 66, 91, 118, 132; Jesus cares for, 61, 107; Bethany and, 114
*Possessed Boy at the Foot of Mount Tabor, The* (Tissot), **83**
*Possessed Man in the Synagogue, The* (Tissot), **64**
*Praotēs*, 128
Prayer, for miracles, 8–10
Priesthood keys, given to Peter, James, and John, 35–36
Primacy of St. Peter, 38
Provision, miracles of: Creation and, 25–26; catch of fish at Capernaum, 26–29; feeding of five thousand, 29–30; feeding of four thousand, 30; fish with coin in its mouth, 30–32
Psychological disorders, 59, 63
Purity, Jewish rules about, 16, 58. *See also* Ritual impurity

*Rabbouni*, 101–2
*Raising of Jairus' Daughter, The* (Polenov), **11**
*Raising of Lazarus* (Richards), **115**

*Raising of Lazarus, The* (Bloch), **104**
Rebuke: of storm, 19–21; of illnesses, 57, 66, 135; of demons, 69, 82; of spiritually deaf and blind, 88; of disciples, 91–92, 96; of Chorazin, Bethsaida, and Capernaum, 121
Recovery, from abuse and betrayal, 81
Re-creation, 20
Repentant thief, 63
Reports, 132
Rescue miracle, calming of sea as, 20–22
Resurrection: healing of infirmities at, 10, 63, 84; Jesus' work finished at final, 55; Jesus' teachings on, 115–16; of Lazarus and Jesus Christ, 117–18. *See also* Dead, raising
*Resurrection* (Chora Church), **8**
Resuscitation, 107–8, 109, 112
Revelation, 95
Revelation, book of, 18, 35, 75, 95
Ricci, Sevastiano, **44**
Richards, J. Kirk: *Healing*, **2**; *Christ among the Lepers*, **47**; *Sight Restored*, **94**; *Raising of Lazarus*, **115**
Rich young man, 103
Rigdon, Sidney, 95
Ritual impurity: from lepers, 46; from menstruating or hemorrhaging women, 58; from dead bodies, 74. *See also* Purity, Jewish rules about
Ritual observance, 122
Road to Jericho, 103, **113**
Romans, as military occupiers, 37, 68
Royal official's son, healing of, 42–45

Sabbath, 55, 56, 60–61, 96–99
Sacrament, 30
Sadducees, 109
*Saint Peter Attempts to Walk on Water* (Boucher), **24**
Saliva, 90, 94, 97–98
Salvation: through Atonement, 22, 121; healing and, 46–49
*Ṣārāʿaṭ*, 48
Satan (*Sāṭan*), 71; deliverance from, 66; tactics of, 66, 84–85; overthrowing kingdom of, 68–69; exorcisms as victory over reign of, 79; and healing from abuse, 81
Schizophrenia, 67
*Schöpfung, Die* (Haydn), 6
Scott, Richard G., 81
Sea, 76
Second Coming, 35
*Šēdîm*, 71
*Śeʿîrîm*, 71

*Selēniazomai* (*selēniazetai*), 82
Self-righteousness, 123
*Sēmeia kai terata*, 3, 43
*Sēmeiōn* (also *sēmeia*, *sēmeion*), 3, 5, 15, 42, 52, 91, 112, 133, 135, 136, 148n3. *See also* Signs in John
Senses, restoration of. *See* Blind, healing; Deaf, healing
Sensory processing disorder (SPD), 84, 139
Seven, 30, 72, 148n36
Seventy, 30
Sheol, 109
Shunem, 106, 108
Sickness: as type of Fall, 43–44, 53–54; sin as perceived cause of, 50, 67, 92; in ancient world, 51; unseen, 59
*Sick Waiting for Jesus to Pass By, The* (Tissot), **10**
Sight, restoration of. *See* Blind, healing
*Sight Restored* (Richards), **94**
Signs in John: water turned into wine, 15–19; walking on water, 19–25; feeding of five thousand, 29–30; healing of nobleman's son, 42–45; healing of lame man at Pool of Bethesda, 52–55; healing of man born blind, 96–100; raising of Lazarus, 112–18
*Šiloaḥ*, 99
Siloam, Pool of, **96**, 99
Simon Peter. *See* Peter
Sin: sickness associated with, 50, 67, 92; condemnation for, 121–22
Six, 16
Smith, Hyrum, 91
Smith, Joseph: on Creation, 5; on priesthood keys given to apostles, 36
Smith, Joseph Fielding, 36
Social conventions: regarding leprosy, 46; regarding blood afflictions, 58, 59; regarding Gentiles, 80, 82; regarding funerals, 107; Jesus' love supersedes, 123
Socrates, 109
Solomon, 101
Son of David, 88–89, 101
Son of widow of Nain, raising of, 106–8
*Soudarion*, 118
Source criticism, 14, 22, 41, 128, 132–33, 147n32
Sources, multiple attestation of, 136–37
*Sōzō* (also *esōzonto*, *sōthēsetai*, *sōson*, *sesōken*, *sōthē*), 20, 22, 25, 46, 58, 63, 110, 112, 118

Spiritual deafness and blindness, 87–88, 99–100
Spiritual death, 116, 119
Spiritual gifts, 121
Spiritual life, 116, 119
*Splanchna*, 30
*Splanchnizomai* (also *splangnistheis*), 30, 149n9
Stereotypes, gender and racial, 123
Stone water pots, 16
Storm, calming of, 19–25
Storms and tempests, symbolism of, 19, 21–22, 23, 25
Strauss, David Friedrich, 136
Strong man, parable of, 79
*Sukkôt*, 96, 99
Sulam, 106
Summaries, 131–32
Susanna, 56, 152n12
*Swine Driven into the Sea, The* (Tissot), **74**
Synagogue: woman healed in, 60; at Narazeth, 66; devil cast out from man in, in Capernaum, 68–69; as sacred space, 74
Syrophoenician woman, 79, 80–82

Tabgha: church at, **29**; feeding of five thousand at, 29–30
*Ta idia*, 14–15, 146n3
*Talitha cumi*, 111
Talmage, James E., 4, 18–19
Talmud, 92
*Tamea*, 100
Teiresias, 92
Temple (Jerusalem): and miracle of fish with coin in its mouth, 31, 32; cleansing of, 37; and Feast of Tabernacles, 96; Jesus passes through mob in, 136
Temple tax, 32
Temptation, 66, 67, 85
Ten lepers, healing of, 46–47
*Thambos*, 146n12
*Thauma*, 3
*Thaumasion*, 3
*Thaumazō*, 146n12
Thayne, Emma Lou, 78
*Therapeuō* (also *etherapeusen*, *etherapeuthē*), 79, 82
"There Is a Balm in Gilead," 45
Thief, repentant, 63
*Thygatrion*, 80
Tiberias, 43
Tissot, James: *In the Villages the Sick Were Brought unto Him*, **xii**; *The Sick Waiting for Jesus to Pass By*, **10**;

*Christ Stilling the Tempest*, **14**; *Christ Walking on the Sea*, **22**; *The Accursed Fig Tree*, **37**; *The Healing of the Officer's Son*, **42**; *He Did No Miracles but He Healed Them*, **42**; *Healing of the Lepers at Capernaum*, **46**; *The Palsied Man Let Down through the Roof*, **50**; *The Woman with an Infirmity of Eighteen Years*, **59**; *The Man with the Withered Hand*, **61**; *All the City Was Gathered at His Door*, **62**; *The Possessed Man in the Synagogue*, **64**; *The Man Possessed of a Devil in the Synagogue*, **69**; *The Swine Driven into the Sea*, **74**; *The Blind and Mute Man Possessed by Devils*, **77**; *The Possessed Boy at the Foot of Mount Tabor*, **83**; *The Blind of Capernaum*, **88**; *Jesus Heals a Mute Possessed Man*, **90**; *The Blind Man Washes in the Pool of Siloam*, **99**

Titian, **34**

Titles and roles of Jesus Christ: Creator, 1, 15, 18, 19, 20, 25, 32, 39, 43, 52, 75, 128, 137; Savior, 1, 102, 135; Divine Word, 5, 7, 14, 15, 19, 44, 52; Man of Galilee, 5; Babe of Bethlehem, 7, 19; Incarnate Word, 7, 14, 18, 39, 43, 44, 52, 122, 128; Word made flesh, 15, 18, 122; Sustainer and Provider, 32, 39; Judge, 37, 39; Living Water, 55; Son of David, 88–89; Light of the World, 96–97, 99; Resurrection and the Life, 112, **114**, 115; Great I Am, 122

Tombs: empty, 18, 103; man dwelling among, 72; as place of ritual defilement, 74; of Lazarus, 114, **116**; of Lazarus and Jesus Christ, 117–18; Garden Tomb, **118**

Touch, used in healing, 89, 90, 94–95, 97–98

Transfiguration, 32–36

*Transfiguration of Christ, The* (Titian), **34**

Trials: faith through, 23, 25; unseen, 59. *See also* Storms and tempests, symbolism of

*Tribute Money, The* (Massacio), **32**

Truth, 95

Twelve apostles, 35–36, 148n45

Tyre, 80, 121

Unbelief, 84

Unseen illnesses, 59. *See also* Depression

Visions, of Jesus Christ, 35

Vocations, support in, 27

Water: turned into wine, 15–19, 39, 43, 52, 68; symbolism of, 19; walking on, 19–25; and healing of man born blind, 96, 99

Watts, Isaac, 31

Way, the, as early term for Christian Church, 102

Weakness, 49–50

Wedding at Cana, 16–19, 147n7

*Wedding at Cana* (Bloch), **17**

Wedding feast, symbolism of, 18

"Where Can I Turn for Peace?," 78

Widowhood, 107

Widow of Nain, raising of son of, 106–8

Wilberg, Mack, 31, 78, 110

Wine: symbolism of, 15–16; water turned into, 15–19, 39, 43, 52, 68; role of, in messianic banquets, 16–18; miracles providing, 26

Withered hand, healing of man with, 60

Woman caught in adultery, 121–22

*Woman of Canaan, The* (Copping), **80**

Woman who was a sinner, 70

*Woman with an Infirmity of Eighteen Years, The* (Tissot), **59**

Women: Jesus' attitudes and interactions with, 55–60, 61; cultural restrictions upon, 58, 60; conventions against touching unrelated, 60

Word, Jesus Christ as incarnate, 7, 14, 15, 18, 19, 39, 43, 44, 52, 122, 128

*Yəhôšūa`*, 29–30

YHWH: as Creator, 5; Israel's covenant relationship with, 18; power of, over elements, 19, 20, 21; reveals himself to Moses, 25; provides for all creation, 25–26; as healer, 51; law of, 122–23; Jesus Christ as, 136. *See also* Jehovah; Jesus Christ

Young, Al, **58**

*Zaō (zē)*, 44

Zarephath, 106, 108

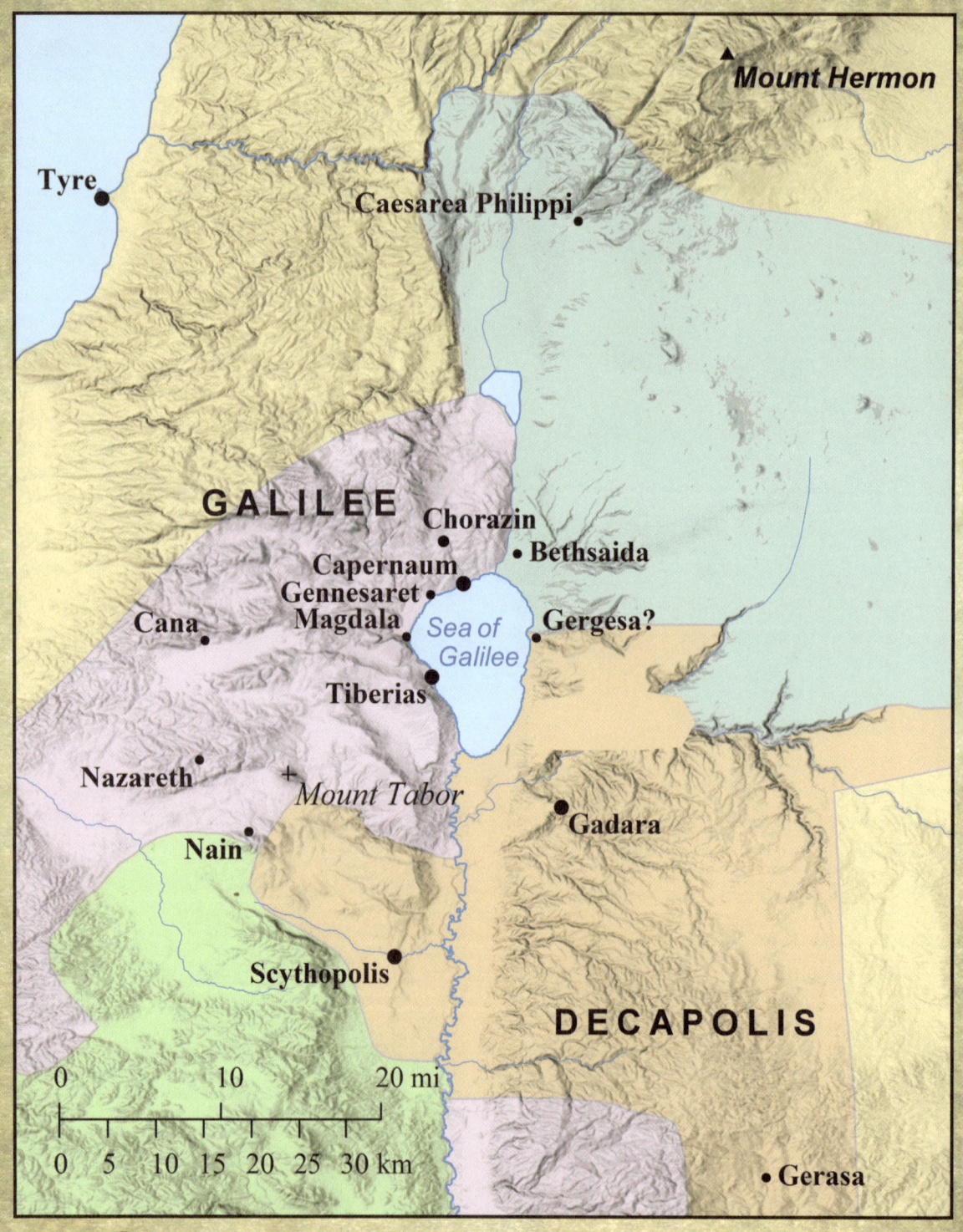

GALILEE AND THE NORTH DURING JESUS' MINISTRY